During the first four decades of the twentieth century, no issue attracted greater attention among political leaders, businessmen, and lawyers than the public regulation of corporations. Control over corporate securities was of central concern.

In tracing the origins of securities regulation back to the Progressive Era, Mr. Parrish casts light upon major questions inherent in American reform movements: Who sought regulation and for what purposes? What were the relationships between government and the business community, between the regulator and the regulated? The author concentrates on the New Deal as he examines the complex legislative struggles that produced the nation's first comprehensive securities laws. He details the influences of particular interest groups, Congressmen, and President Franklin Roosevelt. Utilizing, among other sources, the personal papers of Felix Frankfurter and James M. Landis, Mr. Parrish assesses the role of Roosevelt's talented legal advisors in shaping the Securities Act, the Securities and Exchange Act, and the Public Utility Holding Company Act. Finally, he explores the early history of the Securities and Exchange Commission, and, in so doing, demonstrates the successes and failures of New Deal reform and the processes of administrative decision-making.

Mr. Parrish is assistant professor of history at the University of California, San Diego.

Yale Historical Publications, Miscellany, 93.

Yale Historical Publications
Miscellany, 93

SECURITIES REGULATION AND

THE NEW DEAL

by Michael E. Parrish

New Haven and London, Yale University Press

1970

Copyright © 1970 by Yale University.

Library of Congress catalog card number: 70–118735
International standard book number: 0–300–01215–2

Designed by John O. C. McCrillis,
set in Times Roman type,
and printed in the United States of America by
The Carl Purington Rollins Printing-Office of
the Yale University Press, New Haven, Connecticut.

Distributed in Great Britain, Europe, and Africa by
Yale University Press, Ltd., London; in Canada by
McGill-Queen's University Press, Montreal; in Mexico
by Centro Interamericano de Libros Académicos,
Mexico City; in Australasia by Australia and New
Zealand Book Co., Pty., Ltd., Artarmon, New South
Wales; in India by UBS Publishers' Distributors Pvt.,
Ltd., Delhi; in Japan by John Weatherhill, Inc., Tokyo.

To my mother and the memory of my father

Contents

Acknowledgments

I wish to express my gratitude to the individuals and institutions who have assisted my efforts. Historians of the Roosevelt period are always indebted to the men and women who, with extraordinary patience and expertise, manage the President's library at Hyde Park. I add my appreciation, particularly to Elizabeth Drewry and Philip C. Brooks. Mrs. William McKee permitted me to use the papers of her father, James M. Landis, in the Library of Congress. To her and to John C. Broderick of the Manuscripts Division I give thanks.

George A. Strait and the staff of the Harvard Law School library rendered valuable assistance by making available portions of their Landis collection and Felix Frankfurter's personal papers. Judith A. Schiff and her capable co-workers in the Yale University library provided office space and unusual courtesy in the face of many tedious requests. I also wish to thank Boris Bittker, of the Yale Law School, for allowing me to examine the papers of Jerome Frank. Buford Rowland, chief of the legislative branch of the National Archives, guided me through Congressional materials, and David L. Thomas of the University of Virginia added his special knowledge of the Carter Glass collection. A grant from the University of California, San Diego, enabled me to complete my research during the academic year 1968–69 with greater dispatch than would have been possible under other circumstances. For this support and for the encouragement of Armin Rappaport I am grateful. Miss Joyce R. Chastain was a gracious and energetic typist. To my wife Caryl I owe the index and three years of equanimity during which I frequently lost my own.

Finally, I wish to acknowledge the sustained contribution of John Morton Blum who, through scholarship and teaching, inspired my interest in the Roosevelt years and American political history. His knowledge and judgment prevented numerous blunders, both factual and stylistic. I thank, too, Alexander Bickel for his enthusiasm, conversation, and helpful criticism. Any shortcomings in the manuscript are my own.

M. E. P.

La Jolla, California
January 1, 1970

List of Abbreviations

CDR	Commerce Department Records, Record Group 40, National Archives
CGP	Carter Glass Papers, University of Virginia
CICR	Capital Issues Committee Records, Record Group 158, Federal Records Center, Suitland, Maryland
FDRP	Franklin D. Roosevelt Papers, Hyde Park
FFPH	Felix Frankfurter Papers, Harvard Law School Library
FFPLC	Felix Frankfurter Papers, Library of Congress
HJP	Hiram Johnson Papers, University of California, Berkeley
HLSP	Henry L. Stimson Papers, Yale University
HTP	Huston Thompson Papers, Library of Congress
JFP	Jerome Frank Papers, Yale University
JMLPH	James M. Landis Papers, Harvard Law School Library
JMLPLC	James M. Landis Papers, Library of Congress
NPPCR	National Power Policy Committee Records, National Archives
SCR	Senate Committee Records, Record Group 46, National Archives
TDR	Treasury Department Records, Record Group 56, National Archives

Introduction

Twentieth-century reform movements have held considerable fascination for American historians. Source materials are numerous and varied. So, too, has been the conflict over the historical remains of particular reformers, the movements they led, and their public policies. Controversy about the meaning and significance of Populism, Progressivism, and the New Deal, although frequently sharp, has seldom been banal, because it has attracted many resourceful scholars. We who mine the narrow veins owe a great deal to the bolder prospectors who laid claim to the richest territory and mapped it with imagination. I gladly acknowledge my intellectual debt to real pioneers, particularly Richard Hofstadter, Arthur Schlesinger, Jr., Samuel P. Hays, Gabriel Kolko, and Robert Wiebe. Although not agreeing upon the answers, they have asked the right questions: Who were the reformers? What motivated their actions? And, finally, what were the consequences of reform? I have asked similar questions about a single issue: securities regulation. My answers, I hope, will help to illuminate a portion of the larger debate: the relationship between American businessmen and reform.

This study grew out of the recognition that although businessmen had not totally dominated public government in the United States, the activities of businessmen and the problems created by their activities had largely fixed the agenda of our politics. The interaction between businessmen and government therefore seemed crucial to an understanding of the politics of reform.

Felix Frankfurter once told Franklin Roosevelt an anecdote which he believed summarized his own contribution to the New Deal and the basic thrust of FDR's disparate programs.

Thomas Reed Powell, a colleague at the Harvard Law School, found himself one evening in the company of eminent legal and financial magnates who dominated the conversation by complaining about Frankfurter's alleged radicalism. Powell listened quietly for a while, but finally his patience gave way. "Felix, a radical?" he protested. "Hell!! The damn fool is wearing out his heart trying to make capitalism live up to its pretensions." Frankfurter's anecdote is pertinent to more than the New Deal. It touches a central theme of the complex development which historians have called the progressive movement. That central theme has been the use of governmental power, often federal power, to create an economic environment that was both reasonably predictable and reasonably humane. Although Americans at different levels of political influence and perception disagreed violently over the substance of these goals and over who should implement them, a vast majority subscribed to the general idea that they could be achieved without abandoning the price system or abolishing the private corporate form of enterprise. Whether or not one agrees with the aspirations of the more radical Populists, Wobblies, Socialists, Technocrats, and Communists, or simply deplores their harassment by vigilante groups and public officials, it requires extraordinary historical imagination to portray them as palpable threats to the American consensus. That consensus, however much particular scholars malign it as naïve and misguided, did in fact elect Taft not Bryan, Wilson not Debs, FDR not Thomas. To this extent, at least, even our reform tradition has been conservative.

Franklin Roosevelt's administration, the Congress, and a diverse business community, all fervent spokesmen for capitalism as a rampart of democracy, engaged in a seven-year struggle over how best to preserve capitalism. Securities regulation was only a skirmish on that larger battlefield. And yet, as a case study, an inquiry into securities regulation casts light not only on the New Deal and the forces working for and against it, but also on the nature of federal political and economic reforms in the twentieth century, of which the New Deal comprised a major episode. National progressivism and the New Deal were essentially responses to a single, continuing circumstance of our social development: Americans created a de facto national economy, capitalist in style and corporate in form, before they devised responsible institutions, public or private, which could govern that economy with a modicum of justice and foresight. An earlier Roosevelt perceived this situation when he spoke of the need "to secure by proper legislation and executive action the abolition of the grave abuses which . . . obtain in connection with the business use of wealth under our present system —or rather no system—of failure to exercise any adequate control at all." That situation persisted long after the second Roosevelt. It persists today, but the first system of national control over corporate finance began with FDR.

For many New Dealers like Frankfurter, and for Roosevelt himself, financial regulation was central to the New Deal. Making capitalism live up to its pretensions necessitated a restoration of public confidence in the governing symbols and basic currency of the economic order—investment securities. Long before FDR's first term, American enterprise rested upon a foundation of paper and transactions involving that paper. In addition to bankers' acceptances, bills of exchange, promissory notes, and other forms of commercial paper, the nation's industrial activity had become dependent upon a bewildering array of financial and organizational tools: bonds, debentures, cumulative and noncumulative preferred stock, and common stock, some with par value and some without. These were the idioms of an economy both capitalistic and corporate, that was propelled by mobile, liquid, divisible, and impersonal property.

Roosevelt's administration, inheriting the wreckage of the great crash, turned many of its initial energies toward reviving and restructuring institutions intimately connected with the paper foundations of the economy: the banking system and the securities market. The Emergency Banking Act, the Glass-Steagall Act, and the Federal Securities Act shared executive and legislative precedence with measures directed toward agricultural and industrial recovery. Banking reform, however, did not require unique national regulatory machinery. Legislation, with the exception of the Federal Deposit Insurance Act and an amendment enlarging the role of the Reconstruction Finance Corporation, built upon the existing Federal Reserve System. In addition to a basic administrative outline, the banking legislation of the New Deal applied policies drafted during the closing months of the Hoover administration and utilized two decades' experience in the management and mismanagement of the nation's commercial credit. In contrast, no fund of continuous, national administrative experience informed the original conception of federal securities regulation. No machinery comparable to the Federal Reserve served as a focus for reform and reorganization. Although commercial paper had been under national and quasi-public control for two decades, supervision of the more exotic forms of corporate property remained decentralized among forty-eight states, private institutions such as the Investment Bankers Association, stock exchanges, individual investment firms, and other professional organizations. These narrow, isolated, and fragmentary regulatory efforts contributed to the debacle of 1929. Moreover, the constituencies that nurtured them often proved intractable under FDR's regime.

During Roosevelt's first two terms, the federal government devised a legislative and administrative program designed to gain new mastery over vital areas of the securities market and corporate finance. The New Deal's program blended public and private decision making and responsibility. It rehabilitated a disorganized and demoralized financial community. I will examine important aspects of that program, including the breakdown of private and state regulation before 1933; Roosevelt's commitments and the impact of his talented advisers; the power of individual congressmen and the idiosyncrasies of others; the friction among administrators and departments; and the role of particular interest groups. These forces, in various combination, shaped the scope and content of securities regulation and influenced the structure of American capitalism for years to come. It was a conservative revolution which nonetheless horrified a great many conservatives.

1

Roots of Reform

Efforts to regulate corporation securities in the United States flourished initially during the first two decades of the twentieth century. Securities regulation, like other efforts of the time to impose legal restraints upon the burgeoning economy, drew upon a wide spectrum of motivations and touched a plethora of interest groups. State legislatures, incited to action by genuine and spurious complaints from investors, filled statute books with "blue-sky" laws, designed ostensibly to protect innocent widows and schoolteachers from the depredations of roving financial hucksters. These same state legislatures were responsive frequently to the blandishments of parochial businessmen and securities dealers who, threatened with the loss of local capital and markets to national corporations, encouraged particular "blue-sky" laws if they frustrated potential competition from out-of-state corporations and financial intermediaries. Many reputable investment bankers, alarmed by the activities of both unscrupulous promoters and zealous legislatures, banded together in the Investment Bankers Association to resist unwanted regulation, to promote professional status, and to insure legitimate profits. Finally, a few reformers and financial magnates, alarmed by the waste of resources involved in the chronic purchase of worthless securities and disenchanted with state regulation, flirted with the idea of federal supervision over investment funds.[1]

1. Harry F. Kohn, "The Blue Sky Law," *Technical World* 17 (March 1912): 36–45. The epithet "blue sky" was attached to the laws by one midwestern state legislator who, during the course of heated

Unfortunately for the proponents of comprehensive federal control, legislative successes were achieved first on the state level. Moral fervor, not regulatory acuity, guided many of these efforts. Joseph N. Dolly, state bank commissioner of Kansas, drafted and administered the first state "blue-sky" statue. Responding to a rash of land, mining, and insurance company frauds, the Kansas legislature voted in 1911 to regulate the sale of securities by out-of-state corporations. All companies not chartered in Kansas that wished to raise capital in the state were required to file a petition with the state banking commissioner setting forth their assets, liabilities, and future business plans. The commissioner could grant a license to sell the company's securities, if the enterprise "provided for fair transaction of business and in his [the commissioner's] judgment promised a fair return on the securities." The Kansas statute exempted only United States government bonds, Kansas municipal bonds, notes secured by Kansas real estate, state and national bank notes, and shares in Kansas building and loan associations. The Kansas law, defensive and negative in purpose, began a trend toward similar legislation in other states. These regulatory efforts, because of their narrow, sporadic, and unrelated character, ultimately created as many problems as they solved.[2]

---

debate, declared that if securities legislation was not passed, financial pirates would sell citizens everything in his state *but* the blue sky.

2. Gilbert E. Brach, "The Blue Sky Law," *Marquette Law Review* 3 (1918–19): 143; "Uniform Sale of Securities Act," *Columbia Law Review* 30 (December 1930): 1189–98; *Law Notes* 25 (June 1921): 45. Railroads and other public utilities were, of course, the first enterprises to have their securities supervised by the states and municipalities. Supervision often included control over the amount of financing as well as disclosure of assets and liabilities. For an analysis of the salutary and otiose aspects of these earlier statutes see William Z. Ripley, "Public Regulation of Railroad Issues," *American Economic Review* 4 (September 1914): 541–64; Leo Sharfman, "Commission Regulation of Public Utilities," *Annals of the American Academy of Social and Political Science* 53 (May 1914): 1–18; Arthur V. Ayres, "Governmental Relation of Securities Issues," *Political Science Quarterly* 28 (December 1913): 586–92.

Progressive spokesmen were divided over the utility of initial state securities legislation. Many hailed the enactments. They tended to agree with Iowa's attorney general who declared that his state's statute, patterned after the Kansas legislation, had the very simple purpose of protecting "the humble, honest citizens of the state" from being "plundered and despoiled of their small earnings . . . by the alluring machinations of the deceptive, misleading, and fraudulent devices which the unscrupulous, cunning, and deceitful 'Get-Rich-Quick-Wallingford's' of our day practice." No state legislation, wrote one commentator, "has met with more general acceptance . . . than the . . . blue-sky laws." Another reformer, after documenting the financial knavery perpetrated upon "helpless females," recommended the Kansas panacea to every state. His verdict summarized much naïve progressive thinking on the subject: "Funny how simple are the solutions of these intricate problems. Just stop it. That's all." Some friends of regulation, however, questioned the wisdom of these initial regulatory outbursts. In the United States, one lamented, "the science of investment is probably less well understood than in any other civilized country in the world." There was little reason to believe state legislatures held a monopoly of understanding.[3]

No group pondered the impact of state efforts more than the newly organized Investment Bankers Association. The IBA was a product of the trend toward business and professional institutionalization through voluntary association characteristic of the progressive era. Organized in 1912, the association sought to embrace within its membership the functions connected with the underwriting, distribution, and trading of public and private securities. With an initial membership of 392, the IBA announced its dedication to "promoting the influence of investment banking, to safeguard the offerings of investment houses . . . and [to] the mutual protection of legitimate invest-

3. William B. Shaw, "Progressive Law-Making in Many States," *Review of Reviews* 48 (July 1913): 88–90; Kohn, "Blue Sky Law," p. 39; *William R. Compton Co. v. Allen,* 216 Fed. 547. See also editorials in *Harper's Weekly,* August 12, 1911, p. 22; May 10, 1913, p. 24.

ment bankers and the public against irresponsible dealers in investment securities." The association's principle objective, however, was to secure greater uniformity in state and federal laws, governing the issuance, purchase, and sale of securities. "Millions upon millions of the savings of people of moderate means are each year falling into the clutches of the get-rich-quick promoter and the bucket shop," L. B. Lawrence of Guaranty Trust told IBA organizers, "and it is only by a campaign of education, and by proper legislation, that this waste of resources can be stopped, to say nothing about diverting some small profit into the pockets of legitimate dealers."[4]

The Investment Bankers Association did not advance a consistent legislative program during or after the progressive period. In part this was the result of the complex state and regional interests built into the IBA's national organization. But general economic trends also played a crucial role in determining the association's position on securities regulation. Initially, the IBA opposed state license statutes. Instead, it advocated simple fraud laws, which did not require prior registration of securities, demand full disclosure, or permit a veto by state administrators. Rebuffed by the legislatures and by the courts, the IBA swung briefly behind federal legislation, either in the form of a national incorporation law or a national securities law similar to the British Companies Act. The association's desire for a federal incorporation statute was disingenuous, resting as it did upon the certain knowledge that such legislation could not gain congressional approval. On the other hand, a federal securities law elicited IBA support if, as in British practice, the registration data remained limited, personal liabilities proved consistent with common law definitions of fraud, and the opportunities for administrative interference were remote. Erratic economic growth and anxiety over fluctuating profits influenced the association's attitude toward state and federal regulation before the middle of the 1920s. Shaped

4. Investment Bankers Association, *Proceedings of Annual Convention* (1912), p. 192; ibid. (1913), pp. 1, 38.

to IBA standards, securities regulation was one method for controlling a chaotic business environment. Support for federal regulation evaporated when the American economy became more buoyant during the 1920s. Then, the prospects of lucrative business and the willingness of individual states to revise their laws to the association's satisfaction reduced IBA interest in federal legislation. Expediency, in short, was the main propellent of their policy.

Following enactment of the Kansas statute, the Investment Bankers Association commenced a broad attack upon the problem of securities regulation. It attempted to raise the prestige of the profession by making association membership synonymous with respectability. In addition, the IBA sought to improve self-regulation by controlling access to membership through a system of recruitment based upon recommendations from local and regional members. "We have been suffering from social poverty," President George B. Caldwell said; "we not only did not know enough of our own people, but did not know enough about the business of those engaged in investment banking." Finally, the association endeavored to influence the content of state securities laws. The IBA bitterly contested the original regulatory-license statutes, while rhetorically endorsing legislation to suppress "the irresponsible promoter and the dealer in spurious securities." The association's vehement denunciation of particular state statutes was not totally unjustified. Many proposed laws were presented in a haphazard manner. Blue-sky bills were often introduced by legislators who had a feeble grasp of the nature and character of the business they proposed to regulate.[5]

Because the association was poorly organized during the years before World War I, it won a few legislative skirmishes but lost the major war against license statutes based on the Kansas model. Except for important litigation, the IBA's influence remained decentralized. State lobbying, like membership recruitment, fell to state members who not infrequently

5. IBA, *Proceedings* (1913), pp. 18, 48–49, 54; ibid. (1914), pp. 67, 78.

worked against national IBA policy. The central legislation committee, burdened with analysis of many state and national laws touching investment banking, could not give continuous direction to the association's policy on state securities legislation.

The IBA drafted a "model securities act" between 1913 and 1915 and sought to impress its virtues upon states then writing legislation. It was a fraud act based largely on sections of the federal postal laws. The model act granted powers of investigation, injunction, and prosecution to state officials charged with enforcement. All registration and license laws were stigmatized by the association as "crude paternalistic measures." The model fraud act was presented as "fair and practical . . . [it] will prevent distribution of wild-cat securities and . . . protect investors." The association won a partial victory in 1913 when Maine incorporated the fraud provisions in its first securities act. But this victory was overshadowed by other provisions. Unlike the Kansas, Michigan, and Ohio laws, the new Maine act did not require the registration and licensing of each proposed issue of securities. Instead, individual dealers were required to register and granted a license after an investigation of "their business character and repute and the character of the securities in which they dealt." Maine's act, according to the IBA, was preferable to mandatory registration of specific issues, but the association continued to fight for a fraud act without registration of either issues or dealers. New Hampshire, Virginia, Minnesota, and West Virginia adopted fraud provisions before 1918, but all added other forms of regulation based on the Kansas or Maine precedents.[6]

In those states where its membership was large and active, the association could forestall securities legislation. New York's assembly passed a license law in 1913, which the association quickly labeled as an "extreme type of . . . radical legislation."

6. IBA, *Proceedings* (1913), pp. 55, 165–66; ibid. (1915), p. 186; Robert R. Reed, "Blue Sky Laws," *Annals of the American Academy of Social and Political Science* 88 (March 1920): 180.

The IBA's powerful New York constituency persuaded the state senate to kill the measure "without further comment in the legislature or in the press." The IBA could not, however, reverse or stop the tide of license statutes. It suffered a major defeat in 1917 when the United States Supreme Court, after six years of exhausting litigation, upheld the registration-license laws of Ohio, Michigan, and South Dakota. All three were patterned after the Kansas law. The 1917 decision gave a green light to similar state regulatory efforts.[7]

Robert R. Reed, the IBA's chief counsel, summarized the association's first decade of legislative frustration. Pursuing what it called a "cooperative approach" to regulation, the IBA attempted to influence the legislative recommendations of state bank commissioners and attorneys general. However, a committee of attorneys general, writing a common statute for Michigan, Ohio, and South Dakota, excluded IBA representatives from all conferences and, as Reed complained, "practically refused . . . cooperation and drafted a new proposed act . . . without time or opportunity for discussion." The attorneys general, their efforts upheld by the Supreme Court, did not believe in "government by discussion." Reed, speaking for the IBA, pronounced all of the state laws "hopelessly crude and unworkable." The perspective of Reed and other IBA partisans was jaundiced by political defeat. Yet several of their complaints and objections had merit. State laws covered an administrative field that could be patrolled only by several hundred trained administrators. The states had not begun to provide adequate manpower and, as a result, little effort had been made to apply the laws impartially. Administrative favoritism, even bribery, were common. And although legislation discouraged fly-by-night promoters in some states, it also drove out conservative dealers. State officials, according to Reed and others, could not cope with "the complications and corporate

7. IBA, Proceedings (1913), p. 166; *Hall v. Geiger-Jones Co.*, 61 U.S. (L. ed.) 480; *Caldwell v. Sioux Falls Stock Co.*, 61 U.S. (L. ed.) 493; *Merrick v. Halsey*, 61 U.S. (L. ed.) 498.

machinery of large speculative or fraudulent interstate flotations."[8]

In addition, Reed and many IBA members found state regulation intolerable because of its restrictions upon interstate investment operations. Large New York and Chicago investment houses were forced to revise their mailing lists and distribution machinery in order to avoid diverse, onerous license requirements in ten or twenty states. Investors in blue-sky states were frequently denied high-grade securities. At the same time, fraudulent promoters found various methods of evading state laws. Reed proposed two possible solutions. Either the federal government had to enact a national incorporation law to control the creation of corporations, or the federal government had to enact a blue-sky law "reasonably adapted to the constitutional purposes of preventing fraud and deception in interstate flotations." His own preference was a federal statute similar to the British Companies Act, which did not require government approval of specific issues, but did include the filing of financial data.[9]

Other legal spokesmen for the IBA condemned state license regulation and, like Reed, called for federal legislation. Ohio's law, according to the president of the Cleveland Bar Association, was "a welter of exceptions and definitions . . . a piece of dictionary gone mad." Registration-license laws were objectionable because they allowed state functionaries, usually short-term political appointees, to determine what securities could be sold in the state. Regulation was reduced to "a matter of expediency and a battle ground between the selfishness of the bureaucrat and the selfishness of the security dealer. . . . No precedents will be established. One administrator will succeed another and the lawyer will continue in the dark." The Cleve-

8. Reed, "Blue Sky Laws," pp. 178–85. For a complete text of the state laws in 1920 see also Robert R. Reed, *Blue Sky Laws: Analysis and Text,* passim. On the state incorporation dilemma see Adolph A. Berle, *Studies in the Law of Corporation Finance,* pp. 188–92, and passim.

9. Reed, "Blue Sky Laws," pp. 184–85.

land bar, too, called for "a Federal act," which would follow "the provisions of the English Companies Act." Like the British law, federal legislation should require the filing of an official prospectus; the disclosure of profits to promoters and discounts or commissions paid to underwriters; and details of all property acquired by the corporation within two years of the formation of the corporation. Further, the purchaser of securities should be given the right to rescind his purchase if any statement in the prospectus was untrue. Adequate penal provisions should punish the use of false statements or the omission of material facts, and an adequate force of specialists should be engaged to detect fraud. Under this type of regulation, "the buyer would not be buying blindly, but would form his own judgment in the light of the true facts." Either there had to be total state approval or the investor had to select his own securities, but "as long as the law is permitted to rest upon these two conflicting principles, there will be confusion and constant change."[10]

Federal regulation, given the diversity of state statutes and the excessive paternalism of many state administrators, had a strong attraction for some investment bankers and lawyers with national as opposed to local interests. They could not but be dismayed by the statement of one state administrator who said it was best to prevent national corporate issues from draining away local capital: "Hardly any sales . . . made in this state have turned out profitable [sic] to the investor. There are always safe investments at home which ordinary people would do better to put their money in." Nor could they take comfort from the confusion that plagued interpretation and administration of some state laws. Minnesota's attorney general, explaining his state's legislation, said a security had to be classed as fraudulent "where the purchaser . . . does not have a fair chance to gain by the investment. It is not sufficient that the money invested be secured against loss; there must be a fair chance to gain." But, he added, "this does not mean that the

10. A summary of the Cleveland Bar Association proceedings may be found in the *Ohio Law Reporter* 18 (February 28, 1921): 515–24.

[Minnesota] commission attempts to remove ordinary business hazards or limit the right to engage in speculative ventures."[11]

Members of the investment banking profession and many of their legal representatives did not express an isolated sentiment when advocating federal supervision. Numerous segments of the business community, including commercial bankers, railroad leaders, manufacturers, and food processors, looked frequently to federal regulation during these years to fulfill general needs, special interests, and vague hopes. For some, intervention by the federal government implied possible escape from discriminatory and conflicting state jurisdictions. For others, federal regulation contained the bewitching promise of instant economic stability. And for still others, federal regulation held out the vision of triumph over commercial rivals. But indefinite goals and vague aspirations tended to produce federal legislation that was itself indefinite and vague and whose results even ardent proponents found hard to assess for years to come.[12]

The first concrete proposal for federal securities legislation

11. Forrest B. Ashby, *The Economic Effect of Blue Sky Laws*, p. 24; William L. Stoddard, "Blue Sky Situation," *Outlook*, January 27, 1926, pp. 147–50; Montreville J. Brown, "The Minnesota 'Blue Sky' Law," *Minnesota Law Review* 3 (February 1919): 159–61. The Minnesota law, resembling many state statutes for control of railroad securities, permitted the commission to determine the amount and type of stock issued by corporations in the state and to fix promotional and underwriting fees.

12. The relationship between businessmen and the federal government during the progressive period is a subject of intense historical controversy. Who initiated regulatory efforts and for what purpose? To what extent did particular businessmen and reformers share identical goals but clash over implementation of those goals? Contrasting interpretations are, to some extent, a reflection of the diversity of business-political objectives and of the confusion that plagued contemporary businessmen and political leaders. In the case of securities regulation, it seems clear that state politicians, responding primarily to inchoate abuses, were the initiators. Formation of the IBA and its regulatory demands was largely a response to this activity. On the larger debate see Robert H. Wiebe, *Businessmen and Reform: A Study of the Progressive Movement*, pp. 1–15, 206–24; Gabriel Kolko,

came from the Investment Bankers Association and from individuals concerned with the national management of credit and investment funds during the wartime emergency of 1917–19. Like other experiments in national planning before 1933, the need to utilize and direct all economic resources on a national basis received powerful impetus from war mobilization.

The Capital Issues Committee, created by Congress and composed of Treasury, Federal Reserve, and private banking representatives, adopted such a national regulatory posture during its brief existence. The CIC, given a vague mandate to approve all private and public financing, found it lacked specific power to compel submission to its jurisdiction, to enforce its findings, or to curb fraudulent securities issues. Regulatory efforts by the committee, the states, and the IBA broke down completely. "In no years in the past have these people [fraudulent dealers] been so bold and so unscrupulous." W. H. Maxwell, Jr., of the IBA's fraudulent advertising committee complained to William G. McAdoo, "and because of the tremendous difficulty in securing competent evidence . . . the business of selling fraudulent stocks and bonds is one of the safest . . . in the country." Traffic in doubtful securities, the CIC chairman Charles Hamlin said, "is . . . general throughout the country."[13]

The Triumph of Conservatism, pp. 1–56, and passim; John Braeman, "The Square Deal in Action: A Case Study in the Growth of the 'National Police Power,'" in John Braeman, Robert H. Bremner, and Everett Walters, eds., *Change and Continuity in Twentieth-Century America,* pp. 35–80; Gabriel Kolko, *Railroads and Regulation,* passim, Robert W. Harbeson, "Railroads and Regulation, 1877–1916: Conspiracy or Public Interest?" *Journal of Economic History* 27 (1967): 230–42.

13. W. H. Maxwell, Jr., to William G. McAdoo, April 5, 1918, CICR, Box 001; Charles S. Hamlin to F. H. Curtis, September 9, 1918, CICR, Box 266; William Willoughby, *The Capital Issues Committee and War Finance Corporation,* pp. 9–39. On the CIC and the collapse of regulation see Hamlin to John S. Drum, August 14, 1918, and F. H. Goff to Bernard Baruch, July 19, 1918, CICR, Box 266; Maxwell to Paul M. Warburg, April 12, 1918, and Warren S. Hayden to Hamlin, July 5, 1918, CICR, Box 001.

The Capital Issues Committee and its local officials attempted to discourage enterprises that were palpably unsound. But without adequate enforcement machinery, the committee was "unable to deal effectively with many enterprises whose promoters or managers remained deaf to every appeal to their patriotism." In its first report to Congress in 1918, the CIC urged federal supervision after the war "by some public agency . . . in such a form as to check the traffic in doubtful securities, while imposing no undue restrictions upon the financing of legitimate industry." Federal supervision was necessary in order to fill "a crevice in our financial structure through which flows a constant torrent of funds in utter wastage." The CIC recommendations echoed the suggestions of private bankers who staffed its local committees.[14] "As our work increases in volume," John H. Rich told Hamlin,

> I am astonished at the number of fraudulent, indifferent and actually bad propositions that come before us. . . . Work of this scope and value should be continued in some form after the war. . . . Once having taken the position of inspecting offerings of securities, the Government should not turn back from the plow but should continue some appropriate form of supervision that will be more effective than the present operations of the Blue Sky Commissions.[15]

In its final report, the CIC once again called attention to the continued distribution of worthless securities which represented "sheer waste and net loss . . . not only of dollars but of morale, confidence, and the incentive to save." State regulation, the CIC noted, had been effective only to a limited extent, principally where a company had organized to operate and sell its securities in the state of its creation. The committee recommended new federal legislation broader than the existing fraud statutes enforced by the Post Office and Justice departments.

14. *Report of the Capital Issues Committee* (House Doc. 1485, 65th Cong., 3d sess., 1918), pp. 1–3.
15. John H. Rich to Charles S. Hamlin, September 13, 1918, CICR, Box 266.

These two departments, the committee noted, "do not and cannot act until after fraud has been perpetrated. The purpose of . . . [new] legislation should be to prevent the perpetration of fraud."[16]

The year 1919 appeared auspicious for federal legislation. At its annual convention, the Investment Bankers Association's legislation committee endorsed some form of federal securities regulation. Like the CIC, the association's committee urged the creation of a "machine which . . . would suppress offerings of fraudulent and misrepresented securities at their very outset rather than attempt to punish those responsible for their perpetration upon the public." Administrative expenses would be large, but the committee emphasized the benefits of uniformity, efficiency, and smooth investment operations. "It has become almost impossible for the investment bankers to comply promptly with the statutes of the various states," the committee said, "and if the Federal government in conjunction with the . . . several states would enter into a close working arrangement it would permit . . . information, when required, being filed in one place, preferably Washington, and would save a great multiplicity of work and expense." The committee viewed federal regulation as a device to eliminate marginal operators and to rationalize interstate investment activities.[17]

The IBA committee's proposals represented a significant modification of the association's previous insistence upon punitive fraud statutes. The complete futility of that philosophy had been demonstrated during the wartime emergency, as had the defects of state regulation. Yet the committee could not mobilize a majority of the association behind its recommendations for a federal law. When federal legislation, based upon the British Companies Act, reached the Congress between 1919 and 1921, the IBA helped to prevent its enactment.

The initial measure, written by Bradley Palmer, counsel for the Capital Issues Committee, and by Huston Thompson, a member of the Federal Trade Commission, was introduced by

16. *Final Report of the Capital Issues Committee* (House Doc. 1836, 65th Cong., 3d sess., 1919), pp. 1–3.
17. IBA *Proceedings* (1919), pp. 122–24.

Congressman Edward Taylor of Colorado. Taylor's bill, in many respects similar to the legislation later drafted by Thompson for Franklin Roosevelt in 1933, required registration of all security issues using the mails or instrumentalities of interstate commerce. A new bureau within the Treasury Department would administer the statute. But the Taylor bill, characterized by Thompson as "prophylactic and preventive rather than paternal," incurred the hostility of the IBA. The association objected to the requirement of detailed information on income statements and balance sheets for all issues and to the personal liability provisions which, they claimed, exceeded the common law. In addition, the bill encountered opposition from new Republican administrators in the Treasury Department. Speciously, they attacked the bill as both too lenient and too burdensome: "This plan relies chiefly upon mere publicity to restrain issues. . . . Legislation of this character is no barrier to the rogue." But, Treasury experts added, "such provisions . . . constitute an almost impossible burden on many legitimate transactions. The necessity of elaborate statistical detail, to be verified under civil and criminal liabilities, will present a very real obligation to persons of responsibility." The legislation also threatened Republican fiscal austerity. It would require a new bureau and necessitate "appropriations which . . . would not be justified at this time." The Palmer-Thompson-Taylor measure did not leave the House Judiciary Committee.[18]

Almost simultaneously, however, the Investment Bankers Association supported an innocuous measure introduced by Illinois Congressman Edward Denison. The Denison bill sought federal enforcement for all the laws and administrative rulings of the states relating to securities regulation. In this form it received the IBA's condemnation as "the most dangerous pro-

18. *Congressional Record*, 65th Cong., 1st sess., 58, p. 16; House Judiciary Committee, *Federal Blue Sky Law* (66th Cong., 1st sess., 1919), pp. 11–12, 19, 25; Treasury Department, memorandum, January 10, 1921, TDR, Box 17; Huston Thompson, "Regulation of the Sale of Securities in Interstate Commerce," *American Bar Association Journal* 9 (March 1923): 57–59; IBA, *Proceedings* (1919), p. 125.

nouncement that has been made in legislative halls in . . . memory." The Treasury Department, too, ridiculed the original Denison bill. "Legislation of this character," said Secretary Andrew Mellon, "would in effect subject transactions . . . to the diversity of rules involved in the laws of forty-eight different states . . . and would involve the Government enforcement agencies in the insuperable task of enforcing these infinitely diverse laws."[19]

Following a conference with IBA leaders, Denison submitted a revised bill which carried the association's blessing. This proposal was a skeleton fraud statute, without provision for registration of issues, barren of liability mechanisms, and without federal enforcement of existing state laws. Nearly all interstate offerings would have been exempted. "If these same provisions can be worked out into a uniform [state] act," IBA representatives said, "[we] will have gained more than . . . this Association ever thought possible." The Treasury Department, now hostile to any legislation, dismissed the second Denison bill. Mellon, a man with considerable financial perspicacity, thought the measure worthless. "It would," he told the chairman of the House Interstate Commerce Committee, "leave untrammeled all dealings in securities in the exempt list however dangerous they might be to the investing public." Mellon, despite this insight, did not provide further leadership by suggesting a meaningful solution to the regulatory problem. He recommended simply that the attorney general "investigate . . . securities, and, if he [finds] evidence of fraud . . . issue a summary order forbidding . . . sale, under heavy penalty." This approach was only slightly less inane than the Denison bill. Despite House approval and intensive lobbying by the Investment Bankers Association, the Denison proposal died in the Senate Finance Committee.[20]

19. *Congressional Record,* 67th Cong., 1st sess., 61, pp. 92, 2740; House Interstate Commerce Committee, *Blue Sky Bill* (67th Cong., 1st sess., 1921), pp. 5–62; IBA, *Proceedings* (1921), p. 258; Andrew Mellon to Samuel E. Winslow, July 19, 1921, TDR, Box 17.

20. House Interstate Commerce Committee, *Blue Sky Bill* (67th Cong., 2d sess., 1922), pp. 1–120; IBA, *Proceedings* (1922), pp. 206–

The IBA then endorsed a measure introduced by Congressman Andrew Volstead. This, too, was a fraud statute. It empowered the attorney general to investigate, after complaint, fraudulent practices in the sale of securities and to issue an injunction if "the results of the investigation justified." The House Interstate Commerce Committee did not give the bill a hearing.[21]

After these short excursions into the federal legislative arena, the IBA drew back. The measures that gained its support, the revised Denison or Volstead bills, were ludicrously inadequate. Only the Taylor bill, which the association opposed, offered a real alternative to regulation otherwise punitive in intention and occasional in enforcement. As an epilogue to national progressivism, World War I had mobilized briefly concern for federal securities regulation. And though barren of legislative results, the experience of controlling a war economy had left remnants of conviction and policy that could be revived during a greater domestic catastrophe after 1929. Meanwhile, the issue of securities regulation returned to the states where, to the satisfaction of the IBA, it remained until 1933. Pliny Jewell, IBA president, summarized the association's new attitude when he declared in 1927: "There is no need of Federal legislation. . . . With most of the states already with adequate specific laws, with the assistance of the postal authorities, and our basic common law . . . nothing further is needed."[22]

07; Andrew Mellon to Samuel E. Winslow, February 23, 1922, TDR, Box 17. The revised Denison bill exempted securities listed on the New York, Chicago, and Boston stock exchanges and all issues junior thereunto. See IBA, *Bulletin* 10 (March 15, 1922): 1–10.

21. *Congressional Record,* 66th Cong., 1st sess., 59, p. 3106; IBA, *Proceedings* (1922), pp. 206–07.

22. IBA, *Proceedings* (1927), p. 48. For a provocative study of the philosophical and practical relationships between World War I economic mobilization and the New Deal see William E. Leuchtenburg, "The New Deal and the Analogue of War," in Braeman et al., *Change and Continuity,* pp. 81–143.

2

The Collapse of Self-Regulation

Two developments sharpened the opposition of the Investment Bankers Association to national securities regulation during the 1920s: (1) success in forcing the modification of state regulation and (2) sufficient business prosperity to eliminate the fear of excessive competition from disreputable promoters. Instead of working for comprehensive national regulation, the IBA placed complete faith in its own ability to discipline the securities industry and sought to promote uniform administration on a state-by-state basis. The association's new strategy embraced three objectives. In thirty-six states with registration mechanisms, the association did not attempt to remove the statutes, but worked instead to amend the laws "from time to time so as to make them more workable." The IBA opposed additional legislation in those states with nonregistration fraud laws. In states without specific legislation, the association worked to secure laws without registration requirements.[1]

From the bankers' viewpoint, some states became more important than others. It did not matter if Oklahoma or Mississippi passed registration laws, but it mattered a great deal if New York followed this regulatory procedure. Registration and license laws, the IBA realized, could be tolerated "unless . . . there is to be some legislation of that kind in really creditor states." The association devoted large resources to the task of keeping New York State, the major securities market, free from registration or license laws. The New York legislature,

1. IBA, *Proceedings* (1921), p. 283.

with IBA encouragement, enacted a fraud measure in 1921 known as the Martin Act. It gave the state attorney general power to investigate fraudulent practices in the sale of securities, and the right to issue subpoenas and to seek injunctions against suspected individuals. Thereafter, the association hailed New York's statute as a monument to regulatory intelligence, although one incredulous attorney general, cognizant of the basic defect in fraud laws, remarked: "Just how [we are] to discover in advance who is going to perpetrate fraud is not made clear in the act." Without registration, there was little information available to the enforcement agency.[2]

The IBA and its New York allies successfully defended the Martin Act against modification until 1932 when individual dealers were first required to register with a new state securities bureau. The association helped to defeat legislation that would have required the registration of securities issues. This proposed amendment to the Martin Act, the IBA said, contained "an oppressive and wholly impracticable schedule of information." Before 1932, the association and the New York Stock Exchange also sidetracked proposals designed to license dealers, to regulate the Exchange's ticker service, and to examine the financial records of investment firms.[3] The Martin Act, in short, enabled the IBA, its corporate clients, and the New York Stock Exchange to enjoy the best of two worlds. It helped to police bucket shops and fraudulent dealers who drained away business. At the same time, the Martin Act allowed the IBA, corporations, and Exchange members to avoid the responsibility of registration or disclosure. With unconscious irony, one student of the Martin Act said: "The large body of . . . security dealers in the state [of New York] have been unfailing in their sponsorship and support of the Act and its administration. . . . There has never been the slightest effort on the part of orga-

2. William C. Breed, "Public Regulation in Origination and Distribution of Securities," *Investment Banking* 3 (February 21, 1933): 186–96; New York State Bar Association, *Bulletin* (1929), p. 389.

3. *New York Times,* February 21, March 13, March 17, 1922; IBA, *Proceedings* (1923), pp. 44–45; *New York Times,* June 17, 18, 29, 1932.

nized security dealers or recognized stock exchanges to oppose either the Act or its enforcement. It has never been charged with hindering legitimate business or driving business from the state."[4]

The association revamped its policy-making and lobbying machinery during the 1920s in an effort to secure greater influence upon state securities legislation and administration. Beyond New York, IBA activities were directed primarily at states that insisted upon registration of either securities or individual dealers. Rhetorically, the IBA continued to berate these statutes for requiring "a vast amount of detailed information on sound securities." Practically, the IBA worked assiduously to mitigate the severity of many laws against nationally known corporations, to correct what it euphemistically called "mistaken administration," and to promote uniformity in registration requirements. Policy making and lobbying were centralized under a special committee headed by Arthur G. Davis. The new committee was charged with encouraging state legislation and administration that provided equality for all IBA members. This remained a difficult task. The Davis committee continued to encounter local and regional rivalries among members. Nonetheless, Davis's group raised the banner of uniformity and equality against the "insular selfishness" of many members who worked to maintain state laws and administrative rulings that harassed other IBA members or discriminated against their securities. "There should be no sectionalism in any law regulating the sale or distribution of securities," Davis said. "Good securities should be eligible to flow into one section of the United States with the same ease as in any other section. There should be no favoritism against good securities in any locality."[5]

The Davis committee experienced success in promoting state

4. Ambrose V. McCall, "Comments on the Martin Act," *Brooklyn Law Review* 3 (April 1934): 197–203; Lawrence P. Simpson, "The New York Blue Sky Law and the Uniform Act," *New York University Law Quarterly* 8 (March 1931): 465–74.

5. IBA, *Proceedings* (1924), p. 118; ibid. (1925), p. 31; ibid. (1926), pp. 129–30.

uniformity through both legislation and administrative rulings. Indiana and Minnesota, after IBA urging, exempted from registration and license requirements all securities listed on the New York and Chicago stock exchanges. Other states, under association pressure, adopted the practice of "registration by notification," or "temporary approval" for the securities of corporations listed on exchanges or with a record of stable earnings. These registration procedures greatly facilitated wide distribution of national issues and favored national syndicating machinery perfected during the decade. On other occasions, however, Davis's committee still faced the recalcitrance of members who wished to protect local markets from national issues and national syndicates. Discriminatory legislation increased slightly after 1927 during the years of fierce competitive activity. Virginia's IBA members were typical offenders against the Davis doctrines. They secured legislation that imposed a one-year residency requirement upon all dealers operating in their state and incurred the association's displeasure for creating "a barrier to the proper distribution of sound securities."[6]

By 1929, however, Davis could report that sixteen states had so modified their laws as to achieve uniformity in the registration of securities. "A vast advance," he said, "over the seemingly hopeless confusion which existed a few years ago." These sixteen states required identical financial data and standardized the forms used for registration. Moreover, the trend of administration was toward standard exemptions and the exemption of standard transactions in many states. Securities of corporations listed on exchanges, securities of utilities subject to separate state regulation, securities with a continuous history of earnings—all received standard exemptions. Sales to other corporations and isolated sales by one investor

6. IBA, *Proceedings* (1926), p. 120; J. Edward Meeker, "Preventive vs. Punitive Securities Laws," *Columbia Law Review* 26 (March 1926): 318–28; Forrest B. Ashby, "The Influence of Securities Regulation upon Standards of Corporation Financing," *Michigan Law Review* 26 (June 1928): 880–81.

to another were often exempted transactions. Even Michigan, a state with the most searching registration requirements, bowed to IBA arguments and exempted securities listed on the New York Stock Exchange. Davis, disregarding the enmity of a few delegates, praised the association for adopting a national perspective and for supporting legislation that permitted securities freely to cross state lines. "The time was," he said, "when each such [state] law was peculiar unto itself. No semblance of uniformity, even between two or more states, either in statutes or practice and procedure, existed." The tenacious lobbying efforts of Davis's committee had overcome regulatory diversity and brought the association a large measure of commercial, if not organizational, unity. The committee's next task, according to Davis, would be to simplify further the registration forms of all the states and to expand the categories of exempted securities.[7]

The IBA's efforts received strong support during the decade from the National Conference of Commissioners on Uniform State Laws and from the American Bar Association. The Committee on Uniform State Law of the Michigan Bar Association expressed the sentiments of both groups when it reported in 1928:

> We have a stupendous number of statutes and decisions emanating from our legislatures and courts, but . . . there is an inexcusable divergence between the various states. . . . Such a situation is extremely disconcerting to general business. . . . The paper boundary lines of the states are nothing but obstacles of inconvenience and nuisance to the average business man. . . . Notwithstanding the almost universal complaint and public ridicule of this situation the honorable legislatures seem very slow to adopt what is a comparatively easy solution, namely, uniform state laws.[8]

7. IBA, *Proceedings* (1929), pp. 79–81, 90–96. Also see Ashby, "The Influence of Securities Regulation," pp. 881–83.
8. Michigan Bar Association, *Proceedings* (1928), p. 221.

The National Conference in 1922 delegated the problem of uniform securities legislation to a committee on uniform commercial acts. The latter submitted a model act the following year. The committee abandoned the license approach of many states in favor of registration for brokers, dealers, and nonexempt securities. This model act proposed administration by autonomous state securities commissions. It exempted securities listed on exchanges but proposed to give state commissions power to approve all other issues. Since the committee draft contained no standard for exercising approval, the measure came under severe criticism from the conference and from the American Bar Association.[9]

Eight years elapsed before a revised model act received the approval of the American Bar Association. The text, when approved, incorporated many of the ideas encouraged by the IBA over the past decade. Securities listed on the New York, Chicago, and Boston stock exchanges, the Chicago Board of Trade, the New York Curb Exchange, "and any other recognized and responsible stock exchange," received complete exemption from registration. Furthermore, a dual system of registration was proposed for issues not exempt under the exchange loopholes or through an automatic exemption accorded to government issues and the securities of state banks, building and loan associations, and public utilities under state supervision. An issuer who could demonstrate three years of continuous operation and two years of average annual net earnings on bonds or stock might register by notification. Registration by more rigorous qualification was reserved for what the act called "speculative" issuers. Only this latter group would be required to submit detailed balance sheets, income statements, copies of a prospectus, and advertisements.[10]

Guidelines for granting and withholding registration re-

9. National Conference of Commissioners on Uniform State Laws, *Handbook and Proceedings* (1922), p. 113; ibid. (1923), pp. 230–43; American Bar Association, *Reports* (1923), p. 708.

10. National Conference, *Handbook and Proceedings* (1930), pp. 235–66.

mained blurred under the proposed uniform act. State commissions could withhold or revoke registration if the issuer was of "bad business repute," or if the enterprise was "not based upon sound business principles." The proposed uniform act thus contained vestiges of the original license statutes. However, recision and liability provisions were more conservative than existing state laws. Both fell upon individual dealers who made false or misleading statements, not upon the issuing corporation. A two-year limit on civil damage suits insured limited redress for unwary purchasers.[11]

The proposed uniform act reflected a decade's experience with securities regulation and mirrored the progress made by the Investment Bankers Association toward obtaining legislation and administration tailored to its own narrow needs. The IBA, despite local and regional conflicts, valued a national securities market and shaped its basic regulatory demands around efforts to make that market as free as possible for corporations in search of national capital. Various state rulings and the proposed uniform act reflected this strategy by granting broad exemptions to issuers who could secure endorsement from allegedly reputable, expert institutions such as the New York Stock Exchange or to issuers whose accountants, bankers, and lawyers could demonstrate a sustained period of earnings. As a consequence, securities regulation, decentralized among the states, underwent further fragmentation as state commissions in effect delegated enormous power and responsibility to private institutions and voluntary associations. Although IBA-induced uniformity may have been a virtue, the extent to which states abandoned formal regulatory powers to private organizations was one more indication of the extravagant confidence displayed during the decade by all levels of government in the ability of private decision making and self-regulation to manage effectively vast areas of the American economy. This attitude influenced more than state securities regulation; it also afflicted the resolution and nonresolution of

11. Ibid.

other significant issues, including monetary policy, trade practices, labor relations, railroad consolidation, agricultural prices,
and water power development. But self-regulation often became a euphemism for private despotism, industrial anarchy,
or economic drift.[12]

Although state-by-state regulation evolved satisfactorily for
many IBA members, some state administrators criticized the
decentralized methods of control. The stock market crash
tended to vindicate these opinions. Very few states devoted
sufficient resources to continuous administrative supervision
during the decade. Most placed the arduous task of securities
regulation within a preexisting administrative framework. By
1933 only eight states had developed separate commissions
devoted full time to the labor of securities analysis, investigation, and regulation. In forty states, administration usually
rested with overburdened, underpaid, and often unspecialized
agencies, including bank superintendents, railroad commissions, secretaries of state, attorneys general, state auditors,
insurance commissions, bank examiners, or general license
directors. Many administrators, inexpert in their task, con-

---

12. Robert P. Lamont, President Hoover's Secretary of Commerce,
summarized the decade's convictions when, before the stock market
crash, he told representatives of the stricken anthracite coal industry:
"It seems to me the difficulty should be worked out within the industry itself. I happen to know one or two of the leaders in it—they
are sound, able and fair men who should be able to find a solution.
I don't see how the Government can do very much." Near the nadir
of the depression, Lamont expressed the belief that "the principle of
allowing every industry to regulate itself is still worth trying a little
longer. . . . This should be done by each industry working through
some organization of its own,—without Government interference"
(Robert P. Lamont to Jackson E. Reynolds, July 10, 1929, and
Lamont to John S. Crout, May 27, 1931, CDR, Boxes 3, 10). See
also Albert U. Romasco, *The Poverty of Abundance: Hoover, the
Nation, the Depression,* pp. 10–23 and passim; Ellis W. Hawley,
"Hoover and the Bituminous Coal Problem," *Business History Review*
42 (Autumn 1968): 247–70; George Soule, *Prosperity Decade: From
War to Depression, 1917–1929,* pp. 132–46; Robert Sobel, *The Great
Bull Market: Wall Street in the 1920s,* pp. 49–58, 113–28.

tinued to be short-term political appointees who rotated in and out of office without developing a coherent, sustained policy. As one critic of the situation remarked: "Any commissioner or examiner who can intelligently pass on the soundness of all the security offerings in any of our great financial centers must be a man of extraordinary capacity, and it is too much to expect that such a man will be available in all the forty-eight states, or perhaps even in any one of them."[13]

The greatest regulatory defect, from the standpoint of some state administrators, remained large interstate flotations, either of a fraudulent or a legitimate nature. Through the use of the mails, the telephone, or the telegraph, it was possible to conclude sales contracts in New York or New Jersey and circumvent the registration-license requirements of other states. Early in its existence, the IBA, despite sympathy for regulation of fraudulent issues, told its members that they could feel safe in "ignoring the laws, for the purpose of making offerings by mail, and . . . it would be well . . . to close all transactions . . . outside the blue sky state." In this spirit, fostered partly by the association, evasion became a well-developed art, practiced not only by reputable firms but also by the less reputable.[14]

In addition, a few reform-minded state administrators became justifiably alarmed over the burgeoning number of exemptions granted to corporations listed on exchanges or subject to the jurisdiction of other state regulatory agencies. A state utilities commission, for example, might supervise the rates and financing of local operating companies, but both the utilities commission and the state securities commission had little or no control over the growing network of interstate

13. Breed, "Public Regulation," pp. 186–96; Ashby, *The Economic Effects of Blue Sky Laws,* p. 45; Watson Washburn, "Anti-Fraud Legislation," *Michigan Law Review* 31 (April 1933): 771. There were, of course, exceptions to this generalization, particularly in states such as Wisconsin, Michigan, and Illinois. But competent administrative personnel remained a vexing problem which even irritated the bankers. See IBA, *Proceedings* (1931), p. 181.

14. IBA, *Proceedings* (1915), p. 118.

holding companies, construction combines, management firms, and investment trusts whose remote policies often dictated the financial structure of operating companies. The market crash also demonstrated the folly of granting exemptions to corporations listed on stock exchanges. Enterprises controlled by Samuel Insull and Ivar Kreuger provided clear proof, said one member of Wisconsin's commission, "that [exchange] listing in many . . . cases was for the purpose of avoiding [state] regulation."[15]

The market crash and depression led states to jettison regulatory devices encouraged by the IBA. State after state, following 1929, revised its statutes and rulings in the direction of more stringent registration requirements and fewer exemptions. The temper of state legislatures, Arthur Davis ruefully told the association in 1931, "has been a little more critical, a bit more antagonistic, than I ever have noted before. . . . There has been some tendency toward paternalism and regulation for the sake of regulation." The association fell into despair as even conservative states such as Massachusetts tightened up registration requirements. The IBA's state uniformity crusade collapsed under the weight of depression-inspired statutory amendments and administrative revisions. "No one with any certainty can tell what the . . . laws are going to be," Davis complained. "This matter is in a state of flux. . . . You can go right down the list and you will find there are [now] many different types of laws. No one can tell whether or not this type works or that type works." The association proposed several artificial programs: an impartial investigation of all

15. For a cogent analysis of the problems that plagued Wisconsin's commission, by all accounts one of the more aggressive, see David Lilienthal to Felix Frankfurter, February 9, 1933, Roll 8, FFPH. For the complaints of other commissions see Olga M. Steig, "What Can the Regulatory Securities Act Accomplish," *Michigan Law Review* 31 (April 1933): 780–82; National Association of Securities Commissioners, *Proceedings* (1931), p. 163; Hans J. Klapbrunn, "Regulation of Interstate Security Sales," *University of Chicago Law Review* 1 (May 1933): 88–90; Mitchell Dawson, "Blue Sky Blues," *American Mercury* 25 (March 1932): 353–61.

state laws combined with further attempts at promoting uniformity. It spurned new federal legislation and called instead
for larger appropriations and more vigorous action by the
Post Office Department to curb security frauds.[16]

The IBA, its corporate clients, and the stock exchanges had
assumed a heavy burden of managerial and moral responsibility for the national securities industry during the 1920s.
They had sought and secured a large measure of self-regulation through statutory and administrative exemptions on the
state level. This responsibility, prior to 1929, did not exceed
their pretensions, but it was incommensurate with their organizational development and with their fund of economic intelligence. When combined with the defects of formal, public regulation which they, too, had fostered, the internal weakness of
these private groups contributed to the speculative boom and
retarded their capacity to govern a vital area of the economy.
During the course of the decade, conservative members of the
financial elite, in addition to the more radical critics of investment banking, had perceived the breakdown of self-regulation.
It was both an institutional and an intellectual crisis; the IBA
and the New York Stock Exchange were at the center of the
crisis.

Members of the IBA, the nation's most knowledgeable financial association, were often unaware of how various parts
of the investment system operated, ignorant of their own particular function, and ill-prepared to analyze the relationship
between functions. This situation arose from the rapid transformation of the investment banking business in the years
before 1929 and, above all, from the new forms of property
that investment bankers were called upon to evaluate and
manage. Although equity securities, in the form of common
and preferred stock, made their appearance before the 1920s,
that decade witnessed a sudden increase in their use as financial
and strategic weapons by industrial and public utility com-

16. IBA, *Proceedings* (1929), p. 147; ibid. (1930), pp. 40–41; ibid.
(1931), pp. 177–80; ibid. (1932), pp. 156–57.

panies. These new forms of property, when combined with the equities of investment trusts and holding companies plus the centrality of stock exchanges, altered the investment banker's function. At the same time, in the opinion of some IBA members and numerous critics, many investment bankers had neither the technical resources nor judgment to serve as competent managers of the new property.[17]

The IBA's Business Conduct Committee, reporting shortly before the market crash, illuminated the basic problem of many members. The committee marked 1927 as the end of an era in which corporations financed their operations mostly by bond issues and commercial bank loans. The work of the average investment banker had centered previously upon the buying and selling of fixed obligations "judged largely according to the proportion of the obligations to the [real] property owned." Massive equity financing created a different environment. Investment firms that two years before would not deal in securities other than mortgage-secured bonds were bewildered by the new property. Even the largest investment houses, after developing nationwide branch offices staffed by personnel trained to sell bonds, found their organizations obsolete. Association members, accustomed "to look carefully at the intrinsic value of properties and to have their buying . . . on a safe margin against these values," discovered they now needed

---

17. On the nature and impact of the new property see Adolph A. Berle and Gardiner C. Means, *The Modern Corporation and Private Property,* pp. 62–77, 280–97, and passim; William Z. Ripley, *Main Street and Wall Street,* pp. 16, 83, 86–87, 131; Arthur S. Dewing, *Corporation Securities,* pp. 125, 136–37, 237; Dewing, *Corporation Finance,* rev. ed., passim; Gardiner C. Means, "The Diffusion of Stock Ownership in the United States," *Quarterly Journal of Economics* 44 (August 1930): 561–600; Sobel, *The Great Bull Market,* pp. 88–95. The same situation plagued commercial banking, but here, because of greater numbers and geographical dispersion, the incidence of financial ignorance reached even greater proportions. See, for example, American Institute of Banking, *Bulletin* 12 (July 1930): 283; New Mexico Bankers Association, *Proceedings* (1930), pp. 63–65; Michigan Bankers Association, *Proceedings* (1931), pp. 80–99.

new data on management and projected earning power rather than on real property and tangible values. Numerous members, the committee warned, "will have to alter the entire current of their thinking."[18]

A serious information lag, according to the Business Conduct Committee, harried the association and its members. "Even the houses which pretend to supply good information are apt to have only a general idea on a large part of the market and to specialize in their detailed knowledge in a few companies." With 1,450 issues traded on the New York Stock Exchange alone, the committee noted, "it is obviously impossible for any ordinary house to give even superficial information.... The average house has none too much money to spend on statistical departments." Bewildered IBA members tended to agree with the committee's shocking analysis. Confessions of incompetence reached indecent proportions prior to the market debacle. "We, here, and our customers," said one member, "are groping around to find out what our equities are worth.... There is no yardstick at all for us to go by." Another member, who did not relish the admission "that we are all ignorant," nevertheless felt certain "we are all quite densely ignorant of our own business . . . we have been 'chasing rainbows' and looking for Santa Claus instead of for facts."[19]

The IBA's organizational and intellectual crisis was of long standing, although it appeared to have arisen suddenly in the fall of 1929. Through the decade, despite presidential rhetoric extolling the association's professional sagacity, individual members and committees remarked on the weaknesses of the IBA. These were weaknesses of internal organization and self-regulation which the association did not begin to overcome before 1929. "Strange as it may seem," the IBA's Industrial Securities Committee reported two years before the crash, "some organizations selling securities do not understand the real points of variation between different types of audits, yet

18. IBA, *Proceedings* (1929), pp. 182–87, 197, 201.
19. Ibid., p. 201.

because of the complexities of industrial earnings, it is most necessary." But with regard to improving the quality of audits contained in circulars and prospectuses, the same committee announced it would "follow tendencies rather than . . . exercise any arbitrary power. . . . No one . . . [in the association] desires to assume exacting labors of this kind."[20]

The failure of the association to insist upon intelligible income statements and balance sheets in circulars had been a long-standing grievance of some members. As early as 1920 a special committee headed by the eminent Harold Stanley revealed the need for reform. Stanley decried the lack of consistent information in prospectuses. It appeared to his committee that the material contained in most circulars had been determined "by what the companies gave out or by the facts that would especially appeal to investors, rather than . . . in accordance with a schedule of required information." This situation should not be allowed to continue, the committee warned, because "in some cases the distributing banker knows no more about the issue than does his customer." Stanley noted that some of the largest corporations objected to disclosing full information even when urged to do so by the IBA members. Prophetically, he suggested the possible consequences of such timidity: "Unless the bankers who sell the highest grade of securities give at least such information as an intelligent investor requires . . . the demand for this information may lead to a national registration plan of some kind which will oblige companies, issuing securities, to put on public record information probably in greater detail than bankers or investors would ordinarily require."[21]

20. IBA, *Proceedings* (1927), pp. 48–51, 146–47.

21. The Stanley committee compiled a devastating critique of the disclosure policies of IBA members and their clients. In the case of utility offerings, the committee found "it is exceptional to have a balance sheet included" in the prospectus. Income statements of all companies fared little better. The committee noted: "It is frequently the practice to give average earning over a period of years without showing the fluctuations which make up this average." Information on the distribution of dividends and depreciation policy were usually absent. See IBA, *Proceedings* (1920), pp. 161–65.

Reforms came grudgingly, when they came at all. The IBA's Public Service Securities Committee expressed regret in 1923 that "adequate financial information . . . is not yet being released." This committee submitted a model circular for all public utility holding company issues which included: consolidated balance sheets and income statements for all subsidiary companies, covering earnings, expenses, maintenance expenditures and reserves, fixed charges, dividend record, assets, and capitalization. A year later, the same committee noted that some members had taken the recommendations seriously. "It is equally apparent from the offerings of other houses that either the recommendations . . . have not been brought to their attention or that they have not carefully studied the principles defined therein." Throughout the decade, IBA committees filed wholesome reports on the need for accurate, uniform disclosure. These same committees compiled model circulars, urged their immediate adoption by members, and bemoaned noncompliance. A laissez-faire attitude characterized enforcement of the recommendations. After drafting one model circular, the Industrial Securities Committee decided to send a copy to all members with the intention of promoting "a general, if gradual, improvement in the . . . circulars presented to investors." The word "police," said IBA President Henry Hayes, "is an unsavory one." Neither the board of governors nor individual committees, he assured the membership, would ever attempt "to regulate unduly our private business."[22]

Pious declarations and subsequent inaction continued even

22. The Industrial Securities Committee, following a further study of circulars in 1928, found that statements of earnings "have been a trifle ambiguous not to say misleading." Voting rights were seldom set forth. Balance sheets were usually obsolete at the time of publication. Identical depreciation charges were subject to wide latitude in treatment. This committee announced a policy of future meetings with the American Institute of Accountants. "It is not presupposed that this will entail very many occasions for action," the committee said, "but . . . such contact will be of benefit to the Association." See IBA, *Proceedings* (1925), p. 278; ibid. (1926), pp. 260–61; ibid. (1928), pp. 86–87, 91–95.

though the economy became further entangled in the new property. While deploring the fact that many investment trusts did not segregate real income from trading profits, the Investment Companies Committee declared it would resist "any legislation which will provide a form or standard which unreliable managements may comply with and thereby use as a cloak to gain public confidence." Lamentations and angry accusations became more pronounced after the market crash. The Public Service Securities Committee, noting that compliance with its recommendations had not improved, blamed the secrecy of holding company managers. In a futile gesture, it urged members to boycott such companies. The stock market debacle, according to the Industrial Securities Committee, should teach members to be "fully informed as to the use to which . . . money is to be put," but the same committee noted that only a few circulars then under review divided fixed assets into intelligible categories. Even fewer segregated inventories or liabilities, and, in a number of cases, no balance sheet was included in the circular. Despite annual IBA pronouncements, meaningful coordination with the American Institute of Accountants remained on a rhetorical level.[23]

The Investment Bankers Association, reluctant to coerce either members or clients, proved to be an ineffective mechanism for self-regulation of the national securities market. Unable to provide full disclosure for customers, IBA members were themselves often untutored, perplexed servants of the new property. Claiming financial omniscience, the association became a victim of its own flatulent oratory because good intentions could not disguise forever an attenuated enforcement program.

Stock exchanges were the only other private associations with sufficient expertise, influence, and organization necessary to perform regulatory functions. Unlike the Investment Bankers Association, the exchanges, above all the New York Stock Exchange, had never encouraged even minimal regulation of

23. IBA, *Proceedings* (1930), p. 156; ibid. (1931), pp. 147–51; ibid. (1932), p. 233.

their activities by the state or the federal government. An abortive attempt was made in 1914, following the Pujo investigation, to bring about such regulation. This legislation, written by Samuel Untermeyer, the Pujo counsel, and supported by Senator Robert Owen, proposed to give exchanges two options: they could voluntarily incorporate under state laws, or they could submit to the jurisdiction of the Post Office Department under penalty of losing use of the mails for their quotations. If they elected the second alternative, the exchanges would have to revise their charters and bylaws to meet certain federal standards. These standards included comprehensive listing requirements for securities traded on the exchanges; a minimum 20 percent margin for all transactions; limitations upon the practice of hypothecating customers' securities for short selling operations; and disclosure of all trading by directors and officers of listed corporations.[24]

Proponents of the legislation were not inspired by radicalism or animus toward the exchanges. Untermeyer, a caustic critic during the Pujo investigation, said he had no patience with "agitators, demagogues, and ignoramuses . . . who regard the [New York Stock] Exchange as a sort of gambling den . . . whose activities should be suppressed." For him, the New York Exchange was "a wholesome public necessity." The bill did not propose continuous administrative supervision of the exchanges by the federal government. Once the postmaster general had approved new charters and bylaws, the exchanges themselves would enforce federal standards. Despite the bill's moderation, spokesmen for the exchanges characterized it as an attempt to drive the business of buying and selling securities "out into the street." President Wilson, who did not grasp the details of the bill, refused to add it to his legislative agenda. Senator Owen, presiding over a rump meeting of the Banking and Currency Committee, secured a favorable vote, but he

24. Senate Banking and Currency Committee, *Regulation of the Stock Exchanges* (63d Cong., 2d sess., 1914), pp. 555–64; *Congressional Record,* 63d Cong., 2d sess., 51, p. 1498; *New York Times,* January 20, 23, 1914; *Wall Street Journal,* January 20, 1914.

could not overcome the parliamentary tactics of the Democratic majority leader, Gilbert Hitchcock, once the bill reached the full Senate. Hitchcock, who said the measure violated the First Amendment, mustered enough votes to have it recommitted to committee. He also quashed the favorable committee report. The bill did not rise to the surface again.[25]

Given the broad exemptions granted during the 1920s by states to securities listed on exchanges, it was vital that these institutions provide not only a marketplace for the new property, but also a mechanism for its analysis and prudent management. Unfortunately, the values of the marketplace were dominant until after 1929. Only then did the exchanges embark upon limited programs of reform and reorganization. The exchanges were reluctant to enforce standards of disclosure upon listed companies for fear of losing securities to other exchanges or to over-the-counter markets. This reluctance led the New York Stock Exchange to follow a policy of ad hoc reform, suitable for coping with separate crises but ill-adapted to the high regulatory responsibilities generously delegated to it by the individual states.

E. H. H. Simmons, president of the New York Stock Exchange, often elucidated that institution's philosophy of regulation. At the heart of the problem, as Simmons saw it, were charter-mongering state legislatures which wrote shameless incorporation statutes and then expected the New York Stock Exchange to control the mischievous progeny. Many corporations were listed on the New York Exchange, but it was not the Exchange's function to impose national standards of financial disclosure through its listing requirements. Some companies listed on the Exchange reported earnings annually; others reported semiannually. According to Simmons it was

25. Samuel Untermeyer, "Speculation on the Stock Exchanges and Public Regulation of the Exchanges," *American Economic Review* 5 (March 1915): 25, 50–51, 58–61; *Wall Street Journal,* January 20, 1914; *New York Times,* March 21, June 4, 26, 1914; Senate, *Regulation of the Stock Exchanges,* pp. 458–520; *Congressional Record,* 63d Cong., 2d sess., 51, pp. 11075, 11116–17, 11166–72.

impossible for the New York Stock Exchange "to verify . . . the accuracy of the statements made to it in the listing application," and even if it were possible, the Exchange should not undertake the task. "The New York Stock Exchange," he said, "is a private organization, and as such is not a suitable means for the performance of an obviously public function. . . . It is by no means equipped to undertake any policy of controlling American corporate practice." Who, then, should perform these public functions? Simmons believed the matter could best be handled by local better business bureaus and by righteous enforcement of antifraud laws.[26]

The New York Stock Exchange, like the IBA, failed to maintain control over the new property. As a few critics at the time recognized, the market crash did not occur from greed alone or only because predatory individuals exploited ignorant investors. The crash occurred, in part, because institutions, including the Investment Bankers Association and the New York Stock Exchange, lacked the will, the ability, and the administrative apparatus necessary to regulate greedy and predatory individuals. In 1917, stock issues constituted less than one-third of all listings on the New York Stock Exchange. By 1926 stock issues had risen to 43 percent of all listings. In that same year, the total value of equity shares listed exceeded the total value of listed bonds. "The fact that securities representing business equities should have so rapidly overtaken in their aggregate value the securities representing corporate indebtedness," the Exchange reported, "is an interesting indication of the continuing business prosperity of this country." It was also an indication of the new burden placed upon the Exchange's antiquated regulatory machinery. In 1926 the Exchange's eight-man listing committee approved 300 new stock applica-

26. E. H. H. Simmons, *Listing Securities on the New York Stock Exchange,* New York, March 23, 1926, pp. 12–23; Simmons, *Security Frauds: A National Business Liability,* New York, September 20, 1927, pp. 14–15; Simmons, *Security Frauds and Business Prosperity,* New York, November 2, 1927, pp. 3–11; Simmons, *Security Swindling: Its Menace and Its Cure,* New York, February 24, 1925, pp. 10–15.

tions. This figure rose to 571 new applications in 1928 and 759 new applications in the first nine months of 1929. Even the Exchange was forced to admit a "strain" upon its small investigative staff. In a masterpiece of understatement, the Committee on Listing noted that "the situation [is] rendered all the more complex and difficult to analyze because of the sudden creation of many and large security holding companies and investment trusts." Nevertheless, the listing committee continued to approve an increasing volume of securities for trading after cursory examination. Between 1925 and 1929 the Exchange, deluged by new offerings, faced an organizational crisis sufficient to overwhelm the most efficient and aggressive administrative body. Regrettably, the Exchange was neither.[27]

In 1923 only one-fourth of the corporations listed on the New York Stock Exchange filed quarterly earning statements. This figure had risen to barely one-half by 1933. In the latter year, 308 listed companies continued to report annually, although the Exchange had urged the virtue of semiannual statements since 1927. If the frequency of reports varied widely, the content of reports was equally diverse. Recommendations by the listing committee were never retroactive. Lawrence Sloan of Standard Statistics noted in 1927 that 57 percent of the listed corporations failed to report either gross income or gross sales. Depreciation policy was usually not included; reserves were lumped together; inventory figures were recorded without stating the method of valuation or the nature of the goods carried; earned and capital surplus were usually combined in one figure.[28]

Beginning in 1929, the New York Stock Exchange attempted to improve its disclosure policy and regulatory posture. The Exchange included in new listing applications a provision forbidding the treatment of stock dividends as earned income;

27. New York Stock Exchange, *Report of the President* (1925–26), p. 5; ibid. (1926–27), pp. 18, 56; ibid. (1927–28), p. 25; ibid. (1929–30), pp. 5, 64.
28. Lawrence H. Sloan, *Corporate Profits: A Study of Their Size, Variation, Use and Distribution in a Period of Prosperity*, p. 62.

required companies to disclose indirect and direct holdings in unconsolidated subsidiaries; and called for either consolidated earning statements or separate statements from all subsidiaries indicating intercompany profits. The majority of listed companies, however, was not bound by these salubrious innovations. Informally, the New York Stock Exchange attempted to encourage other reforms. Companies were urged to desist from the practice of constantly revising depreciation charges in relation to earnings and from writing off unamortized bond discounts and expenses against capital surplus in order to avoid embarrassing charges against income. Following the IBA, the New York Stock Exchange began consultations with the American Institute of Accountants. The recommendations of their joint committee did not receive approval from the Exchange until October 1933. By that time, initiative had passed to the federal government and new efforts had begun in the search for securities regulation national in impact, continuous in application, and expert in administration.[29]

But new regulation, demanding only honesty and fair play from individual investment bankers, stock exchange members, and corporations, would not be sufficient. Organizational debility, as well as moral fraility, was a major weakness of American capitalism. This was apparent in the area of state securities legislation and administration where confused, fragmentary efforts by public governments and by private associations had become the rule rather than the exception. The Roosevelt administration would have to surmount this legacy of failure by creating fresh institutional arrangements and by infusing old organizations with new vitality and direction.

29. Frank P. Smith, "Accounting Requirements of Stock Exchanges, 1933," *Accounting Review* 12 (June 1937): 145–53; Alfred L. Bernheim and Margaret G. Schneider, eds., *The Security Market,* pp. 584–609.

3

Foundations of National Control

The principal architects and supporters of the 1933 Federal Securities Act were political moderates who labored against the counselors of deliberate procrastination and the advocates of rash innovation. They struggled to arrest economic demoralization, to attack the most blatant abuses, and to prevent more drastic financial regulation. "I was a moderating influence among the draftsmen of the Securities Act," Felix Frankfurter, Harvard law professor and Franklin Roosevelt's first choice for solicitor general, explained. "An examination of the proposals before I was asked to enter the situation . . . and the one that passed . . . will leave no doubt in your mind of that." Congressman Sam Rayburn, chairman of the House Interstate Commerce Committee, urged his colleagues to pass the legislation and warned of the consequences if no action were taken: "When a people's faith is shaken in a business the business becomes halting and lame. . . . only one thing can follow in the wake of this destroyed confidence . . . the evils that attend socialism, bolshevism, and communism." Senator Duncan Fletcher, chairman of the Senate Banking and Currency Committee, said the measure had three purposes: "To prevent further exploitation of the public . . . to protect honest enterprise, seeking capital against the competition afforded by questionable securities [and] to restore confidence . . . in sound securities.[1]

1. Felix Frankfurter to Henry L. Stimson, February 20, 1934, HLSP, Box 324; *Congressional Record,* 73d Cong., 1st sess., 77, pp. 2919, 2983.

The winter of 1932–33 had been a crisis for American capitalism and for the transient forms of property that dominated industrial organization in the United States. At its nadir, the depression threatened to destroy public veneration for the institutions of America's paper economy and for the paper itself. "The word 'securities' had almost become obsolete," wrote Frank A. Vanderlip, former president of the National City Bank of New York. "The page of stock-and-bond quotations might well be headed Quotations of Risks and Hazards. To call them securities . . . is ironical. . . . Isn't it about time that we began thoughtfully to examine some of the fundamentals of our . . . investment theories and methods?" Gardiner C. Means, the distinguished economist, noted that more than half of the wealth of the United States was represented by stocks, bonds, warrants, debentures, notes, and mortgages. "An intangible form of wealth represented by pieces of paper," he said, "has thus been replacing tangible forms." Corporate securities alone amounted to more than $160 million. In order to place the buyer of securities on a par with the buyer of horses and second-hand cars," Means concluded, "it is . . . necessary that he have access to the relevant information. And recent events have shown that only compulsion can insure his receiving it."[2]

For the new president, securities regulation was as much a question of morality as one of economics or rational financial control. Legislation was only required, Roosevelt believed, "when evils are not eradicated by people in the business in which the evil exists." He often told the apocryphal story of a small village in New York State where 110 out of 125 families, all wage earners, met misfortune in the stock market. One hundred and nine families lost their savings, and half of them lost their homes or their dining room furniture. He blamed the New York Stock Exchange and investment bankers for these personal disasters. In Albany and Columbus, during the campaign, Roosevelt called for federal legislation "to inspire truth

2. Frank A. Vanderlip, "What about the Banks?" *Saturday Evening Post,* November 5, 1932, pp. 3–4; *New York Times,* April 9, 1933.

telling" in the marketing of securities, to regulate holding companies that sold securities in interstate commerce, and to supervise stock exchanges.[3]

Following the election, Roosevelt gave the task of formulating securities legislation to Samuel Untermeyer, the venerable and still zealous Pujo investigator. Untemeyer, who had attempted for two decades to secure public regulation of the New York Stock Exchange, readily accepted the task. In Raymond Moley's opinion, this Don Quixote of financial regulation "had more knowledge and more constructive ideas about reform than anyone else." Moley's faith was misplaced. Untermeyer spent most of his time attempting to secure the position of chief counsel to the Senate Banking and Currency Committee. The committee, under Florida's aging Senator Fletcher, was prepared to open the most sensational phase of its long inquiry into the financial misconduct of American entrepreneurs. Untermeyer hoped to repeat his Pujo performance. Forensics, not legislative draftsmanship, remained his forte. By the second week of March 1933, Untermeyer had produced nothing more than a modified version of his 1914 proposal to regulate stock exchanges through the Post Office Department. Even Roosevelt and Moley, who did not pretend to be experts in this field, thought it unwise to assign the postal bureaucracy important regulatory functions. Roosevelt, unwilling to offend so famous a progressive, allowed Untermeyer to continue reworking his stock exchange bill. For more salient and immediate legislation, however, FDR turned to Daniel Calhoun Roper, the bucolic South Carolinian, who headed the Department of Commerce. Roper delegated the work to two middle-level administrators in his department, Walter Miller, head of the Foreign Service Division, and Ollie M. Butler, a departmental attorney. Then, on March 13, Roper asked for additional assistance from Huston Thompson, the former chairman of the Federal Trade Commission.[4]

3. FDR to Fred I. Kent, March 27, 1934, PPF 744 FDRP; Raymond Moley, *The First New Deal*, p. 307.

4. Moley, *First New Deal*, pp. 308–11; Arthur M. Schlesinger, Jr., *The Coming of the New Deal*, p. 440; Huston Thompson, Diary,

Thompson, a courtly Westerner, was an old Wilsonian Democrat with a states-rights bias, antipathy for large-scale governmental or business organizations, and a passionate belief in legislation as the automatic governor of economic conduct. Fifty-eight years old in 1933, Thompson had served his apprenticeship in the political wastelands of Colorado as assistant attorney general from 1907 to 1909. Named by Wilson as assistant attorney general of the United States in 1913, he held that post until 1918 when the president appointed him to a seven-year term on the Federal Trade Commission. He served as chairman from 1920 to 1921 and again from 1923 to 1924.

Thompson's political outlook had hardened in the ideological molds cast by a rural, provincial Democrat party under William Jennings Bryan and Wilson. In addition, he had been touched by Louis Brandeis's more sophisticated, yet basically provincial, attitude about economic and social organization. Both viewpoints found expression in the securities legislation he helped to draft for the Capital Issues Committee in 1919. At that time Thompson had opposed federal incorporation as a solution to the problem of securities regulation because this method would involve a large staff of federal employees and because it would conflict with the jurisdiction of individual states. Thompson's draft of the Capital Issues Committee bill required prior registration for all securities sold in interstate commerce and created a special bureau within the Treasury Department to act as a record-keeping depository. But actual administration of the statute fell to the states. Federal officials would play a residual role to state commissions.

Thompson abhorred big business as much as he abhorred big government. "From every part of our land," he told a group of Southern lawyers in 1926, "there is a demand that the Federal Government shall assume more control, and individuals and groups are surrendering their rights and thrusting them into the hands of those at Washington . . . until we have an

---

March 13, 1933, HTP, Box 1. A copy of the revised Untermeyer bill may be found in the JMLPH, *SEC,* II.

army of federal employees that is staggering in its size." Some
businessmen encouraged this trend, Thompson said, but they
were representative of "special privilege . . . clamoring, now
that it has built up its great monopolies, for Government to assume control and direction of the business of the industrial
life." In order to reverse this trend, he urged relentless application of the Sherman Antitrust Act, "the greatest law . . . that
has ever been enacted." The Sherman Act, properly enforced,
would foster more business competition and preserve entrepreneurial freedom. The expansion of bureaucratic organizations
in government and business alarmed Thompson as it did other
Americans. Like Brandeis, he feared the erosion of economic
individualism, which he associated with personal morality,
dignity, and initiative. "It must be obvious," Thompson said,
"that when one hundred individual competing corporations are
absorbed into one great combination . . . there are many less
chances open to our children in the business world to become
the heads of individual units." The children of America should
not be doomed to hold "subordinate positions and be satisfied
underlings in the business and professional world."[5]

Miller and Butler prepared the first draft of possible legislation. Thompson studied the measure for several days, con-
sulted Charles Hamlin of the Federal Reserve Board, Oliver
Sweet, director of finance for the Interstate Commerce Commission, and even Justice Brandeis. He presented the proposed
bill to FDR, Moley, Roper, and economist Charles Taussig on
March 19. Roosevelt criticized the length and detail of the
draft and specifically asked the removal of "that part of the bill
permitting the [Federal Trade] Commission to refuse directly
the sale of foreign government securities." They all agreed to

5. Huston Thompson, "Regulation of the Sale of Securities in
Interstate Commerce," *American Bar Association Journal* 9 (March
1932): 157, 184; Thompson, "The Meaning of Public Welfare," North
Carolina Bar Association, *Reports* 28 (1926): 154–68; Thompson, "International Trade Commission," *American Bar Association Journal* 8
(1922): 509–10. For a perceptive discussion of Brandeis see Richard
Abrams's introduction to Louis D. Brandeis, *Other People's Money*,
pp. vii–xliv.

keep the bill separate from Untermeyer's project. The Coloradan made the necessary revisions overnight, and FDR quickly accepted the final draft. Thompson showed the measure to congressional leaders, and Roosevelt told the press on March 21 that securities legislation would soon be introduced.[6]

Moley, the following week, wrote FDR's special message to Congress. The President recommended legislation for federal supervision of traffic in investment securities. The federal government could not "and should not take any action which might be construed as approving or guaranteeing that newly issued securities are sound in the sense that their value will be maintained or that the properties which they represent will earn a profit." But the federal government must insist that "every issue of new securities . . . be accompanied by full publicity and information and that no essentially important element attending the issue shall be concealed from the buying public." Such legislation, the message concluded, "should give impetus to honest dealing . . . and thereby bring back public confidence."[7]

Roosevelt's message received a warm response in some financial circles. The market crash and depression had convinced many ardent free-enterprisers that something should be done to dispel popular outrage and to prevent future catastrophes. "Such legislation, obviously, is in the interest of the commonweal," said *Financial Age,* "and will go a long way to prevent the plundering of the public. . . . The sooner this legislation is on the books the better." The *Wall Street Journal,* after a hasty analysis of the bill, concluded that "The . . . measure is in the main so right in its basic provisions . . . the country will insist upon its passage."[8]

Unfortunately, the legislation which everyone eagerly endorsed was a jerry-built structure. Thompson's bill, approved

6. Thompson, Diary, March 19, 20, 21, 1933, HTP; *Wall Street Journal,* March 24, 1933.

7. *Congressional Record,* 73d Cong., 1st sess., 77, p. 937.

8. *Financial Age* 67 (April 1, 1933): 250; *Wall Street Journal,* March 31, 1933.

by FDR and sponsored initially by Rayburn and Senator Henry
Ashurst of Arizona, reflected the confusion that had bedeviled
securities legislation since the progressive period. The Thompson
claimed many ancestors for the bill, including the abortive
Taylor and Denison proposals of 1919–22, the Martin Fraud
Act of New York, the Uniform Sale of Securities Act, the
British Companies Act, and the French Securities Act. He
neglected to add that the bill bore some resemblance to many
state laws. "You see," he told Rayburn's committee, "we have
a number of precedents . . . that have had approval of high
authority." But the bill's diverse lineage proved to be its greatest defect.[9]

Basically, the Thompson bill was a disclosure statute, designed to prevent the interstate sale of securities not previously
registered with the Federal Trade Commission. In this respect,
the proposal followed the earlier Taylor bill, many state laws,
the British Companies Act, and the Uniform Act in favoring
a preventive rather than a punitive method of regulation. But
the Thompson bill, unlike the Uniform Act and many state
laws, closed significant loopholes. Stock exchange listing would
not exempt securities from registration, nor would regulation
by state public utility commissions. Corporations with a history of earnings and reliable debt service on senior securities
were not exempt from registering future issues. In addition to
the registration mechanism, however, the Thompson bill contained an antifraud provision similar to the Martin Act (section 13) and brought federal enforcement behind existing state
regulations as provided for in the old Denison bill (section 14).[10]

9. House Interstate Commerce Committee, *Federal Securities Act*
(73d Cong., 1st sess., 1933), p. 11.

10. Section 13 of the Thompson bill provided: "That it shall be
unlawful for any person, firm, corporation, or other entity in any interstate sale . . . of any security . . . willfully to employ any device,
scheme or artifice to defraud. . . . Whenever it shall appear to the
[Federal Trade] Commission that the practices investigated constitute
a fraud or an attempt to defraud . . . it shall transmit such evidence
. . . to the Attorney General, who may in his discretion bring action

Registration constituted the heart of the bill. By requiring the filing of information relative to a corporation and its securities before issue, the Thompson measure sought to prevent fraudulent transactions rather than punish fraud after the fact. The registration statement, signed by the corporation's executive officers and directors, required several classes of information. These data did not exceed in breadth or detail the material required under the proposed uniform state act: the capitalization of the issuer, including authorized and paid-up amounts of capital stock; a description of the voting rights, preferences, and dividend rights of each class of capital stock; the amount of funded debt; a current balance sheet; an income statement covering the preceding fiscal year; the name of the underwriting syndicate; the public offering price per share and the net amount returnable to capital investment; the purposes for which the proceeds of the issue were to be used; and the amount of all commissions and other remunerations paid to the corporation or the underwriting syndicate. In addition to the formal registration statement, all securities sold in interstate commerce were to be accompanied by a prospectus containing information similar to that contained in the registration statement.[11]

Thompson's legislation, in order to encourage complete and accurate disclosure in the registration statement, provided for

---

. . . to enjoin the continuance of such practices or transactions." Section 14 provided: "That is shall be unlawful . . . to carry or cause to be carried . . . in interstate commerce . . . any offer to sell . . . in any State . . . where at that time it is unlawful to sell . . . such security or securities." For the text of Thompson's bill (H. R. 4314 and S. 875) see House Interstate Commerce Committee, *Federal Securities Act,* pp. 1–9, or Senate Banking and Currency Committee, *Securities Act* (73d Cong., 1st sess., 1933), pp. 1–9. Also see Thompson's analysis of the bill in the *Congressional Record,* 73d Cong., 1st sess., 77, p. 938. Cf. text of Uniform Act, National Conference of Commissioners on Uniform State Laws, *Handbook and Proceedings* (1930), pp. 235–66.

11. House, *Federal Securities Act,* pp. 3, 51.

both civil remedies by individual purchasers and revocation of registration by the Federal Trade Commission. Section 9 provided that

> every person acquiring any securities specified in such [registration] statements . . . shall be presumed to rely upon the representations set forth in the said statement. In case any such statement shall be false in any material respect, any person acquiring any security to which such statement relates, either from the original issuer or from any other person, shall have the right to rescind the transaction and to obtain . . . any and all consideration given or paid for any such securities . . . either from any vendor knowing of such falsity or from the persons signing such statement. . . . Any persons acquiring any securities to which such statement relates shall also have the right to obtain damages . . . from any one or more of the signers of the statement in which such falsity occurs, or from any person who authorized the statement to be made.

Section 6 provided that

> the [Federal Trade] Commission may revoke the registration of any security by entering an order to that effect, if upon examination into the affairs of the issuer . . . it shall appear that any such issuer or person . . . had violated any of the provisions of this Act . . . has been or is engaged or is about to engage in fraudulent transactions . . . is in any other way dishonest . . . is not conducting its or their business in accordance with law . . . that its or their affairs are in unsound condition or insolvent . . . [or] that the enterprise or business of the issuer . . . is not based upon sound principles.[12]

The liability provisions were broader than the same provisions in the Uniform Act. The latter attached liability only to sellers, not to the corporation, officers, and directors. The revocation section, on the other hand, was copied verbatim

12. Ibid., pp. 5, 7.

from the Uniform Act. The sweeping grounds for revocation also followed the language in many state statutes and reflected their concern to protect investors from high-risk enterprises.

Although Thompson's bill granted substantial powers to the Federal Trade Commission on the matter of revocation and imposed heavy liabilities, the measure did not look in the direction of flexible administrative regulation. Thompson anticipated that the measure, like his ideal Sherman Act, would be largely self-enforcing. The bill's brevity, particularly in the area of the FTC's functions, reflected a belief in simple legislative palliatives rather than creative administration.[13]

For two weeks, Thompson and his colleagues defended their efforts before the House Interstate Commerce Committee and the Senate Banking and Currency Committee. Sections 9 and 6 came under withering attack in both committees. Thompson did not help the bill by demonstrating a shocking ignorance of its language. He insisted that the measure was concerned only with disclosure. "The Commission," he said, "is not going to pass upon whether the security itself is good or bad." Ollie Butler maintained that no attempt would be made to prevent the sale of speculative issues. House members found this difficult to believe after reading section 6. Rayburn thought the standards for revocation too vague. "If you were going to pass upon whether or not a man's business was based upon sound principles," he said, "you would want quite a corps of the ablest economists in the land to sit around you. . . . It is quite a hazard, is it not, realizing the personnel in the past of some of these Commissions?" Butler's only defense was that twenty-two states had revocation clauses in their statutes; ten states used exactly the same language; and thirteen states went further to authorize revocation for "bad business repute." Revocation, in Butler's opinion, was no worse than an injunction under the fraud laws.[14]

13. National Conference, *Handbook and Proceedings*, pp. 255–56, 262–63.

14. Senate, *Securities Act*, pp. 86, 241–51; House, *Federal Securities Act*, pp. 126, 136.

The liability section encountered even greater opposition. Senator Thomas Gore, the sixty-two-year-old former Populist, thought the absolute liability imposed upon directors by section 9 would "paralyze business entirely." Michigan's Senator James Couzens was of the same opinion. "You," he scolded Thompson, "as a director of General Motors could not investigate all their plants . . . you could not count all the automobiles, you could not value all their buildings . . . you could not check all their accounts receivable. . . . That is a thing that just cannot humanly be done." Representative James Parker said directors "cannot count every piece of steel and every machine." And, he added, "if this law was in effect I would resign as director from some of the companies I happen to be in."[15]

The fears of some congressmen were not chimerical. Many of the bill's more passionate advocates wanted the legislation to attack "big business" generally. Section 9, according to Butler, was based on the belief that there were "entirely too many directors." The curse of the present situation, he said, echoing Brandeis, "is the curse of bigness." Alexander Holtzoff, a special assistant to the attorney general, opposed any relaxation of directors' liability, as did Robert E. Healy, the FTC's acerbic chief counsel. "Who is going to suffer?" Healy asked. "The honest director, who made the statement, and whose corporation got the money, or the purchaser, who did not make any mistake, and lost his money? This bill will cause directors to act with a greater degree of care." Butler even objected to exempting from civil liability a director who "in good faith makes a misstatement. That would destroy the effect of the entire act." Professor William O. Douglas of the Yale Law School thought section 9 "doubtless will drive many directors out." But that, he said, "will be highly commendable."[16]

15. Senate, *Securities Act,* pp. 204, 210; House, *Federal Securities Act,* p. 122.

16. Representative Schuyler Merritt was the only committee member who agreed with Butler that "the fewer they [directors] are . . . the better it will be for them and for the country." See House, *Federal Securities Act,* pp. 117, 123–24, 246; Senate, *Securities Act,* p. 204; *New York Times,* April 9, 1933.

Thompson and Butler, near the conclusion of the House hearings, introduced amendments modifying section 6. The Federal Trade Commission would not automatically revoke registration if the issuer's affairs were in "unsound condition," or not based upon "sound principles." The other standards for revocation remained, however, and Butler even persuaded FDR to endorse the amended section. The Thompson group rejected suggestions for a "cooling-off period" between the time of registration and the time of sale. They agreed to exempt from registration all securities then outstanding and all commercial paper, but they refused to modify a comma or period in section 9.[17]

Although Thompson's bill dismayed some legislators, it horrified investment bankers and their legal advisers. Since the progressive period they had generally opposed all legislation involving prior registration and disclosure. Antifraud statutes had become their standard answer to the conundrum of regulation. By 1933, however, many investment bankers anticipated positive benefits from federal legislation, provided it met their demands. "Gentlemen," William Breed, counsel for the Investment Bankers Association, told Rayburn's committee, "we want a model law, a law that will be effective . . . and prevent the sale of bad securities." The IBA would welcome a federal law, Breed claimed, because "before an investment banker can offer any security for sale nationally he must qualify that security according to the terms of . . . 42 different state laws." If Congress enacted a model law which the states in turn adopted, Breed said, "think what it would mean to the investment banker. . . . It would help them in every particular."[18]

Breed and Frank Gordon, president of the IBA, explained the content of their model federal law. They recommended a

17. *New York Times,* April 4, 9, 1933; *Wall Street Journal,* April 4, 1933; Senate, *Securities Act,* p. 241; House, *Federal Securities Act,* pp. 50, 130, 221.

18. House, *Federal Securities Act,* p. 176; Senate, *Securities Act,* pp. 124–25.

national Martin Act to punish fraud. The Federal Trade Commission would "know who the crooks are. They [the FTC] will be able quickly to distinguish between spurious security and a good security." Breed's conception of regulation was naïve and terrifying: The Federal Trade Commission should have power "to go into a man's office . . . determine if there is anything fraudulent . . . sieze the books, walk straight up to the court, and on a simple affidavit, get an injunction against the security being issued." The IBA approach, of course, eliminated the necessity for registration.[19]

But the bankers modified their strategy when it became apparent that neither congressional committee would settle for a fraud law without registration. The IBA then began to concentrate its opposition against the liability and revocation sections. They hoped so to weaken these provisions that registration and disclosure would be meaningless. The strategy was excellent since sections 6 and 9 had already drawn condemnation from key committee members. The liability provisions of the Thompson bill, Breed said, would "open up more litigation by crooked and unprincipled people than any legislation you could pass." He predicted a "mass exodus" of directors if section 9 remained unchanged. "It is," he concluded, "a prescription with a lot of poison in it and a great injury to the public."[20]

Breed and other financial spokesmen urged the adoption of a liability section consistent with the common law and the British Companies Act. If Congress insisted upon a registration statute, Breed said, it should not contain a revocation section and the liability of directors should be "broadened so as to follow generally the English Act and also our own common law and the decisions of our courts." Directors would be liable, in other words, only for the exercise of diligence and good faith. Thompson's measure, according to Arthur Dean of Sullivan and Cromwell, was a "hopeless confusion of ill-assorted provisions." Congress should write new language and

19. House, *Federal Securities Act*, p. 169.
20. Senate, *Securities Act*, pp. 175–77; House, *Federal Securities Act*, p. 169.

follow the English model in respect to liability for the registration statement. Directors could then rely on the reports of accountants or engineers and "they [directors] are protected if they have reasonable grounds to believe that the statements . . . made were true."[21]

The bankers' legal technicians, despite rhetorical attachment to the British Companies Act and the common law, wanted something more. How much more was baldly revealed in a memorandum of amendments presented to Senator Fletcher. The IBA demanded elimination of section 6. Investor recision rights under section 9 were to be dropped. And the signers of the registration statement would not be liable for damages if they proved either.

> as regards any untrue statement purporting to be a statement of a public or chartered accountant, engineer, appraiser, lawyer, or other expert . . . such person had reasonable ground to believe that the person making such statement . . . was competent to make it and that it was obtained and accepted in good faith

or

21. Senate, *Securities Act,* pp. 151, 175; House, *Federal Securities Act,* p. 177. The British statute, amended in 1929, limited directors' liability for data contained in the registration statement to "due diligence." Furthermore, British investors were required to prove reliance upon the registration statement in damage suits. Many hostile lawyers and businessmen became hysterical over the Thompson bill because of its departure from these standards of British practice. Eustace Seligman, another member of the powerful Sullivan and Cromwell firm, thought the liability provisions were "revolutionary . . . and without precedent in Anglo-Saxon law." James Brown, president of the New York Chamber of Commerce, demanded that the section be revised "so that officers and directors . . . could rely on expert opinion and be relieved of liability when acting in good faith." Although the Thompson bill did exceed the liability provisions of the British law, most critics conveniently ignored the fact that the British statute was also a general incorporation law which imposed uniform national standards upon all English companies. See *New York Times,* April 1, 19, 1933; *Washington Post,* April 5, 1933.

> as regards any untrue statement not purporting to be
> made on authority of an expert . . . such person had
> reasonable ground to believe and did . . . believe that the
> statement was true.

Furthermore, no signer would be held liable for failure to disclose information in the registration statement if

> he proves that he in good faith exercised due diligence
> and was not cognizant of the matter not disclosed; or he
> proves that the failure to disclose such matters arose from
> an honest mistake . . . or the matter not disclosed was in
> respect of a matter which, in the opinion of the court
> dealing with the case was immaterial or was otherwise
> such as ought, in the opinion of that court, reasonably
> to be excused.

Faced with the certainty of a registration and disclosure statute, the bankers and their legal retainers wanted extraordinary protection against "crooked and unprincipled people" who might seek to use it. The Thompson bill, like most legislative efforts, satisfied few individuals other than its creators. Banking, business, and legal opposition did not greatly exceed that of congressmen and senators. The *New Republic,* usually a zealous advocate of financial regulation, characterized the measure as "more pitiful than pitiless . . . loosely drawn and entirely inadequate." Even a fervent New Dealer like David Lilienthal had to admit that it was "a pretty amateurish piece of drafting."[22]

The major initiative for a new bill came from Rayburn. Since his earliest days in the House, the taciturn representative from Bonham, Texas, had demonstrated a persistent concern for federal regulation of corporate securities. In 1914 he sponsored legislation to give the Interstate Commerce Commission supervision over railroad financing. Although this attempt

22. Memorandum by Paul V. Keyser and William C. Breed for Investment Bankers Association, Senate, *Securities Act,* appendix, pp. 335–41; *New Republic,* May 24, 1933, pp. 29–30; David Lilienthal to James M. Landis, April 15, 1933, JMLPLC, Box 6.

failed, the Rayburn proposals were incorporated into the
Transportation Act of 1920. In 1933 he retained his enthusiasm for comprehensive regulation of all corporate securities sold in interstate commerce. But Rayburn was not prepared to dissipate his influence for a measure which he personally felt to be defective and which many of his colleagues
looked upon as too radical. On April 5, at the conclusion of
House hearings, he told Moley the Thompson measure would
have to be drastically revised or put aside entirely. Moley
turned to Felix Frankfurter who arrived in Washington on
April 7 with a retinue that included James M. Landis, Benjamin V. Cohen, and Thomas G. Corcoran. Roosevelt, informed of the deteriorating situation, eased Thompson out of
the picture by persuading him to oversee pending government
litigation against Muscle Shoals power companies and Henry
Ford. By Saturday night, April 8, the Frankfurter group had
produced a new bill.[23]

Frankfurter's entourage presented a striking contrast to the
Thompson group and to other men around President Roosevelt in 1933. The newcomers exuded youth and intellectual
brilliance. Further, their arrival presaged the growing importance of a new constituency within the Democratic party
and American government: the professional, quasi-academic
expert. This was not wholly an innovation. During earlier
progressive years, state and national leaders, including Robert
LaFollette and Theodore Roosevelt, had utilized extensively

23. On Rayburn see Arthur S. Link, *Wilson: The New Freedom,*
p. 426. According to Moley and James Landis, the movement to revise Thompson's bill began with Rayburn. Moley, however, had sent
Rayburn a bundle of complaints from bankers and lawyers. Thompson
saw FDR and Moley as the major proponents of revision. Moley, according to Thompson, said "parties had told the President . . . the
Bill as I had drafted it was too stringent, and they had called in
Frankfurter because he . . . was . . . in the eyes of the administration
the leading lawyer of this country." See Moley, *The First New Deal,*
pp. 311–12; James M. Landis, "The Legislative History of the
Securities Act of 1933," *George Washington Law Review* 28 (October
1959), 33–34; Thompson, Diary, April 7, 8, 13, May 5, 1933, HTP.

the specialized talents of academicians and other professionals in the areas of conservation and business regulation. Wilson's traditional Democratic coalition found room for Brandeis and Frankfurter. Herbert Hoover, too, gave social scientists an expanded role in federal programs. But Franklin Roosevelt's administration greatly enlarged and deepened the participation of this constituency within government and absorbed its commitment to disinterested, informed public service.[24]

Felix Frankfurter had never held elective office. His major public responsibilities before 1933, including positions in the office of the United States Attorney for the Southern District of New York, the War Department, and the War Labor Board, were without great drama. On the War Labor Board, however, he began a close, lifelong friendship with Franklin Roosevelt. Like Brandeis, he was a "people's lawyer," without a tangible, institutionalized political base. Most effective as an informal adviser, he gave his energy during the 1920s to unpopular and wearisome causes: labor legislation, Sacco-Vanzetti, and public utility regulation. The law and teaching were his profession and his passion; in the practice of both he demanded competence and social relevance. From him, Harvard law students learned both the profession and the passion.

Although only one representative of a diverse, complex alliance known as the New Deal, Frankfurter may have been its most influential member. Few would leave a larger imprint upon its legislative record, and none was more catholic in interest or ability. Taxation, government spending, collective bargaining, holding companies, and social security were all within the ambit of his concern. Intellectually, he combined the broad generalities and idealism of the social critic with the hard logic and precision of a legal technician. He was per-

24. See for example, Samuel P. Hays, *Conservation and the Gospel of Efficiency,* passim; Barry D. Karl, "Presidential Planning and Social Science Research: Mr. Hoover's Experts," *Perspectives in American History* 3 (1969): 347–409; Richard S. Kirkendall, *Social Scientists and Farm Politics in the Age of Roosevelt,* passim; Richard Polenberg, *Reorganizing Roosevelt's Government, 1936–1939,* passim.

haps the only New Dealer who effectively bridged both the *New Republic* and Wall Street; the world of Arthur Dean and that of John Flynn. And the three men he brought to Washington were equally remarkable.

Benjamin Cohen, thirty-nine, was the eldest of the three. In 1933, Landis was thirty-four, Corcoran thirty-three. They were men whose social and political outlooks were unscarred by the old ideologies and alignments of Populism or progressivism. Cohen had been a precocious child, one who, according to legend, neglected marbles for Descartes and Herbert Spencer. The son of a comfortable Muncie, Indiana, Jewish family, he received a Ph.B. in economics from the University of Chicago in 1914 and a J.D. degree the following year. Cohen, according to professor Harold Moulton, was "the most brilliant student I ever taught." After receiving a law degree at Harvard under Frankfurter in 1916, he served as secretary to Federal Circuit Court Judge Julian W. Mack in New York. In Mack's office, Cohen first acquired skill at unraveling the complicated legal and financial webs woven by some corporations. He mastered the subtleties of receivership and other forms of business warfare. During World War I, he worked as an attorney for the United States Shipping Board; later became counsel for the American Zionists; helped to negotiate the Palestine mandate at the Paris Peace Conference; and met John Maynard Keynes. In New York City after the war he was known as a lawyer's lawyer who specialized in the intricacies of corporate reorganization. In addition, he was an unpaid counsel to the National Consumers League and drafted their model minimum wage law for New York State. Usually disheveled in appearance, always reserved in speech, Ben Cohen's gentle exterior camouflaged a quick and incisive legal mind.

Tommy Corcoran was, personally and intellectually, a blend of the incongruous. Facile as any Wall Street lawyer, resourceful as any Irish ward heeler, he had mastered Greek and Latin and read Dante and Montaigne to Justice Holmes for whom he had clerked. On the piano he could play and sing to operettas of Gilbert and Sullivan without a score. A native of Pawtucket, Rhode Island, he received a B.A. degree from Brown University in 1921, and a law degree from Harvard in 1925 where, with Frankfurter, he coauthored law review articles on the Supreme Court. Corcoran served one year with Holmes and then joined the New York firm of Cotton and Franklin in 1927. Like Cohen, he specialized in corporate reorganizations. The years from 1927 to 1932 in New York law offices provided bountiful experience in this branch of business metaphysics. In 1932 when Eugene Meyer needed a skilled lawyer on the staff of the Reconstruction Finance Corporation, he turned to Frankfurter for recommendations. Corcoran got the job. The RFC episode broadened Corcoran's grasp of practical business affairs. He spent his time untangling the labyrinth of investments that had strangled American bankers after the stock market crash. No less skilled in legal craftsmanship than Cohen, he nonetheless deserved the reputation as an abrasive and ruthless political fighter. Irish wit or sentimentality seldom submerged his boundless ambition.

James McCauley Landis, son of Presbyterian missionaries, Phi Beta Kappa graduate from Princeton in 1921, and professor of legislation at the Harvard Law School, was more academically oriented than either Cohen or Corcoran. Except for one year as Justice Brandeis's secretary, he had lived the routine existence of a young faculty member in Cambridge. For Landis, until the move to Washington in 1933, involvement had meant a clever retort in the *Harvard Law Review,* finding suitable Wall Street positions for his best students, and participating sporadically in state and municipal politics. Although he lacked the rich business experience of Frankfurter's other protégés, Landis came equipped with superb theoretical tools, sufficient flexibility to master the give-and-take of actual legislative battles, and a willingness to work long hours. Like Corcoran he was eager to serve the New Deal and impatient to extend his own influence. Like Cohen and Corcoran he was fired with idealism and highly skeptical of the American businessman's capacity to serve as sole guardian of the public interest.[25]

Cohen, Corcoran, and Landis were needed additions to the struggle for securities legislation. They were, first of all, more cosmopolitan in outlook than either administration draftsmen or congressional leaders. They had matured within the large bureaucracies, public and private, that came to dominate American life in the three decades after 1900. Accustomed to the analysis and management of complex business and legal affairs, they were inclined to seek solutions to particular problems within a flexible administrative framework rather than through simple legislative proscription. But from Frankfurter, they had also come to share Brandeis's attitude that large organizations, public and private, could deaden individual responsibility and retard innovation. These were attitudes, as Frankfurter said, "founded on deep convictions regarding the manageable size for the effective conduct of human affairs." The Frankfurter group believed in the necessity of an expanding and dynamic federal government. They were not willing, however, to see one power center extinguish all others. In 1912 Frankfurter had broken with Theodore Roosevelt and the Progressive party over precisely this issue. Thereafter, he often quoted Brandeis in defense of governmental and social pluralism: "the States should not be hampered in dealing with evils at their points of pressure. . . . If legislation is to deal with realities, it must address itself to important variations in the needs, opportunities and coercive power of the different elements in the states." Not all social and economic ailments could be cured in Washington, he told William O. Douglas of the Yale Law School. "I was a hot Hamiltonian when I went to Washington in 1911, but the years in the government service and all the rest of the years watching its operations intently have made

25. William E. Dorman to James M. Landis, January 22, 1930; Landis to John J. Burns, September 27, 1933; Landis to S. Pearce Browning, December 5, 1932; and Browning to Landis, September 30, 1932, JMLPLC, Box 5.

me less jaunty about devices for running a whole continent from Washington. This isn't theory but fear that the big fellows will thus be relieved from the effective controls that we can fashion against them without putting all our eggs into one basket." The securities legislation that Frankfurter and his followers prepared would encompass many of these attitudes: recognition that the intricate machinery of modern business and finance could be regulated only through comprehensive and yet flexible national administration; individual freedom to make investment decisions; and preservation of existing state regulation.[26]

Even before Thompson's measure had been introduced in Congress, Frankfurter and Landis discussed the many subtle problems raised by attempts at legislative control of financial activities. Here was a problem, Frankfurter told Landis, "not only of policy but of drafting in effectuating policy." He lamented the tendency of state legislatures to confront regulatory difficulties with encyclopedic statutes which frequently narrowed administrative discretion. He knew the danger of "excessive generality," but he felt that astuteness in formulating broad guidelines could prevent evasion and at the same time encourage creative administration. The English Companies Act provided a possible model. But, he warned, the English statute should not be followed slavishly. Above all, liabilities should extend beyond the vague concept of due diligence. On March 22, 1933, Frankfurter recommended to Moley the services of Bernard Flexner, a former general counsel for Samuel Insull's Middle West Utilities, as one "particularly qualified to help in perfecting such a bill." Flexner, according to Frankfurter, "knows all the holes that must be filled

26. Felix Frankfurter, "The Early Writings of O. W. Holmes, Jr.," *Harvard Law Review* 44 (March 1931): 717; Frankfurter, "Mr. Justice Brandeis and the Constitution," *Harvard Law Review* 45 (November 1931): 50–51; Frankfurter, "The Task of Administrative Law," *University of Pennsylvania Law Review* 75 (May 1927): 614–21; Felix Frankfurter to William O. Douglas, January 16, 1934, FFPLC, Box 10.

. . . and . . . to what extent methods adequate for England will be inadequate and not sufficiently protective in this country."[27]

Frankfurter's draftsmen, hoping not to irritate Thompson, described their new bill as "perfecting amendments." They met with the House committee on April 10. Rayburn, sufficiently awed by the presentation, asked Landis and Cohen to continue working on the bill with Middleton Beaman and Allan Perley, legislative advisers to the House.[28]

The April 10 proposal was a new departure, despite the euphemism of "perfecting amendments." A major defect of the Thompson measure lay in its conception of regulation. Corporations and their directors, according to the Thompson bill, raised money by selling securities. Therefore, one prevented abuse by controlling corporations and their directors. The Frankfurter group understood that regulatory problems could be more circuitous. Modern financial and business activities, they recognized, involved a series of interrelated functions. These functions, performed by separate professional and interest groups, were interdependent. Yet a registration statute, in order to force thorough disclosure, should apportion liability on the basis of separate responsibility for separate functions. While the liability provisions in the Thompson bill were rigorous, they were not sufficiently broad. The provisions did not technically include underwriters and members of the distributing syndicate, or distinguish between these two groups and their distinct functions. Why provide absolute liability for directors and ignore entirely the professional responsibilities of accountants, engineers, appraisers, lawyers, and other experts? The April 10 draft scaled down the liabilities but shaped them to the realities of modern business and finance. In addition, the revocation section was deleted. Instead, a thirty-day waiting period would intervene between the filing of the registration

27. Felix Frankfurter to James M. Landis, March 23, 1933, FFPH, Roll 7; Frankfurter to Raymond Moley, March 22, 1933, FFPH, Roll 8. See also Landis to Hollis R. Bailey, October 26, 1932, JMLPLC, Box 1.

28. Landis, "Legislative History," pp. 37–38.

statement and the date of issue. The Federal Trade Commission could evaluate the registration statement during this period and order modifications of the statement. Furthermore, the commission "at any time" could, after notice and hearing, issue a stop order suspending the effectiveness of the registration statement if it appeared that the statement "includes any untrue statement of a material fact or omits to state any material fact."[29]

Landis, Cohen, Beaman, and Perley struggled for ten days before producing another draft. "The House legislative counsel [Beaman] is very persnickety," Frankfurter complained to Roosevelt, "and so the process is a bit slow." This was a crucial period in the bill's history, punctuated by controversy over the scope of information to be disclosed in the registration statement and marred by disagreements between Landis and Cohen. The latter had devised a detailed schedule of information for inclusion in the text of the bill. Landis for one was content to omit many specific items from the statute and trust to the vigilance of the FTC. Landis's belief in regulation through a broad administrative mandate made him skeptical of statutes that contained detailed requirements. He felt that Cohen's schedule would impose an unnecessary straitjacket on the Federal Trade Commission. Cohen, too, was an advocate of flexible administration. But past experience in the New York business community made him fearful of statutory loopholes. Tempers flared. "Teamwork," Cohen said, "is impossible." He thought of stepping aside and asked Frankfurter to arrange a graceful exit. Only the latter's stern intervention kept the team together. Frankfurter urged Rayburn to keep the schedule of information in the bill. Moley was asked to lecture Landis, "who in his intensity has not been wholly wise in his relations with Ben." And Cohen was told rather bluntly that "for the sake of [a] job," he must not leave "until the ship is in port."[30]

When the first subcommittee print emerged on April 21, it

29. The above analysis is based on the April 10 printed draft in the Landis Papers, "Securities Act of 1933," JMLPH.

30. Felix Frankfurter to FDR, April 17, 1933, FFPH, Roll 7; Landis, "Legislative History," p. 38. Memorandum of telephone

contained Cohen's schedule. Whereas Thompson's bill had enumerated nine classes for disclosure, Cohen's enumerated thirty-two, including

> a list . . . of all material contracts, not made in the ordinary course of the business, including all management contracts, profit-sharing arrangements, and contracts for the giving or receiving of technical or financial advice or service. . . . The names of . . . all persons owning more than 10 percent of any class of stock or more than 19 percent in the aggregate of all stock. . . . A statement of the securities of the issuer covered by options and the names of any persons holding more than 10 percent of such options. . . . The remuneration paid the directors . . . officers or other persons, exceeding $25,000 per year.

The commission was also given full power to define accounting and trade terms used in the act and to prescribe the methods to be followed in the preparation of accounts. Rayburn was optimistic after seeing the April 21 version. "I believe," he told Frankfurter, "we are going . . . to get out a good, workable bill." Thompson was less happy. "The brain trust crowd," he complained to FDR's secretary, "has ruined my Bill."[31]

Thompson's measure, despite his pessimism, remained very much alive. Before a second House subcommittee print could be prepared, the Senate Banking and Currency Committee reported favorably on the Thompson version. The revocation section had been modified to provide for a hearing. The committee believed, however, that "immediate revocation will . . . save the public . . . heavy losses." The liability section had not been modified. It remained absolute and fell only upon issuers and directors. "If a director can excuse himself by saying that

conversation between Frankfurter and Benjamin V. Cohen, April 13, 1933; Frankfurter to Sam Rayburn, April 14, 1933; Frankfurter to Cohen, April 14, 1933; Frankfurter to Raymond Moley, April 15, 1933, all in FFPLC, Box 67.

31. Subcommittee print no. 1, April 21, 1933, and Felix Frankfurter to Sam Rayburn, April 22, 1933, both in FFPH, Roll 7; Thompson, Dairy, April 21, 1933, HTP.

he has in good faith relied upon an accountants' statement,"
the committee said, "then the investor will continue in the
same position from which the Nation is struggling to extricate
him." Frankfurter's entourage attempted to delay the Thompson version until Rayburn's committee could report a new
House bill. Their intermediary, Senator James Byrnes, failed
to convince the chairman, Fletcher. He succumbed to the arguments of Butler and Miller, who, not surprisingly, remained
convinced of the original bill's superiority.[32]

Failing to prevent the Senate report, Frankfurter and his
colleagues attacked the Thompson measure with fury. "It is
really a very bad bill," Frankfurter told Moley, "and unfair to
the President's purposes." Landis and Cohen dismissed it as
"partly innocuous and partly unconstitutional." They objected
to the vague provision for hearings before revocation, the
limited number of individuals subject to liability, and the insurer liability attached to all statements approved by directors.
Moreover, disclosure under the Thompson version remained
inadequate. They hoped the Senate would postpone further
action.[33]

The second House subcommittee print of April 29 was
basically the bill Rayburn formally introduced on May 3 and
the House passed on May 5. The important civil liability standards (section 11) had reached final form. Civil suits for recision and damages could be instituted by investors "in case
any part of the registration statement contained, at the time it
became effective, an untrue statement of a material fact or
omitted to state a material fact." Every person signing the
registration statement, directors, accountants, engineers, "or
any person whose profession gives authority to a statement

32. *Regulation of Securities* (Senate Rept. 47, 73d Cong., 1st sess.,
1933), pp. 3–5; *Congressional Record,* 73d Cong., 1st sess., 78, p.
24304; Felix Frankfurter to Raymond Moley, April 27, 1933, FFPH,
Roll 7. Moley blamed the hasty Senate action on Rayburn for "not
nursing [Duncan] Fletcher more carefully" (Benjamin V. Cohen to
James M. Landis, May 5, 1933, JMLPLC, Box 4).

33. Felix Frankfurter to Raymond Moley, April 27, 1933; James M.
Landis and Benjamin V. Cohen to Frankfurter, April 28, 1933; Frankfurter to Moley, April 28, 1933, all in FFPH, Roll 7.

made by him," and every underwriter and dealer could be sued. Only the corporation was unconditionally liable. All other persons could avoid liability if they sustained one of two burdens of proof:

> that as regards any part of the registration statement not purporting to be made on the authority of an expert . . . he had, after reasonable investigation, reasonable ground to believe and did believe that the statements therein were true and that there was no omission to state a material fact; and as regards any part of the registration statement purporting to be made on the authority of an expert . . . he had reasonable ground to believe and did believe . . . that the statements therein were true and that there was no omission to state a material fact, and that the registration statement fairly represented the statement of the expert . . . or was a fair copy of or extract from the report or valuation of the expert.

The standard of reasonableness, defined by the statute, would be that "required of a person occupying a fiduciary relationship." This definition significantly altered the liability provisions of the British statute. Those who claimed to be fiduciaries, Frankfurter noted, should not object to assuming responsibilities commensurate with their pretensions. In addition, individual dealers who sold securities by a prospectus or oral communication that included an untrue statement of a material fact or omitted a material fact would be liable for recision and damages if they did not sustain the same burdens of proof. The prospectus, required to accompany each offer to sell, would have to include substantially the same data as the registration statement. Unlike the British law, purchasers would not be required to prove reliance upon the registration statement or the prospectus.[34]

Subcommittee members insisted upon several changes before the bill went back to the full committee. Over the objec-

34. Subcommittee print no. 2, April 29, 1933, FFPH, Roll 7. Cf. *Federal Supervision of Traffic in Investment Securities in Interstate Commerce* (House Rept. 85, 73d Cong., 1st sess., 1933), pp. 8–23.

tions of Landis and Cohen, municipal bonds and railroad securities were exempted from coverage, including the anti-fraud provisions. Local politicians, under pressure to borrow new funds for municipal projects, feared FTC scrutiny of city finances, as did dealers in those securities. Rayburn insisted upon the second exemption in order to preserve the independence of the Interstate Commerce Commission. Other narrow but powerful interest groups secured immunity for their securities: building and loan associations, state-chartered banks, homestead and savings and loan associations.[35]

The major threat to the bill did not come from exemptions, but from attempts to dismantle the new liability section. Wall Street lawyers saw the language as destructive of everything sacred in legal history since the witenagemot. Many members of the House committee, on the other hand, called the section too lenient. They threatened to support the Senate version. A phalanx of eminent New York lawyers, at Moley's insistence, were accorded a private committee hearing before the bill went to the full House. All expressed shock and indignation over the liability section and the thirty-day waiting period. They accused Rayburn of undermining the American financial system, but no modifications were made in the bill. Rayburn, utilizing the arguments of Frankfurter, Landis, and Cohen, fought for the language in the April 29 subcommittee print. "To impose . . . an insurer's liability," Frankfurter said, "is to put to serious hazard the constitutionality of the measure. . . . There is ample protection to the public without securing that public interest through vindictive features which the Courts might resent and most likely would not sustain." Having rebuffed Wall Street's legal advice, Rayburn and Frankfurter convinced skeptical committee members that the liability section was adequate.[36]

35. *Federal Supervision* (House Rept. 85), p. 6; Landis, "Legislative History," p. 39.

36. Interview with Benjamin V. Cohen, August 21, 1967; Landis, "Legislative History," p. 40; Felix Frankfurter to Sam Rayburn, May 1, 1933, FFPH, Roll 7.

Frankfurter and Rayburn, attempting to moderate two extremes, succeeded only in alienating both sides. Representative Carroll Breedy of Maine condemned the bill on the House floor. The administration, he said, "has listened to the repretatives of big business." Representative James Mott and others insisted upon a stronger liability section and urged that the FTC be given the authority to approve the quality of all securities. The new bill, he said, was an open invitation to continued financial huckstering. During an acrimonious White House meeting on May 5, Thompson berated Rayburn and Frankfurter for keeping their work secret and for excluding him from the drafting sessions. "Investment bankers," Thompson said, "would be satisfied with the Frankfurter . . . definition of responsibility and . . . it would never work."[37]

Investment bankers, of course, were not satisfied. Wall Street representatives who welcomed Frankfurter's intervention in April regretted it by May. "I am delighted to know that the matter is now in competent hands," Eustace Seligman had said, "as the [Thompson] Bill as originally introduced . . . was a very poor job." But after viewing Frankfurter's product, Seligman concluded that no legislation was necessary, since "bankers of standing and financial responsibility have in every case that I have been associated with gone to extreme caution." Frankfurter could only express regret that men of Seligman's probity had not been connected with all security issues. "Then," he added, sarcastically, "there would be no need for any corrective legislation." These blunt remarks and the bill itself were too much for the Wall Street lawyer. "You," he told his old Harvard friend, "prefer personalities and invective to reasoned argument."[38]

At the instigation of Majority Leader Joseph Robinson, the Senate agreed to delay a vote on Thompson's bill until the new

37. *Congressional Record,* 73d Cong., 1st sess., 78, pp. 2947–48, 2952–53; Thompson, Diary, May 5, 1933, HTP.

38. Eustace Seligman to Felix Frankfurter, April 11, 24, May 15, 1933; Frankfurter to Seligman, April 25, May 10, 1933, all in FFPH, Roll 10.

measure moved through the House. That assembly, exhausted
by a torrent of other New Deal proposals, quickly approved
Rayburn's bill after permitting opponents a brief opportunity
to reveal their ignorance of its contents. Frankfurter's young
men, equally spent, were astonished by the ease with which the
levers of power seemed to respond to their ideas. It was an
intoxicating moment. "Rayburn," Cohen told Landis, "did not
know whether the bill passed so readily because it was so
damned good or so damned incomprehensible."[39]

The Senate insisted upon Thompson's version, but the conferees were given a "free hand in working out what form the
legislation finally shall take." Robinson was of the opinion that
the "House bill is preferable," and he so informed the Senate
negotiators. Despite Robinson's instructions, the conference
session did not open smoothly. Butler and Miller insisted that
the Senate bill be made the working draft of the committee.
When this tactic failed, they presented an entirely new measure
based on the Senate version but also containing portions of the
House-passed bill. Butler and Miller managed to sidetrack the
conference for one day before Rayburn secured an affirmative
vote in favor of the House bill. Although the conference committee produced four revisions, they contained no significant
alterations. The waiting period under section 8 was reduced
from thirty to twenty days. Section 18, a vestige of the Thompson bill, making it unlawful to use the mails to sell securities
in violation of state law, was finally removed. This section had
encountered strong opposition in the House and from the
Frankfurter draftsmen. The conference report, accepted by the
House on May 22, passed the Senate one day later. Roosevelt
signed the bill on May 27.[40]

39. Felix Frankfurter to Joseph T. Robinson, May 7, 1933; Frankfurter to Benjamin V. Cohen and James M. Landis, May 7, 1933,
FFPH, Roll 7; Cohen to Landis, May 5, 1933, JMLPLC, Box 4.

40. Felix Frankfurter to Thomas G. Corcoran, May 7, 1933; Frankfurter to FDR, May 8, 1933, both in FFPH, Roll 7; Joseph T. Robinson to Frankfurter, May 9, 1933, FFPLC, Box 49; *Securities Act of
1933* (House Rept. 152, 73d Cong., 1st sess., 1933), pp. 1–29; *Con-*

"Conservative investment banking, within its appropriate function," Frankfurter said after the bill's passage, "has nothing to fear and everything to gain from the Securities Act." Landis, attempting to mollify a former law student, made the same assessment. "If [security dealers] fulfill in their ordinary business conduct those standards of reasonable competence and prudence," he said, "they need not fear anything, not even the advice of their lawyers." But Frankfurter and Landis were anticipating a future when the Securities Act, like other New Deal measures, was recognized as providing a competitive floor beneath American enterprise; when fraud and chicanery still survived, but not as dependable methods of achieving financial success; and when a new attitude of professionalization, born of this initial statute, permeated not only investment banking, but also the allied functions of directors, accountants, and lawyers. In the fall of 1933, Frankfurter and Landis saw this larger victory. Privately, some members of the banking fraternity recognized the benign aspects of the legislation. "The better educated offices in New York," Cohen remarked, "are becoming reconciled. . . . The head of the National City Company even went so far as to express the opinion . . . that the Act was workable. I only hope that the boys have not discovered some of the holes that we neglected to plug." But most members of the business and financial community saw only an immediate, terrifying defeat. They perceived the demolition of old legal dectrines and the proscription of hallowed business practices. Beaten in the skirmish, many were prepared to resist future innovations and to salvage, either through legislative influence or administrative pressure, bits and pieces of the past.[41]

---

gressional Record, 73d Cong., 1st sess., 78, pp. 2954, 2969, 2979–82, 2995–96, 3000, 3085.

41. Felix Frankfurter to Arthur Perry, September 18, 1933, FFPH, Roll 10; James M. Landis to Donald M. Halsted, June 7, 1933, JMLPLC, Box 6; Benjamin V. Cohen to Landis, June 7, 1933, JMLPLC, Box 4.

Another man who gazed upon the past during the struggle over the Securities Act was California's tempestuous, quixotic senator, Hiram Johnson. He hoped to rectify old abuses by assisting the holders of defaulted foreign investments. Partly to avoid even greater legislative confusion, Roosevelt had decided in 1933 to defer additional proposals for securities regulation. Even stock exchange legislation, he reasoned, could wait. But the President's decision could not curtail independent endeavors by United States senators. Hiram Johnson provided new and complex diversions for the Congress and the President.

4

The Strange Death of Title II

On May 8, 1933, during Senate consideration of the Securities Act, Hiram Johnson introduced an amendment to the pending bill. He asked the Senate to include Title II, which established a Corporation of Foreign Security Holders. Johnson's proposal passed on the same day and went to the conference committee.

Title II instructed the Federal Trade Commission to appoint six directors to the corporation. No director could serve who had, within the past five years, "any interest, direct or indirect, in any corporation, company, partnership, bank, or association which has sold, or offered for sale, any foreign security." Under Johnson's amendment, the corporation was empowered to require information relative to the original or present holders of foreign securities from trustees, financial agents, or dealers in foreign securities; to function as fiscal and paying agent for securities in default; and to borrow money and to pledge as collateral securities deposited with the corporation. In addition to inviting deposits, the corporation could appoint protective committees to represent holders of defaulted foreign securities and "determine and regulate the functions of such committees." The corporation, working alone or with individual protective committees, could negotiate with foreign governments for the resumption of payments on defaulted securities. Negotiated settlements would be binding upon all bondholders after an affirmative vote by 60 percent of the deposited securities. The corporation's activities would be funded for three years by the Reconstruction Finance Corporation.[1]

Senator Johnson, in a speech accompanying the bill, said his amendment would compliment the Securities Act: "We seek now : . . . to shut the door of the stable after the horse is gone. . . . I am trying to give some place the swindled investor may go for the deposit of his particular [foreign] security and receive the aid of the organization thus created." The Federal Trade Commission should have initial control over the corporation, Johnson said, "because you cannot entrust it to the selection of those who in the past have floated these foreign securities and have been the purveyors of them to the American public." Many protective committees were honest, but "others . . . are under the control, absolutely, of the very people who sold the rotten securities, and they make this sort of thing a racket."[2]

Johnson's proposal touched a problem of great magnitude. From 1920 through 1931, investment bankers in the United States floated 1,758 foreign capital issues, both governmental and corporate. These issues represented a face value in excess of $10 billion. With the coming of the depression, interest and sinking-fund payments underwent complete or partial default. In the case of foreign government obligations, $5.3 billion remained outstanding in 1935, nearly $3 billion of which was held by American investors. One-third of the outstanding bonds no longer payed full interest, and Latin American defaults reached the staggering figure of 76 percent. The individual and institutional investment of Americans in defaulted foreign government bonds was immense. Some estimates reached as high as 700,000 investors, including banks, trust funds, churches, hospitals, YMCAs, and cemetery associations. Because of the wide distribution of this type of security during the previous decade, 96 percent of the Ameri-

1. *Congressional Record,* 73d Cong., 1st sess., 77, pp. 2609, 2987, 2995.

2. Ibid., p. 2988. See also Hiram Johnson to Hiram Johnson, Jr., April 1, 1933, HJP, Box 68.

can bondholders owned less than $20,000. The average holding was estimated at $800.[3]

The depression only precipitated financial catastrophe for the bondholders. It toppled an already shaky foreign investment structure erected through the cupidity and folly of American bankers during the 1920s, above all, in Latin America. Dreary testimony before Senate committees documented the conclusion that the activities of investment houses abroad were "one of the most scandalous chapters in the history of American investment banking . . . characterized by practices and abuses which were violative of the most elementary principles of business ethics." Frenzied competition among investment bankers drove them to ignore poor debt records, to fail to study basic economic conditions in issuing countries, and to neglect to ascertain whether loan proceeds were utilized productively. Investment houses issued false and misleading prospectuses; eminent legal retainers drafted spurious loan contracts and later spoke of these same contracts as "boiler plate . . . not worth the paper they are written on." Lavish commissions were paid for the origination of business, often to foreign government officials and their relatives. Working abroad, investment firms duplicated the high-pressure tactics used in America for the flotation of domestic securities.[4]

Beginning in 1931, private efforts were begun to recover part of the losses through formation of American bondholders' protective committees. Two attempts to form a central protective organization failed before 1932, largely as a result of

3. Data compiled from Department of Commerce, "American Underwriting of Foreign Securities," *Trade Information Bulletin,* no. 802, passim; Foreign Bondholders Protective Council, *Annual Report* (1935), pp. 282–85; Securities and Exchange Commission, *Report on the Study and Investigation . . . of Protective and Reorganization Committees,* no. 5 (Washington, 1937), pp. 4–7.

4. Senate Banking and Currency Committee, *Stock Exchange Practices* (Senate Rept. 1455, 73d Cong., 2d sess., 1934), pp. 126–50; Testimony of Allen W. Dulles, *Proceedings before the Securities and Exchange Commission in the Matter of the Readjustment of the Ex-*

the indifference or hostility of major Wall Street bankers.[5] It required prodding from the State Department, harassed by congressmen and embarrassed by Senator Johnson, to mobilize Wall Street's higher echelons and to launch the first serious movement for a private, centralized foreign bondholders' organization during the spring of 1932. The individuals who then came together, with a few additions, coalesced again under the Roosevelt administration, when the senator's Title II proposal aroused them from a second period of lethargy. In 1933, Wall Street found allies within the national government who were anxious to protect the prerogatives of the State Department and of the investment bankers. The New Deal, committed to domestic securities regulation, abandoned American investors holding defaulted foreign securities until 1939 when foreign policy developments necessitated renewed intervention by the federal government.

Hiram Johnson's solution to the problem of defaulted foreign securities had been conditioned by years of internecine conflict with the State Department and by his propensity to attribute

---

ternal Obligations . . . of the Republic of Peru (Washington, 1935), pp. 1139–43; Senate Finance Committee, *Sale of Foreign Bonds or Securities in the United States* (72d Cong., 1st sess., 1933), pp. 462–63, 742–43, 1585–89, 1612–13, 1934–43.

5. The Latin American Bondholders Association, organized and subsidized by Thomas F. Lee, formerly a member of the investment house of F. J. Lisman and Company, failed after three months of delusory activity in 1931. Two separate protective committees, one for El Salvador and one for Colombia, begun under this association's direction, continued to function through Fred Lavis, formerly president of the association and of the International Railways of Central America. Dr. Max Winkler, a writer on finance and international trade, at one time connected with the investment house of Bertron, Griscrom and Company, organized three related associations in 1931, all under the name of the American Council of Foreign Bondholders. Initially financed by the brokerage firm of J. R. McIntosh and Company, the efforts of Dr. Winkler amounted to little more than dubious advice to bondholders and a bimonthly newsletter. Winkler attracted a diverse group of supporters, but none with an entree to the major investment houses. See SEC, *Protective Committees,* no. 5, pp. 52–53.

all of America's social and economic ills to that agency and to Wall Street. Title II followed logically from Johnson's 1931–32 inquiry before the Senate Finance Committee. He had provided a one-man exegesis of the relationship between investment bankers and the State Department. That relationship, according to Johnson, was always conspiratorial. Independent evidence suggests, however, that it was sometimes intimate, occasionally strained, and frequently passive.

Officially, the State Department followed a policy of nonintervention in the area of foreign investments. Both public offerings and private loans required only pro forma approval by the department. Unofficially, the policy was more complex. Investment banking was often an adjunct to diplomacy and, as Senator Johnson darkly hinted, often diplomacy was an adjunct to investment banking. Johnson's insinuations aside, it was often difficult to distinguish bankers from diplomats. The Finance and Investment Division of the Commerce Department, for example, made exhaustive economic studies of Chile, Peru, Bolivia, and Colombia during 1927 and 1928. Early in 1928, the division notified the State Department that Bolivia, in view of its total resources, had already exceeded prudent borrowing limits. It recommended against a pending $23-million bond issue, but encountered intense opposition from the State Department. "There was a good deal of hemming and hawing," Grosvenor Jones, the division's chief, told Johnson, "and . . . we reluctantly gave our consent . . . for the reason that at that particular time our diplomatic relations with Latin America were a little upset. . . . The State Department said that it might result in embarrassment if we turned down this loan proposition." Within five years, after Bolivia had defaulted, only the bondholders remained embarrassed.[6]

In 1927, following United States military occupation of Nicaragua, the State Department had assumed a more direct role. It began efforts to restore Nicaragua's crippled finances

6. Senate Finance Committee, *Sale of Foreign Bonds,* pp. 360, 725, 954–64.

and to prop up the American-supported regime of Adolfo
Díaz until regular elections could be held in 1928. Financial
solvency and prompt elections were tied together in proposals
made to the Nicaraguans and to New York bankers by Henry
Stimson, President Coolidge's special envoy, and Assistant
Secretary Francis White. In addition to a large loan, the plan
called for strict American control of customs, internal revenue,
and the Nicaraguan budget in order to prevent electoral fraud.
These measures guaranteed, according to the State Department, "fair and free elections" in 1928 and were "a condition
which any banker . . . would be entitled to invoke against the
Nicaraguan government." White negotiated with the investment house of J. and W. Seligman and Company, while Stimson
outlined the plan to Nicaragua's representatives. The State
Department's program, underwriting the success of American
diplomacy, American bankers, and Nicaraguan elections, nearly collapsed through the greed of Hambleton and Company,
investment bankers in Baltimore. They offered a $20-million
loan to Nicaragua without the conditions attached by the State
Department. "Should this loan go through," White informed
Stimson, "it would of course upset our whole financial plan."
White, however, was not unduly agitated. "I am personally
. . . acquainted with the two Hambleton brothers who own the
firm," he assured Stimson. "I shall discuss the matter frankly
with them and I know we will have only their cooperation. I
feel sure they will drop the whole matter." Under State Department pressure, the Hambleton brothers abandoned their
efforts. Nicaragua's financial health remained the joint venture
of the State Department and J. and W. Seligman.[7]

7. See Elting E. Morison, *Turmoil and Tradition: A Study of the
Life and Times of Henry L. Stimson*, pp. 270–80, for background on
the Nicaraguan revolution and American intervention. Also see the
New York Times, January 2, March 19, June 11, 1927. On the financial arrangements see memorandum of conference among Henry Stimson, Francis White, and General Frank McCoy, July 1, 1927; Stimson
to Charles C. Eberhardt, July 14, 1927; Stimson to General José
Maria Moncada, July 14, 1927; White to Stimson, July 15, December

Senator Johnson, however, was more concerned with diplomacy as an adjunct to finance. During January 1932, before the Finance Committee, he sought to document an elaborate conspiracy involving the State Department, Colombian loans, Colombian oil, the House of Morgan, and the former secretary of the treasury, Andrew Mellon. Was it mere coincidence, Johnson asked, that during the previous spring the State Department put inordinate pressure upon the National City Bank of New York to facilitate a $4-million loan installment to the government of Colombia? Why, he continued, should Secretary of State Stimson and Assistant Secretary White intervene personally in the matter of a single loan installment? The loan, Johnson asserted, was not the real issue. The real issue was the rich Barco oil concession, regranted to the Colombian Petroleum Company by the Colombian government during the same spring. A one-fourth interest in the Colombian Petroleum Company was held by the Carib Syndicate, controlled by the Mellons and J. P. Morgan.[8]

Colombia's new petroleum law, regranting the Barco concession, had been written by George Rublee. Rublee, according to Johnson, had numerous friends and immense influence in the State Department. Worse yet, he was counsel to J. P. Morgan and Company. The entire State Department, the California senator concluded, reeked of oil. Was not Herbert Stabler, one-time chief of the department's Latin American division, now Gulf Oil's representative in Venezuela? Had not Stimson and White attempted to persuade National City to grant the loan installment on May 16 and again on June 20, the very day when President Olaya of Colombia ratified the new petroleum laws, and had not the installment finally been paid on June 30, 1931? Was not National City justified in delaying

---

6, 1927, all in HLSP, Box 259; *New York Times,* July 10, 24, 29, 1928. The bankers, according to one reporter, were not eager to join the Nicaraguan diplomatic adventure.

8. Senate Finance Committee, *Sale of Foreign Bonds,* pp. 1664–65, 1802–04.

the installment because of irregularities in the Colombian budget? Had not officials of National City expressed surprise, even anger, at State Department intervention?[9]

For Senator Johnson, the picture was clear: President Olaya expected the loan installment in return for the oil concession. When National City delayed payment, the State Department moved to rescue the Mellon-Morgan interests. Ergo: the U.S. Department of State was a tool of Gulf Oil and the House of Morgan.

Johnson overplayed his hand. Looking for a conspiracy, he succeeded only in proving what everyone already knew and what many people deplored: the State Department frequently interceded with foreign governments on behalf of American businessmen. H. Freeman Matthews, assistant chief of the Latin American division, informed the Finance Committee that the oil concession and the National City loan were "quite unconnected." Francis White, although refusing to make dispatches from the Colombian minister public, explained the affair quite plausibly as a routine matter. The department, he said, had attempted to maintain harmonious relations between an American firm (National City) and a foreign government. The ratification of new petroleum laws and National City's payment schedule were a coincidence. Outraged by Johnson's accusations, Stimson appeared before the committee in executive session on January 16, 1932. With the aid of senators Reed Smoot, David Walsh, and David Reed, he "rolled Hiram all over the floor." Two days later, Reed informed the secretary that the "situation in the Committee is all right in regard to Johnson," and at a White House reception, Smoot apolo-

9. *New York Herald-Tribune,* March 5, 1931. Johnson deliberately ignored the fact that Rublee had impressive progressive credentials. He had assisted Louis Brandeis in drafting portions of the Federal Trade Commission statute, served as an FTC commissioner under Wilson, and held the complete confidence of many anti-Morgan reformers, among them Felix Frankfurter. See Melvin I. Urofsky, "Wilson, Brandeis and the Trust Issue, 1912–1914," *Mid-America* 40 (January 1967): 25–27; Felix Frankfurter to William Phillips, March 14, 1933, FFPH, Roll 8.

gized for "the cutthroats in his Committee." Stimson curtly informed Smoot that the committee would not receive "any more of my papers or any more of my witnesses on the subject of international relations." Johnson, too, was embittered by the episode. "The entire force of the administration was utilized against me," he recalled to his son, "and the State Department had the effrontery to appear before the committee in an endeavor to smother me in the disclosures."[10]

Although the hearings concluded peacefully, Johnson announced he would introduce legislation immediately to supervise the financial activities of both the State Department and the bankers. He suggested a Foreign Loan Board, composed of officials from the departments of State, Commerce, and Treasury, to approve all future foreign issues and to impose a registration procedure whereby information concerning both public and private financing would be filed with the Secretary of Commerce. Johnson introduced the legislation two months later. At the same time, he justly condemned the "peculiar system" of the State Department, which he said, "enabled international bankers to foster sales, and . . . to convey the impression that their securities were of a character satisfactory to our government." And he refused to abandon the idea of conspiracy: "Neither by word nor deed is our Government . . . able to do aught for those who hold doubtful securities. . . . It can, however, when the occasion, in its opinion, demands it, act for a Barco concession owned by the Mellon or the Morgan interests in Colombia."[11]

10. Henry L. Stimson, Diary, January 16, 18, 21, 1932, HLSP; Hiram Johnson to Hiram Johnson, Jr., April 1, 1933, HJP, Box 68.

11. Senate Finance Committee, *Sale of Foreign Bonds,* pp. 2123–24; *Congressional Record,* 72d Cong., 1st sess., 75, pp, 6052–62. The Senate Finance Committee, under Democratic control by 1933, reported favorably on Johnson's original bill. Their report attacked the "nefarious practices" of bond houses and blamed the "loose custom" of the State Department for fostering "the wrongs perpetrated upon the American people." Johnson asked that this measure be put aside on May 1, 1933, following the Banking and Currency Committee's report on the Securities Act. A week later he introduced the Title II

Publicly, the senator's accusations had little impact. They provided fresh ammunition for traditionally Democratic and anti-Wall Street organs of opinion, while the Eastern and business press rushed to defend the integrity of the department and the investment bankers. Privately, the inquiry had greater significance. It created a tempest in the Department of State and spurred the diplomats to find new ways of refurbishing their own reputations and the bankers' as well. Johnson's imputations, a rising volume of defaulted foreign bonds, and the activities of individual protective committees, led the department to press for a centralized, private, and reputable bondholders council of its own creation, a council over which it could exercise informal influence.[12]

Secretary Stimson became increasingly alarmed as Johnson pursued the idea of a Barco intrigue. At first the department was merely "getting stirred up" by the senator's campaign to create what Stimson characterized as "general prejudice against foreign loans and foreign bankers." Four days later, however, Johnson had become "serious trouble" and "internal treachery" existed within the department. Someone with a "muddled head and a suspicious mind," the secretary complained, had given the senator "secret pieces of evidence." Before testifying, Stimson concluded that Johnson was "playing the devil," and it was also apparent to the distraught secretary that "a traitor has placed in his [Johnson's] hands all our correspondence between Bogota and the United States and he is misusing fragments of it to excite suspicion." George Rublee, after a long, friendly conversation, felt certain he had convinced Johnson of the department's innocence. Johnson was reported to have accepted Rublee's assurances that the petroleum laws

---

amendment. See *To Provide for the More Effective Supervision of Foreign Commercial Transactions* (Senate Rept. 41, 73d Cong., 1st sess., 1933), pp. 1–2.

12. See, for example, *New York Times,* January 6, 18, 1932; *New York Herald-Tribune,* January 22, 1932; *Business Week,* February 3, 1932; *Washington Post,* January 21, 1932; *Wall Street Journal,* January 23, 1932; *Atlanta Constitution,* January 11, 1932.

and the National City loan payment were unconnected. Although the State Department might assist American businessmen, Rublee told the senator, it had not acted illegally or improperly. Johnson professed himself satisfied and yet, Stimson complained, "he [Johnson] is going ahead and raising hell." The Californian, according to Rublee, "very greatly suspected the State Department," but believed Stimson to be personally above suspicion. This was little consolation to the secretary.[13]

Following the hearings, Stimson instructed Undersecretary William R. Castle to call an advisory council to the State Department in order "to work out . . . the tangled question of America's defaulted bonds." Immediate, positive action was necessary, Stimson noted, because "self-seeking committees have been crowding up and trying to attend to this already." The department might lose control over the situation. Furthermore, some hint of scandal hung over the entire issue. Senator Johnson, the secretary said, "gave . . . our foreign investment bankers a very bad name just at the time when they needed help." Leadership and decision making, for the secretary, were prerogatives of his social class. Although not an abject servant of the financial elite, Stimson nonetheless identified its general welfare with the nation's economic and social health.[14]

The advisory council met on April 15, 1932. In addition to Castle, the State Department delegation consisted of Harvey Bundy and an economic adviser, Herbert Feis. Ogden Mills attended for the Treasury and Grosvenor Jones for the Commerce Department. Five individuals, "known for their ability and disinterestedness," were also invited: Rublee; Thomas N. Perkins, a Boston attorney; Pierre Jay, chairman of the Fiduciary Trust Company; and two economists, Charles P. How-

13. Stimson, Diary, January 9, 13, 14, 15, 20, 1932, HLSP. Stimson and Rublee attributed Johnson's persistence to his general prejudice against the State Department and to the machinations of one Washington columnist who led the senator "to stir up that mare's nest about the Barco concession" (George Rublee to Felix Frankfurter, April 3, 1933, FFPH, Roll 22).

14. Stimson, Diary, June 2, 1932, HLSP.

land of Yale and Edwin Kemmerer of Princeton. Bundy informed the group that the government continued to receive complaints regarding the foreign bond situation. Accusations of government weakness persisted. Moreover, many disreputable lawyers and bankers, their incomes threatened by the depression, were entering the field as chairmen of protective committees and "creating irresponsible associations purporting to protect the interests of the small investor." The time had come, Bundy said, "to create an organization of unquestionable standing," although the State Department could not assume public responsibility for its formation or activities.[15]

The Inter-American Relations Committee, Castle suggested, might form a suitable nucleus for building a larger and broader organization. But since that committee had long been dominated by American Foreign Power, Standard Oil, and American Telephone and Telegraph, Professor Kemmerer objected to the proposal. He thought it would be difficult to appoint a "disinterested" committee. And, how, he asked, would it be financed? Ogden Mills provided one answer: "American industries could initially finance it," he said, "and . . . possibly it might then be carried on by the bankers." The five guests and Alanson B. Houghton, former ambassador to Germany, were asked to draw up a proposed plan of organization. Submitted at the end of May, their report called for the formation of a council of fifteen men, "whose eminence would command the confidence of the country." The council, however, would have only a slight relationship to the actual protective committees. "In normal cases," the report concluded, "the bankers, supported by the investors, will continue to organize committees

15. SEC, *Protective Committees*, no. 5, pp. 62–63. The advisory council had a friends-and-neighbors quality. Perkins and Rublee were classmates at Harvard and served together on the War Industries Board. Perkins, like Jay, was a director of Fiduciary Trust Company. Kemmerer and Rublee had served in Mexico at the same time, the former as financial adviser to the Mexican government, the latter as legal aid to the American ambassador, Dwight Morrow. Jay was a long-time friend of Stimson.

. . . leaving the conduct of foreign negotiations to the sponsor bankers or the proper protective committee." Stimson complimented them for "a conservative and intelligent report." The Latin American Bondholders Association, obviously ignorant of the advisory council's intentions, praised the attempt to form an "association or council . . . entirely independent of the houses of issue."[16]

With the assistance of the State Department, articles of incorporation and bylaws were drafted. A tentative list of fifteen eminent men was compiled. The services of Norman Davis, diplomat, entrepreneur, and presidential adviser extraordinary, were promised as chairman. Despite these efforts, many investment houses remained aloof from the plan to create a central protective council. "No single thing could help the movement more," the State Department complained, "than the support—even the passive support—of J. P. Morgan. That house has continued to remain completely on the fence, from which position its glances have been cool rather than sympathetic." Parker Gilbert, the nestor of international banking, expressed the Morgan firm's attitude to Professor Howland. Although the Morgans would not support the plan, Gilbert was pleased "no one contemplates an organization which would take entire control, forbid or deter the formation of committees containing representatives of issuing houses . . . and exercise a sort of dictatorship, discharging the issuing houses of all moral responsibility and depriving them of all opportunity to assist in retrieving losses." A plan "on any such lines," Gilbert said, "would be absurd."[17]

The absurd, from Gilbert's special viewpoint, took place a year later when Johnson introduced Title II. Because of banker hostility and indifference, the State Department's original plan had remained only a paper organization. Now, Wall Street

16. Memorandum of State Department meeting, April 15, 1932, HLSP, Box 307; SEC, *Protective Committees,* no. 5, p. 64; Stimson, Diary, June 2, 1932, HLSP; *Commercial and Financial Chronicle,* 134 (April 16, 1932): 2825.
17. SEC, *Peru Proceedings,* p. 1202.

faced the unpleasant prospect of a federal corporation, financed by the RFC, under the initial supervision of the FTC, forbidding banker participation, and instructed to "determine and regulate the functions" of protective committees. Although Johnson's project threatened the bankers, it also aroused anxiety and opposition within the Roosevelt administration. To some, among them the President, Johnson's method presaged an unnecessary and unwarranted expansion of governmental responsibility into an area best reserved for private initiative. Not only was Roosevelt then dedicated to reducing expenditures, he was also advocating maximum cooperation with business and finance. Reform, based upon expanded federal responsibility, constituted a part of FDR's attitude in 1933, but he retained a balmy confidence in the benevolence and effectiveness of self-regulation and private decision making. To other members of the administration, among them individuals in the State Department, a new, independent governmental agency appeared as a menace to existing departmental influence and disruptive of entrenched bureaucratic routine. These attitudes ultimately perpetuated the continued independence of the bankers and the Department of State.

Title II had the deceptive appearance of a classic struggle between unsullied reformers and "the interests." Mischievous practices, associated with the flotation of foreign securities, had been exposed. The Corporation of Foreign Security Holders, representing the public interest, would prevent additional abuses. The issues seemed crystal clear, especially to Senator Johnson, yet upon close scrutiny, the issues were not clear at all.

Johnson's proposal had the support, for one, of Lawrence E. de S. Hoover, secretary of the Independent Committee for Holders of Colombian Bonds, organized in November 1932 to seek deposit of $82 million of defaulted Colombian securities.[18] Hoover was an intrepid promoter. Unemployed in 1932

18. Hoover even claimed authorship of the Johnson amendment, but no evidence in the Johnson Papers can support this assertion. See Hoover to Stephen T. Early, September 14, 1933, OF 100-B, FDRP,

after a fruitless attempt to purchase oil concessions in Colombia, he followed the suggestion of a friend and entered the protective committee business. Although he neither owned nor legally represented a single Colombian bond, Hoover formed the Independent Committee for Holders of Colombian Bonds. Former Oklahoma senator Robert L. Owen accepted Hoover's offer to become chairman. Hoover and his colleagues looked upon the undertaking as an entrepreneurial activity. With the exception of Senator Owen, the members advanced funds to the committee and agreed to receive profits based upon their proportionate contributions. The committee attempted to solicit the deposit of defaulted Colombian bonds. Deposit agreements, signed by individual bondholders, entitled the Hoover committee to a lien on the bonds up to 1 percent of their face value "for compensation and expenses."[19]

Between November 1932 and the introduction of Johnson's bill, Hoover and his adventurers experienced limited success. Few Colombian bondholders accepted the committee's services, and without legal possession of the securities, there was little chance of receiving "compensation and expense." By April 1933 the committee had solicited only $520,400. An unpaid bank loan, shrinking contributions from original members and the resignation of others, left Hoover's committee near collapse in the summer and fall of 1933. In addition to these financial woes, the committee encountered the emnity of issuing houses, who refused to divulge the names of bond-

Box 1. Hoover urged the President to support the Title II amendment by attacking the State Department and "some of the financial interests" who opposed the measure. His own highly questionable activities were later documented by the Securities and Exchange Commission, *Proceedings . . . in the Matter of the Institute of International Finance* (Washington, 1935), pp. 296–99.

19. Hoover told SEC investigators in 1935: "It [the protective committee] appealed to me, first, primarily, it was something to do and that I could do myself some good . . . It was not entirely philanthropic." See SEC, *Institute of International Finance,* pp. 302–03, 307–08, 314–15, 500–03.

holders, and competition from a rival protective committee.[20] Hoover's only hope for survival and financial success lay in official government endorsement. That could occur under Johnson's measure with its provision that the corporation recognize and encourage existing protective committees. Here, at last, was a life raft for the financial fishermen. Since the corporation could, theoretically, support other committees in the Colombian field, government approval was not certain. But the alternative remained equally grim: continued rivalry with other committees and possible bankruptcy.

Small, independent promoters like Hoover, insecure financially and lacking organizational power, supported public regulation in the form of Johnson's Title II. They had nothing to loose and everything to gain. The larger and more stable members of the financial community, including many Wall Street firms, preferred self-regulation along the lines of the advisory council recommendations submitted in 1932. Unlike their independent rivals, they were not concerned with trivial "compensations and expenses." They wished to maintain the existing structure of influence developed in the past with foreign governments and domestic investors. Members of the State Department, sensing a challenge to the department's influence and independence, joined in opposition. They, too, felt more comfortable with the existing relationships.

Herbert Feis, a holdover from the Stimson regime as economic adviser to the State Department, and Raymond B. Stevens, a member of the Federal Trade Commission, fought the Johnson measure from within the administration. Outside the government, their allies included Rublee, Jay, and Stimson.[21]

20. Hoover's committee was the second in the Colombian area. William Rosenblatt, a trader for his own account in foreign and domestic securities, organized the first "independent" committee two weeks before Hoover began his enterprise. Neither committee secured the support of issuing houses. Hoover and Rosenblatt continued their speculative odyssey together after 1934. See SEC, *Protective Committees*, no. 5, pp. 93–94, 112, 131–32, 242–43, 245–46.

21. Rublee and Stevens had been intimates since the Wilson days. Stevens helped Rublee and Brandeis on their draft on the Federal

Feis sought to enlist Roosevelt's sympathy immediately after Senate passage of the Johnson amendment. The proposed corporation, he said, would be a "quasi-official body . . . outside of the control of our [State Department] ministers, and more or less ignorant of the state of our relations with that foreign government. The dangers of confusion would be very great." Feis used Mexico as one example of a country where "financial relationships are the very core of the relations with the foreign government." If an outside agency of an official character brought pressure on these governments or made proposals, "the whole conduct of the Department's work would be complicated and confused." Above all, Feis said, "there could be no assurance as to the character of the personnel selected." Roosevelt, temporarily swayed by the argument, wrote identical letters to Fletcher and Rayburn before the conference committee met. He pointed out that the corporation might conflict with the policies of the State Department, other agencies, or the Congress, and involve the government in unwanted responsibilities. FDR noted that the State Department had suggested the selection of personnel "by private and semi-private bodies of good reputation," but he personally was "not wedded to that idea." Armed with Roosevelt's letter, Feis saw Fletcher, Rayburn, and Senator Robert Wagner. He wanted the conference immediately to reject Title II.[22]

Feis had not mobilized solid support in the State Department. Three days after meeting the President, he found it necessary to outline to William Phillips why the department should oppose the measure. He reiterated his arguments to the President, and added: "The task . . . can wisely only be left to

---

Trade Commission statute and later served as a special FTC counsel during Rublee's tenure. Jay, Stimson, and Rublee were delighted to have a sympathetic friend on the FTC during the fight against Johnson. See Pierre Jay to Henry L. Stimson, October 17, 1933, HLSP, Box 321, and George Rublee to Stimson, October 13, 1933, HLSP, Box 320.

22. Memorandum, Herbert Feis to Louis M. Howe, May 10, 1933, OF 100-B, FDRP, Box 12; FDR to Duncan Fletcher, May 20, 1933, OF 242, FDRP, Box 1.

the private interests concerned. That does not mean to the banking interests. Organizations have come into existence and stronger ones will come into existence, which are free of banking control. The Government might help to bring into existence a private organization completely disassociated from banking interests, but also completely disassociated from Government responsibility."[23]

The fate of Title II rested with the conference committee, which included Senator Hiram Johnson. He was not optimistic. "The Administration," he complained, "is going to kick it to pieces in the conference." Roosevelt, he added, "knew nothing of the detail and was accepting the advice of a lot of little two-by-four individuals in the State Department." But events in the conference committee moved Johnson's way. Once agreement had been reached on Title I, its supporters, including Rayburn, did not wish to jeopardize the entire bill by taking a position for or against Title II. No one was eager to enter the Johnson-State Department controversy. Rayburn, however, willing to follow any suggestion from the President, told Johnson to call Roosevelt and decide the issue. James Landis listened to the conversation and, according to his recollection, "the President had no idea as to what to do and ended up by telling Rayburn to do what he thought best." Faced with this deadlock, Landis, with Rayburn's approval, drafted section 211, which provided that Title II should take effect only when the President decided it to be "in the public interest." Middleton Beaman argued that the section was unconstitutional. Rayburn and other conferees, hoping to throw responsibility on the President, accepted the arguments for constitutionality hastily provided by Landis and Cohen. "To our amazement," Landis said, "[Senator Johnson] accepted it without further argument." Roosevelt endorsed section 211, and the conference committee reported favorably on the entire bill. Ignorance lay behind Johnson's sudden capitulation. Clearly, he distrusted Roosevelt and what he called "two-by-four indi-

23. Memorandum, Herbert Feis to William Phillips, May 12, 1933, OF 242, FDRP, Box 1.

viduals in the State Department." Yet acceptance of the Landis section presented the President with a blank check on Title II. Johnson either misread the amendment or did not grasp its implications.[24]

The battle for and against Title II now shifted to the White House. Stevens played the leading opposition role. Writing to the President "as a Democrat," he expressed concern with the "political reaction against your administration," should Title II take effect. He noted that all of the foreign securities then in default had been issued during previous administrations. Stevens did not want Roosevelt's administration to assume an obligation for a situation that developed under Republican rule. Notwithstanding section 211, Stevens said, foreign governments would look upon the corporation as a government agency, and controversies were certain to develop with the State Department. Moreover, any connection with the United States government would make it "more difficult to arrange reasonable and amicable settlements or collections" with foreign states. "A private organization representing bondholders," he said, "can conduct negotiations more efficiently and more successfully." Stevens urged FDR to postpone action on Title II until another method of aiding foreign bondholders could be worked out. Title II, in his opinion, "held little possibility of real help and is certain to have unfortunate consequences both abroad and at home." Other individuals, less

24. Hiram Johnson to Hiram Johnson, Jr., May 14, 1933, HJP, Box 68; James M. Landis, "The Legislative History of the Securities Act of 1933," *George Washington Law Review* 28 (October 1959): 38–39; Memorandum, Henry M. Kannee to FDR, May 23, 1933, OF 242, FDRP, Box 1. The conferees also added section 210 to Title II which specified that neither the corporation nor the protective committees formed with its approval should "claim or assent or pretend to be acting for or to represent the Department of State . . . or to do any act directly or indirectly which would interfere with or obstruct or hinder the policies or policy of the State Department." See *Conference Report on Securities Act of 1933* (House Rept. 152, 73d Cong., 1st sess., 1933), pp. 28–29; *Congressional Record,* 73d Cong., 1st sess., 78, pp. 4080, 4140.

sympathetic to the independence of investment bankers or the prerogatives of the State Department, entertained doubts about Title II. Ben Cohen hoped it would be "amended before . . . put into effect" and Frankfurter disclaimed responsibility for the provisions. "Indeed," he said, "I should be surprised if anything happens about that [Title II] in the near future."[25]

Roosevelt encouraged Stevens to proceed with efforts to create a private organization. The President informed Hiram Johnson that although he had not definitely made up his mind, he was "inclined to agree with . . . Raymond Stevens . . . a real Progressive [who] talks our language." Further, Roosevelt said he hoped to get "somebody thoroughly trustworthy like George Rublee, to organize a Foreign Security Holders Committee on a basis of very low cost to the bondholders and wholly nonprofit-making." The President's suggestions stunned the senator. His response was acid. Stevens, he said, preached a "gospel of timidity and fear . . . not a doctrine of progressivism." If the State Department and Herbert Feis prevailed, Johnson warned, "control of the directors would be with the very men who had originally perpetrated the wrong." The bankers and the State Department were hatching a dark plot. Any private organization, he added, would be manipulated and directed by the international bankers. Beneficial results could only be expected from an organization "over which, if it ever be desirable, the government itself may exercise absolute domination and control."[26]

25. Raymond B. Stevens to FDR, July 28, 1933, OF 100-B, FDRP, Box 1. Stevens informed Roosevelt on August 5 that Rublee and Jay "have taken up the task of creating the Council." The project would be finished within two or three weeks. He assured the President that every effort would be made to keep the matter quiet and to secure men "who particularly appeal to you." Like Feis, Stevens did not have the united support of the FTC. Chairman Charles March favored the Johnson plan. See Stevens to FDR, August 5, 1933, OF 100-B, FDRP, Box 12; Benjamin V. Cohen to Felix Frankfurter, July 31, 1933, FFPH, Roll 10; Felix Frankfurter to Earle M. Elrick, June 8, 1933, FFPLC, Box 49.

26. FDR to Hiram Johnson, July 31, 1933, OF 100-B, FDRP, Box 12; Johnson to FDR, August 26, 1933, OF 100-B, FDRP, Box 1.

Attempts to form the private organization progressed slowly through the summer. Alarmed by this delay, Herbert Feis feared a revival of complaints about defaulted foreign securities. It was urgent, he said, "to consider whether some positive action cannot be taken to put an end to this agitation." Two alternatives remained: "the fostering by official action . . . of an adequate and disinterested private body entirely independent of all special interests, and particularly of banking interests," or the creation of a government agency under Title II. Feis, of course, still found the first alternative more desirable. A small group, he suggested, should draw up a list of proposed directors to form a private organization and arrange for a meeting with representatives of State, Treasury, and the Federal Reserve Board. Feis was vexed by the problem of finances. Rublee, for one, wanted New York banks to put up the money. "This," Feis said, "would defeat the whole idea." But fear of Title II bred logical inconsistencies: Feis now suggested a governmental loan from either the Federal Reserve or the Reconstruction Finance Corporation.[27]

Two weeks later, Stevens informed FDR that he and Feis had worked out a plan whereby the Council on Foreign Relations would sponsor the private bondholders organization. Individuals selected by the old State Department advisory group should be retained, but "new persons of liberal reputation should be added from the far west and middle west." Contradicting himself, Stevens added that because of Senator Johnson's suspicions, "the creation of a private corporation should be connected in no way with efforts begun under the Hoover Administration." The Council on Foreign Relations, Stevens shortly told the President, could not be used. He and Feis had examined the list of officers and found a marked predominance of J. P. Morgan's partners and legal advisers. Stevens then suggested a slightly new approach. The private council could not be set up without the approval of the federal government and, Stevens said, "that approval might as well be

27. Memorandum, Herbert Feis, September 15, 1933, OF 100-B, FDRP, Box 1.

direct as indirect." The quickest method of starting the private organization, Stevens said, would be for the secretary of state, the secretary of the treasury, and the chairman of the Federal Trade Commission to invite to Washington "men whose names have already been considered." They should be told "that the Government considers . . . the creation of a private corporation . . . necessary and that they would be rendering an important public service if they would proceed to form such an organization." Of course, Stevens added, "once formed the Government would not be responsible for it." He urged haste "because of the pressure which is being brought to bear to bring into force Title II."[28]

With great mental dexterity, but little regard for consistency, Feis and Stevens had thrown together a proposal that effectively blurred all distinction between public and private. The only real difference between their plan and Johnson's now rested in the formal declaration of governmental responsibility under the latter and the fact that investment houses and the State Department would have more influence under the former. Stevens' meeting took place on October 20 in the Treasury Department. Those attending, carefully selected by Rublee and Jay, became directors of the Foreign Bondholders Protective Council.[29]

Supporters of Title II, fighting against well-organized and strategically placed opponents, experienced only frustration. Lawrence Hoover and his committee bombarded the President

28. Raymond B. Stevens to FDR, October 5, 1933, OF 100-B, FDRP, Box 1.
29. In addition to Undersecretary of the Treasury Dean Acheson, Secretary of State Cordell Hull, and Chairman March of the FTC, those who attended included Laird Bell, Hendon Chubb, W. L. Clayton, John Cowles, Herman Ekern, Ernest Hopkins, Philip LaFollette, Mills B. Lane, Frank O. Lowden, Orrin K. McMurray, Roland Morris, Thomas Thacher, J. C. Traphagen, and Quincy Wright. Those unable to attend, but who became directors, included Charles Francis Adams, Newton D. Baker, J. Reuben Clark, and Pierre Jay. See Raymond B. Stevens to FDR, October 15, 19, 1933, OF 100-B, FDRP, Box 1; Foreign Bondholders Protective Council, *Annual Report* (1934), p. 10.

and his staff with letters urging utilization of Title II, demanding personal interviews, and damning the State Department. Johnson's plan must go into effect, Hoover said, "in order to protect the interests of the American holders of foreign securities." He deplored the opposition "of some of the financial interests" and expressed shock that "those desirous of creating a private company [have] been so successful in their efforts." Hoover could not understand the position of the State Department "objecting to the creation of this Corporation because they might have to interest themselves at some time to protect the interests of . . . American bondholders." Nor could he see much difference "between the State Department interesting themselves for a private corporation or what they might consider a semi-government organization." Johnson, too, pressed these arguments. Logically, they were correct. But political leverage, not logic, was the important currency in this struggle. Hoover, rather disingenuously, finally accepted the fact. "The banks," he complained to Henry Kannee, "got the bondholders going and now they can get them coming."[30]

Roosevelt gave his blessing to the formation of a private bondholders council. In a statement to reporters he noted the large number of securities in default and the fact that bondholders had no adequate means of contacting each other and negotiating settlements. Here was a task, the President said, "primarily for private initiative and interests." The federal government recognized a duty to defend the interests of its citizens, but "it would not be wise for the Government to undertake directly the settlement of private debt situations." The recent meeting at the Treasury, Roosevelt added, should produce an effective and disinterested organization. It would be, he said, "entirely independent of any special private interest; it is to have no connection of any kind with the investment

30. Lawrence E. de S. Hoover to Louis M. Howe, June 10, 1933, OF 242, FDRP, Box 1. Hoover to Stephen T. Early, September 14, 1933; Hoover to Marvin H. McIntyre, September 29, 1933; Robert L. Owen to FDR, October 12, 1933; Memorandum, Henry M. Kannee to McIntyre, October 11, 1933, all OF 100-B, FDRP, Box 1.

banking houses which originally issued the loans." Roosevelt reemphasized these points to those who continued to urge application of Title II. The Foreign Bondholders Protective Council, incorporated in December 1933 as a nonstock, nonprofit, membership corporation, began to function soon thereafter.[31]

Two years after its creation, the council underwent examination by the new Securities and Exchange Commission during the latter's investigation into protective and reorganization committees. The commission, like many members of the administration before it, concluded that the council was preferable to the arrangements proposed under Title II. The council, however, was evaluated largely on two points: (1) it was nonprofit and (2), unlike other protective committees, the council's protective committees had not engaged in brazen efforts to fleece bondholders. These, of course, were real virtues. But supporters of the private council had not been inspired by larcenous motives in the first place. They hoped to maintain a structure of public and private decision making in the area of foreign finance that insured the independence and separate influence of the State Department and investment bankers. In the pursuit of this larger objective they were successful.[32]

Despite Rosevelt's assurances that the private organization would have "no connection of any kind with the investment banking houses which originally issued the loans," the council quickly came to rely upon issuing houses for financial support. They contributed 60 percent of the $90,000 raised for the

---

31. *New York Times,* October 21, 1933; FDR to Frederick Steiwer, November 6, 1933; Louis M. Howe to W. G. Andrews, November 22, 1933, both OF 242, FDRP, Box 1.

32. SEC, *Protective Committees,* no. 5, pp. 348–55, 736–46. Officials of so-called "independent" committees frequently traded in the deposited securities. The most flagrant abuse, however, was the unilateral revision of deposit agreements by one committee which automatically increased the "fees and compensation" of committee members and attorneys.

council's activities in 1934. Even the lordly House of Morgan contributed $5,000. Financial reliance upon the bankers had been the open intention of many council supporters, although attempts were made to find other forms of financial assistance, most notably by Stevens. But when these efforts failed, it became ridiculous for the Roosevelt administration to continue the charade that the private organization would have "no connection of any kind" with the original issuing houses. Once the possibility of direct government financial aid had been erased, money would flow from some interested constituency. Moreover, issuing houses could no longer remain aloof as many had done in 1932. They faced the alterative of backing the council or accepting government supervision under Title II.[33]

The opponents of Title II had based a substantial part of their case on the need for an organization divorced from governmental influence or responsibility. Any connection with the United States government, they said, would seriously hamper negotiations with foreign governments. The public and private spheres should remain separate. Realistically, no organization, private or public, could avoid cooperation with the United States government, above all the State Department. The council merely substituted informal cooperation and assistance for the more formal governmental commitment contained in Title II. In December 1933, the Brazilian government, with the encouragement of the British, devised a temporary plan of debt settlement which discriminated against American bond-holders. The State Department insisted that the Brazilians consult with the council before formally ratifying the plan. The council's executive committee, "after consulting with various issue houses," designated J. Reuben Clark as its negotiator, even though Clark was then a member of the official State Department delegation to the Pan-American Conference. Harvey Bundy and Pierre Jay combed through the department's list of diplomats in the hope of finding additional council mem-

33. Raymond B. Stevens to FDR, October 15, 1933, OF 100-B, FDRP, Box 1; SEC, *Peru Proceedings,* pp. 1240–44, 1250–57.

bers who would "understand the importance of the work and, in some cases, be sympathetic to sustaining it." At times, the council became brutally frank regarding its relationship to the government. When opening negotiations with Peru, Guatemala, and Chile, the council characterized itself as "organized at the request of the Federal Administration in Washington." The council enjoyed all the prestige and influence of government sponsorship except the formal responsibility of the corporation under Title II. Without government intervention, the council would not have consummated the Brazilian settlement, its only successful negotiation before 1940. And when the issue of debt settlements became more urgent, the role of the government increased further.[34]

Supporters of the private organization also argued against Title II on the ground that the Roosevelt administration would thereby assume responsibility for Republican negligence. Stevens had emphasized that the organization "should be connected in no way with efforts begun under the Hoover Administration." Rigorous adherence to these principles proved difficult. With the exception of Stevens, the group of organizers remained identical; the directors were selected in both instances by Jay and Rublee, and the list remained unchanged except for the addition of "new persons of liberal reputation." Moreover, the directors were only window dressing. Real power resided with the president and vice–president of the council's executive committee. And the executive committee came to bear a striking resemblance to Herbert Hoover's State Department. Jay, Stevens, and Ernest M. Hopkins, president of Dartmouth College, formed the nucleus of the original executive committee, but they resigned within six months and were replaced by professional diplomats: Francis White, J. Reuben Clark, and James Grafton Rogers. As president and vice-president, Clark and White conducted all negotiations with foreign governments. The council became, during its early phase, the

34. Pierre Jay to Henry L. Stimson, December 28, 1933, HLSP, Box 322; Jay to Stimson, January 18, 1934, HLSP, Box 323; SEC, *Institute of International Finance*, pp. 56, 98.

New Deal's device for attempting to liquidate many old deals through the active participation of many old dealers.[35]

The council was a temporary blessing to both the bankers and to the State Department. Issuing houses ceased to form their own protective committees in self-defense against "independent" committees. Instead, they gave support to the council by making bondholders lists available and by encouraging the formation of protective committees under the council's direction. The council responded by discouraging bondholders' suits against issuing houses and by forming protective committees at the bankers' request in order to forestall "independent" committees. The council also served as a useful buffer between the State Department and irate bondholders. The department reciprocated by assisting the council against some "independent" committees.[36]

In many respects, the council's procedures and conduct compared admirably with those of committees beyond its control. Actual bondholders served on its protective committees without compensation; bonds were not solicited; and the one settlement negotiated before 1940 was far better than the settlement imposed upon bondholders by an "independent" banker-dominated committee for El Salvador. In the long run, however, the council was a conspicuous failure and a formidable barrier to effective resolution of the default situation. It did not provide centralized machinery for setting policy or for coping with the debt problem as a whole; and it failed even its

35. Securities and Exchange Commission, *Proceedings . . . in the Matter of Foreign Bondholders Protective Council* (Washington, 1935), pp. 19, 25–26, 218–21; Foreign Bondholders Protective Council, *Annual Report* (1935), pp. 7, 10.

36. The council organized only two protective committees prior to the SEC inquiry. Both were formed at the request of issuing houses "to deter the formation of . . . outside committees or render them ineffectual." The State Department gave assistance to the council notably in its struggle against the "independent" committee of Cuban bondholders led by William Rosenblatt. See SEC, *Protective Committees,* no. 5, p. 185; SEC, *Peru Proceedings,* pp. 1051–53; SEC, *Foreign Bondholders Protective Council,* pp. 862–65.

primary mission: to push vigorously bondholders' claims, when these claims threatened short-term obligations owed to houses of issue or their former affiliates. The council created new protective committees to battle "independent" committees, but the council could not regulate the practices of the "independent" committees. The council harassed "independent" committees and prevented the formation of others, but it could not develop a coherent policy by responding only at the behest of individual issuing houses.[37]

Debtor governments, above all in Latin America, had only limited funds available for exchange. They were eager to use these funds to maintain current, short-term credit. Issuing houses and former affiliates were also more concerned with the present flow of monies than with past, long-term obligations. As a consequence, issuing houses continued to receive regular payment on short-term notes while bondholders remained empty-handed. The council did not urge restraint upon the bankers, many of whom served as council directors. Nor did the council protest to the debtor governments, or make any effort to mediate the situation. J. Reuben Clark stated the council's attitude: "I think there must be a 'live and let live' [policy] with reference to all of these credits." This meant, of course, that some individuals and some institutions continued to live much better than others. By adopting a laissez-faire policy, the council encouraged the continuation of many sepa-

---

37. Bondholders on the council's protective committees were usually institutional representatives (e.g. Aetna Insurance, Hudson Railroad, Princeton University), but the protective committee played only a loose advisory role to the president and vice-president of the executive committee. The council's only fall from grace occurred when the SEC discovered that the Aetna Company had purchased Cuban bonds at depressed prices while Aetna's president served as chairman of the protective committee for Cuban bonds. A place on the same committee had been denied previously to William Rosenblatt because he was regarded as a speculator, having purchased his Cuban bonds at depressed prices. See SEC, *Foreign Bondholders Protective Council,* pp. 261–62, 674, 713–14; SEC, *Peru Proceedings,* pp. 1079–81.

rate policies where issuing houses and the affiliates frequently held the balance of power.[38]

The council was not, however, a consistent servant of the investment bankers, despite their heavy financial support. Many conflicting interests were represented on the council's protective committees and, although some interlocked with major banking houses, not even Aetna Insurance could forever sacrifice its own investments for the goodwill of the National City Bank. Investment bankers supported the council because it served *some* of their purposes: the council discouraged irritating law suits and "independent" protective committees. The council, in turn, supported investment bankers because they served *some* of the council's purposes: reliable operating funds and bondholders' lists. But the welfare of bondholders and the welfare of bankers were also in conflict with other American economic interests. Foreign finance was a no-sum contest: partial payment for the bondholders meant the loss of new credits for the bankers and possible reduction in the settlement of short-term obligations. Direct purchases by debtor governments of American capital equipment often diluted payments to both bondholders and bankers. Every interest group functioned on the principle that gain for one meant net loss to the other. These separate, clashing strategies became a major barrier to all unified plans for assisting in the financial rehabilitation of foreign economies. Departmental rivalries within the American government exacerbated the problem. Each department became, to some extent, the captive of one program or the guardian of one or two interests. The council, however,

38. The Central Hanover Bank and Trust Company, for example, had $15.5 million in short-term credits outstanding at the end of 1933, including loans to Chile, Argentina, and Peru. By 1935, although this figure had been reduced to $4.5 million, the bondholders gained no relief. The Bank of New York and Trust Company had $608,800 short-term credits outstanding in 1933, including loans to Brazil. This debt was reduced to $17,000 by 1935. Council directors Chubb and Traphagen served as president of the two institutions. See SEC, *Protective Committees,* no. 5, pp. 659–60, 690; SEC, *Foreign Bondholders Protective Council,* p. 242.

in alliance with the State Department, became the most serious impediment to financial reconstruction abroad. Instead of growing into an efficient and successful institution for negotiations, as Raymond Stevens and others predicted, the council became a creature of delay and impotence. Predicated upon private initiative and responsibility, the council became increasingly dependent upon government intervention as a ward of the State Department. At the same time, it acted as an obstacle to the Treasury's preferred policies.

Latin America was the battleground. In 1938, a deteriorating European situation brought home to American policy makers the necessity for increasing United States economic assistance to the nations of South America. Without such aid, Secretary of the Treasury Henry Morgenthau believed, Latin America would become "a helpless field for political and economic exploitation by the aggressor nations." Following the Lima Conference in 1938, Morgenthau and his Treasury advisers became the exponents of a coordinated attack upon South America's financial problems. Morgenthau hoped to stabilize the currencies of these countries; to provide funds for limited economic development; and to subsidize the export of American capital goods as a domestic recovery measure. The State Department also recognized the necessity for American economic assistance, but many of its advisers placed the welfare of bondholders above economic development or America's export trade. Feis, for one, thought it "good policy" to inform the South Americans that "if they continue this complete . . . neglect of that bond situation, the American government wouldn't give . . . any financial help."[39]

Morgenthau began modestly in 1939. But his program to stabilize Brazil's currency and to encourage the continued purchase of American exports crumbled against the State Department's intransigence. Brazil received a two-year credit of $19 million from the Export-Import Bank. Yet it faced

---

39. John M. Blum, *From the Morgenthau Diaries: Years of Urgency, 1938–41,* pp. 50–56.

yearly payments of $36 million to American bondholders, and
the State Department would not intercede with the bondholders' council in an effort to scale down the principal or interest.
Nor would the department recommend a larger credit. Rebuffed, Morgenthau toyed with other methods to circumvent
the bondholders and the State Department: a currency loan to
Brazil from the Treasury's Stabilization Fund, or a loan from
the RFC to a Brazilian corporation chartered in the United
States, or even the creation of a Bank of North and South
America. All of these approaches and suggestions produced resistance from the State Department, hostility in the Congress,
and vacillation on the part of the President. "The whole thing
gets down to this," an exasperated Morgenthau told Harold
Ickes, "whether this so-called Bond Holders Committee [the
council] is going to lay down the foreign policy, or whether Mr.
Roosevelt is going to be able to lay it down." "I'm betting on
the Bond Holders," Ickes said, "if the State Department is to
pass on it."[40]

Ickes, however, underestimated the secretary's resourcefulness. Morgenthau adopted a new tactic. Instead of fighting
the bondholders and the State Department, he proposed to
help them reach settlements. In order to clear up the debt situation as a prelude to other programs, Morgenthau decided to
work with the council, reform the council if necessary, and
break the State Department's policy monopoly. He hoped to
enter all debt negotiations personally along with Jesse Jones
of the Export-Import Bank.

Initially, Morgenthau sought cooperation from the State
Department. Undersecretary Sumner Welles agreed that "the
private debt situation should not hold up the program of
cooperative assistance." Welles even supported Morgenthau's
growing belief that "given the existing personnel [of] the Foreign Bondholders' Protective Council . . . there was no prospect of debt settlement being discussed on a practicable basis."
Welles balked, however, at bringing Jesse Jones into future

40. Ibid., pp. 57–58.

negotiations. Morgenthau continued to criticize the State Department's close relationship with the council. Before he would undertake negotiations with Latin American governments, the secretary wanted the State Department "to give me . . . the formula that they will pursue in regard to . . . the debt owing to our private citizens." He thought it "childish" for the department "to say that until these countries will pay 100 cents on the dollar, whether they can or not, we won't do business with them."[41]

By the fall of 1939, Morgenthau had impressed upon FDR and Cordell Hull the need for a comprehensive program. The State Department, Morgenthau proposed, could select suitable Latin American countries and Treasury experts would then design financial programs for them. Debt settlement and new credits from the Export-Import Bank would be tied together, although each negotiation would remain separate. Welles, Morgenthau, and Jones would have primary responsibility for working out the final details of each plan. Morgenthau hoped for unified action. "I don't want to have happen what did in Brazil," he told Jones, "that for three weeks they [the State Department] put the screws on these fellows [from Brazil] while they tried to extract some money for the private bondholders. . . . You can't put the private debt off in one corner and at the same time turn about making a loan to them and then put the screws on these fellows."[42]

Colombia became the target country. Welles informed Morgenthau that United States and Colombian representatives had devised a plan whereby the privately held Colombian debt would be settled on the basis of 3 percent interest with an in-

41. Henry Morgenthau, Diary, re interview between Morgenthau and Sumner Welles, July 24, 1939, 204:255 ff., and 205:66–69, Franklin D. Roosevelt Library.

42. The secretary blamed the bondholders' greed and the State Department's myopia for ruining the political career of Brazil's pro-American chief negotiator and minister of foreign affairs, Oswaldo Aranha (Morgenthau, Diary, 218:34–35).

crease to 4 percent after three years. Colombia would also seek a loan of $10.5 million from the Export-Import Bank. This plan was endorsed at a Treasury meeting on November 22, but no one present could forecast the reaction of the Council of Foreign Bondholders. Welles, for one, felt that unless the council was "radically overhauled . . . it is not going to be able to serve the position for which it was created." It was agreed to "feel them out on the program," and "not encounter their hostility." John Hanes, undersecretary of the Treasury Department and a former stock broker, was asked to get the council "in order."[43]

Hanes met with John Traphagen, who suggested that the council appoint a special committee for the Colombian negotiations and not rely upon the council's executive committee. This pleased Hanes. Francis White, he said, "is the fellow that has been the fly in the ointment. . . . I thought it would be better to have a new chairman represent this particular thing and . . . get off on the right foot." Hanes assured Morgenthau that the council, at least Traphagen, was not anti-New Deal. "We have got to work with these people," Morgenthau agreed, "unless we want to go out and collect the money, which we don't." Traphagen became the council's representative when talks opened with Colombia. Hanes hoped that the debt negotiations could be combined with negotiations on Colombia's loan. Morgenthau and his assistant, Harry White, demanded that each session remain technically separate. They feared the council would "try to use the loan as a lever and extort more money out of Colombia." In the light of the Brazilian experience, this was not a fanciful objection.[44]

While the Colombian negotiations continued under the joint supervision of Welles, Morgenthau, and Jones, other members of the State Department attempted to regain sole direction of future debt settlements. Feis met with Francis White and in-

43. Morgenthau, Diary, memorandum, Welles to Morgenthau, November 13, 1939, 223:343–44; Diary, 223:336–37.
44. Morgenthau, Diary, 224:303–06; 225:127, 252; 226:2–9.

formed him that new negotiations should begin with Brazil. The State Department, Feis said, "had decided to act alone in the matter and not refer it to the Interdepartmental Committee composed of Welles, Morgenthau and Mr. Jesse Jones." White welcomed this approach since the State Department had earlier insisted that any Brazilian settlement include state and municipal bonds in addition to the Brazilian federal debt. The interdepartmental committee, White feared, might force the council to accept less. Although White accused Morgenthau of undermining the council, he wanted government support for "our minimum requirements" in the Colombian negotiations and he "saw no reason why our Government should not . . . let someone in the Embassy represent us [the council] in Brazil." Morgenthau, learning of Feis's intrigue, was furious. In the secretary's opinion, Feis had no business talking to White about Colombia or Brazil. "The State Department," he said "is more anxious to keep . . . matter[s] in their own hands than they are to get the Treasury's assistance." He accused Feis, Welles, and the State Department of attempting a double-cross. Greatly chagrined, Morgenthau informed Hull that the Treasury would not participate in the Brazilian talks "because State and Feis have been doing things . . . behind Treasury's back and [we] don't know what is going on." Shortly, he abandoned all future negotiations.[45]

The Colombian negotiations were concluded in February 1940 when only a temporary, one-year settlement could be reached. Reluctantly, Morgenthau wrote the final compromise formula. Although the principal of the debt was not scaled down, the Colombians would pay only $1.3 million in 1940 as compared to the council's minimum demand of $2.3 million. Ambassador Jefferson Caffery and the State Department assumed total control of the new Brazilian talks in 1940. Even they were forced finally to abandon the council's excessive claims. "The Council should be told," Caffery said, "that

45. Morgenthau, Diary, 232:432–34; 235:380; 236:449.

[Brazil's] last offer was the best and to stand aside and let individual bondholders decide for themselves."[46]

All in all, the Foreign Bondholders Protective Council did not substantially help American holders of defaulted foreign securities during the New Deal years. Temporarily, it stabilized a chaotic situation and curtailed the rate of theft which the Hoovers and Rosenblatts might otherwise have generated. But the council also hindered the resolution of foreign financial problems. By 1940, Senator Johnson's Title II proposal, whatever its imagined defects, appeared in retrospect preferable to the alternative that FDR chose. The corporation, at least, had a mandate to "determine and regulate" the functions of all protective committees. In addition, Title II held out the possibility of a coordinated government effort not only to assist bondholders but also to encourage international currency stabilization and economic development.

Although not an integral part of Roosevelt's program for securities regulation, Title II and the struggle over it, as well as the subsequent activities of the council, demonstrated the persistent influence of private interest groups upon the content of regulatory policy. Unable to dominate areas of government, many private organizations and individuals retained the capacity to frustrate unwanted encroachments of formal government power. Often, by the very fact of their existence, they were able to assume a large measure of public responsibility. In these respects, the New Deal's experience with Title II and with the council foreshadowed other legislative and administrative conflicts in the area of domestic securities regulation.

46. Morgenthau, Diary, 235:342; 239:73–80, 93–94, 294; 240:220; 245:122–23. 263.

5

The Origins of the Securities and Exchange Commission

In April 1933, Richard Whitney, president of the Essex Fox Hounds, treasurer of the New York Yacht Club, president of the New York Stock Exchange, and confidant of the House of Morgan, took a train to Washington. He wished to learn how Franklin Roosevelt felt about the Exchange and what legislative program could be expected from the Democrats. Shortly after his White House meeting, Whitney wrote the President that the New York Stock Exchange stood ready "to acomplish the purposes you have in mind." He suggested that the Exchange might regulate the activities of its members by limiting the extent to which brokers could act as dealers for their own accounts. This, Whitney said, was an "old principle," and a "sound one." Federal legislation, he cautioned, was undesirable because it would undermine the Exchange's own reform efforts. "Any method of statutory regulation," said the Exchange president, "must mean that the persons affected by any action of the Governing Committee of the Exchange would have the right to appeal to the courts or some administrative tribunal." Although Whitney preferred voluntary self-regulation, he could not guarantee when the Exchange might act. Moreover, it was impossible to forecast the attitude of the Governing Committee. Nonetheless, Whitney was prepared, as he told Roosevelt, "to go forward promptly with the formulation of a plan to carry . . . changes into effect . . . [if] such a program would meet your ideas of what the exchanges should do." Roland Redmond, the Exchange's chief legal adviser, also hoped that "sweeping reforms voluntarily adopted might justify the Administration in withholding legislation to see if the reforms are effective."[1]

Roosevelt, who had decided to delay stock exchange legislation for a short time, did not encourage these pleas for self-regulation. Rather, he let the case for government action grow out of the hearings before Senator Duncan Fletcher's Banking and Currency Committee. Fletcher and his colleagues continued to make headlines during the spring and early summer of 1933 by exposing the past misdeeds of the Exchange and the Wall Street financial community. Then, three months after Whitney's visit, following a wave of short-selling, stock prices plummeted in New York. Bear pools were rampant, particularly in "repeal" stocks such as American Commercial Alcohol. Many conservative businessmen, in addition to battered speculators, were shaken by the event. Edward Stokes, president of Trenton's First National Bank and certainly not a radical, blamed the leadership of the New York Stock Exchange for an "act of incendiarism which impairs the value of the securities of banks . . . and throws a cold blanket on business." No country in the world, he said, "permits such a disgraceful condition except America." Other businessmen, echoing Stokes's sentiments, swelled the chorus of denunciation against the Exchange. They clamored for immediate White House action, including demands for a complete shutdown of every exchange. The experience hardened Roosevelt's attitude toward Whitney's institution. "The fundamental trouble with this whole Stock Exchange crowd," he confided later to Adolph Berle, "is their complete lack of elementary education. I do not mean lack of college diplomas . . . but just inability to understand the country or the public or their obligation to their fellow men. Perhaps you can help them to acquire a kindergarten knowledge of those subjects."[2]

1. Richard Whitney to FDR, April 14, 1933, *SEC,* 1934, VIII, JMLPH; Roland Redmond to FDR, April 11, 1933, OF 34, FDRP, Box 1.
2. Senate Banking and Currency Committee, *Stock Exchange Practices* (Senate Rept. 1455, 73d Cong., 2d sess., 1934), p. 55. On the

Still hoping to avoid federal legislation, the Exchange acted. The Governing Committee, following the July debacle, announced a program of "new reforms." Henceforth, all customer's accounts under $5,000 would require 50 percent margin on the debit balance and 30 percent margin for all accounts over $5,000. Margin computed on the basis of a debit balance was something quite different from margin computed on a customer's total account. A 50 percent margin on a debit balance, although sounding harsh, was equivalent to only a 23 percent margin on a total account. This legerdemain fooled no one. The Governing Committee also asked members to report all pools, syndicates, and joint trading accounts "of which they have knowledge beginning August 4." But no pools, syndicates, or joint accounts were reported. "Why," one critic demanded, "did not the Exchange date the period for information from July 4 to July 20 when the market was honeycombed with pools and syndicates, instead of August 4, when the pools [were] fairly well liquidated." A third "reform" prohibited customers' men from soliciting business in the home or from telephoning clients at home. Since most calls were placed to the client's office or club, this "reform," too, was meaningless. The Exchange's conception of effective, voluntary self-regulation only increased the bitterness of critics and demonstrated the urgent need for federal action.[3]

By 1934, many businessmen, while unwilling to support a specific legislative program, endorsed the concept of government regulation. They shared with other Americans a hunger for economic stability and, like Edward Stokes, they viewed the exchanges as disruptive, unpredictable organizations which constantly threatened that stability. Governmental responsibility for the conduct of these organizations was long overdue.

July episode and the violent reaction from businessmen see Edward Stokes to FDR, July 22, 1933, and other letters, OF 34, FDRP, Box 1; FDR to Adolph A. Berle, August 15, 1934, PPF 1306, FDRP.

3. New York Stock Exchange, *Rules,* 15 (New York, 1933), section 6 and passim; *New Republic,* August 16, 1933, p. 21.

The failure of an earlier generation to confront this issue had proved disastrous. As unincorporated, private associations, largely self-governed, the stock exchanges had demonstrated both their usefulness to a sophisticated capitalist economy and their ability to demoralize that same economy. The basic issues were clear, even to businessmen: could the exchanges assume a responsible role in the nation's commercial life; could they promote rather than retard economic growth; and could they conduct their affairs with probity? Three reforms were essential. The sources and volume of credit available for exchange trading had to be subject to broad national control. This would curtail independent, chaotic decisions by numerous private lenders. The Glass-Steagall Act of 1933 had begun to face this problem by restricting call-loans from nonbanking institutions, including insurance companies and other corporations. The federal government should prohibit or regulate exchange practices that encouraged the gathering of fabulous paper profits without regard for the welfare of the exchange, other investors, or the economy as a whole. Among these practices were wash sales, matched orders, pools, and short-selling, or what one angry insurance company executive characterized as "cheap, undignified, and . . . costly manipulations." Finally, federal regulation, in order to encourage investment behavior based upon reliable information and professional analysis, should require uniform, intelligible financial reports from corporations listed on exchanges. But agreement on generalities did not produce consensus among government leaders and businessmen on the details of legislation or the techniques of regulation.[4]

Roosevelt's decision to proceed separately with securities regulation in 1933 had important consequences for the progress

4. Senate, *Stock Exchange Practices*, pp. 5–80; Ferdinand Pecora, *Wall Street under Oath*, passim; House Interstate Commerce Committee, *Stock Exchange Regulation* (73d Cong., 2d sess., 1934), pp. 20, 44–46, 674; Alfred L. Bernheim and Margaret G. Schneider, eds., *The Security Market*, passim; Alfred L. Bernheim and Margaret G. Schneider, *Stock Market Control*, passim.

of stock exchange legislation a year later. The Securities Act had been a product of the Hundred Days. It emerged with fifteen other statutes, all passed during a hectic fourteen-week period. Legislative decision making, given this crushing load, fell even more than usual to small groups of men who had the expertise, seniority, or good fortune to occupy strategic positions. Only a handful of individuals participated actively in writing the Emergency Banking Act, the Agricultural Adjustment Act, the National Recovery Act, or the Securities Act. Few legislators understood fully the details of any two pieces of legislation passed during the Hundred Days. Senator Carter Glass was typical. He made a brief appearance at the House-Senate conference on the Securities Act. When informed that the bill did not mention the Federal Reserve Board, he left and never returned.[5]

The quantity and pace of other legislation during the Hundred Days had a decisive influence upon the drafting and passage of the Securities Act. Rayburn, even under normal circumstances a powerful chairman, dominated the House Interstate Commerce Committee as never before. The ability of Frankfurter and his colleagues to shape the content of legislation depended upon Rayburn's temporary dictatorship and his confidence in their recommendations. Furthermore, the Senate Banking and Currency Committee did not present satisfactory alternatives. Fletcher's staff continued to concentrate upon the sensational Pecora investigation. Investment bankers, faced with other threatening legislation, were divided, surprised by the securities measure, and ineffective as lobbyists. In both houses of Congress, the 1933 legislation had provoked little substantive debate and few amendments.

5. Arthur M. Schlesinger, Jr., *The Coming of the New Deal*, pp. 20–21; Raymond Moley, *The First New Deal*, pp. 154–220; Ellis W. Hawley, *The New Deal and the Problem of Monopoly*, pp. 19–34; Richard S. Kirkendall, *Social Scientists and Farm Politics in the Age of Roosevelt*, pp. 50–60; James M. Landis, "The Legislative History of the Securities Act of 1933," *George Washington Law Review* 28 (October, 1959): 44–45.

A year later, proponents of stock exchange regulation faced a totally different legislative environment. Frankfurter, whose prestige and discipline guided the 1933 act, was absent, a visiting professor at Oxford. The Banking and Currency Committee, having completed its tedious inquiry, was eager to operate at least as an equal with Rayburn's committee. Max Lowenthal and John Flynn, two members of Fletcher's staff, particularly wanted to impress their ideas upon new legislation. With the atmosphere of crisis removed, both committees and Congress as a whole prepared to resume their traditional roles, which included delay and obscurantism. Stock exchanges, as objects of possible legislation, had anticipated congressional action since the spring of 1933. Although riven by internal power struggles, they were better prepared to face a legislative challenge than the bankers had been a year before. Finally, all realistic efforts to regulate the exchanges would have to reach the nation's credit machinery, above all, the Federal Reserve System. This, however, was the political fiefdom of the Federal Reserve Board and Senator Glass, both of whom were contemptuous of the financial competence of outsiders and jealous of their own independence. The legislative milieu was not propitious for those who anticipated both effective and rapid legislation.

James Landis was more than honest when he remarked that "the origins of the Securities Exchange Act are fairly obscure." Roosevelt entered 1934 without solid recommendations for the Congress. Samuel Untermeyer's ubiquitous bill appeared totally inadequate after the market collapse in 1933 because it envisioned a high degree of self-regulation by the exchanges. It did not mention margin requirements or proscribe a single practice. The charters and bylaws of exchanges would simply contain "regulations and prohibitions which in the judgment of the Postmaster General satisfactorily safeguard the public." Given the mediocrity of past and present incumbents in the Post Office Department, this was a mandate dangerous to the public and to the exchanges. Roosevelt, hoping to break the stalemate, had appointed a committee to evaluate the new

Securities Act and to propose exchange legislation. Chaired by Secretary of Commerce Roper and assistant secretary John Dickinson, the committee had a membership so diverse that few recommendations could command a majority. Among others, it included Landis, Berle, and Arthur Dean of Sullivan and Cromwell. In November 1933, before the committee reported, one member, Henry Richardson, a Washington attorney, circulated his draft of exchange legislation. "This bill is to be drawn," Richardson said, "on the theory that in so far as possible each exchange will discipline its own members and conduct its own affairs." Richardson's bill provided for the creation of an independent Stock Exchange Commission appointed by the President. The membership of Richardson's commission guaranteed administrative impotence. Two of the seven members would represent "the general investing public," two "shall be members of some stock or commodity exchanges," one "shall be engaged in agriculture," and one member "shall represent business." The president of the New York Federal Reserve Bank would serve as perpetual chairman. The seven members would have few positive functions. Like Untermeyer's postmaster general, the commission suggested by Richardson would only approve revisions in the charters and bylaws of the exchanges. Richardson's draft anticipated the plan advanced by Secretary Roper and a minority of his committee in early 1934. Roper's recommendations received enthusiastic support from the Commerce Department's Business Advisory Council.[6]

6. James M. Landis to Robert E. Cushman, March 7, 1941, JMLPLC, Box 171; Samuel Untermeyer, Draft of Stock Exchange Legislation, 1933; Henry Richardson, Draft of Stock Exchange Legislation, November 16, 1933, both *SEC,* II, JMLPH. The Roper-Dickinson report, filed with FDR, called for federal licensing of exchanges and the creation of a seven-man Regulatory Authority. The secretary of commerce, the secretary of the treasury, and the governor of the Federal Reserve Board would serve as permanent members. "Self-regulation should be emphasized," the report concluded, "and . . . the governing boards of the exchanges should, in the first instance, formulate . . . fair rules, subject to the veto of the Federal Regulatory

Landis, in addition to this official administration assignment, began to work independently on a stock exchange bill with Cohen and Corcoran. Having examined Richardson's proposal, Landis rejected a regulatory agency that included exchange members or the president of the New York Federal Reserve Bank. A satisfactory commission, in his opinion, needed more autonomy from the financial establishment. Requirements for listing securities on the exchanges could be enforced by the Federal Trade Commission, Landis said, "but the Federal Reserve Board should have some powers," such as jurisdiction over margins. Although not averse to giving exchange governing committees disciplinary power over members, he insisted upon "recourse to a public agency where Governing Committees fail to act." Cohen and Corcoran did not share all of these ideas, but they agreed with Landis on a larger issue: legislation must involve more than the supervision of existing institutions. Frankfurter's three protégés hoped to change significantly the exchanges' internal organization. They received encouragement from Ferdinand Pecora and Lowenthal, members of Senator Fletcher's staff, who suggested that they prepare a bill for the opening of Congress in January 1934. Landis and Cohen gave the preliminary work to two young government lawyers, I. N. P. Stokes and Telford Taylor. Before Cohen put the bill into final form, it had been rewritten thirteen times and subject to advice and criticism from Landis, Corcoran, John Flynn, and Winfield Riefler, a friend of Cohen's, who worked as a statistician for the Federal Reserve Board. Their measure, which Rayburn and Fletcher introduced on February 10, promised not only to revolutionize the role of stock exchanges in American business life, but to

---

Authority." This placed considerable initiative in the hands of the exchanges, since the governing boards would promulgate rules relating to pools, margin, short-selling, floor trading, and disclosure requirements. See Daniel C. Roper, memorandum, February 20, 1934; Business Advisory Council to Roper, March 6, 7, 1934, both OF 34, FDRP, Box 2.

revise drastically the conduct of corporations, their directors, officers, and principal stockholders.[7]

"There is no social philosophy behind this bill," Corcoran told the Senate Banking and Currency Committee. "This is not at all a moral proposal for abolishing stock trading. This [bill] is the result of . . . economic judgment." Actually, the draftsmen of the first Rayburn-Fletcher bill, above all Cohen and Flynn, had made important social, moral, and economic judgments: (1) credit for exchange trading should be severely restricted; (2) the activities of individual exchange members

7. James M. Landis, memorandum, November 8, 1933, *SEC,* VIII, JMLPH; Schlesinger, *Coming of the New Deal,* pp. 456–57; House, *Stock Exchange Regulation,* p. 82. The tentative bill which Stokes and Taylor gave to Cohen on February 1 invested total administrative control in the FTC. It gave that agency sweeping powers to regulate exchange activities. The commission would license exchanges that adopted trading and listing requirements set forth in the statute. They were also required to adopt and enforce all subsequent FTC rules. Although the bill did not set a fixed figure for margin trading, the commission was required to establish the minimum equity below which no account could be maintained, the minimum percentage which the value of collateral should bear to the total price of the securities carried, and the basis on which securities would be valued for the purpose of determining margin. Short sales were subject to FTC control, including complete prohibition "in periods of emergency," or below "the highest price at which the security . . . has been sold during the day or below the price of the last sale of the security." Directors and officers of listed corporations were prohibited from carrying margined accounts and from executing short sales. Pools, wash sales, and matched orders were forbidden. Exchange members and their firms were required to confine themselves either to dealing for their own accounts or acting as brokers for others "except as may be permitted by the Commission." Specialists fell under the same ban. The bill also included a schedule of information required from all corporations seeking trading privileges. The Stokes-Taylor draft took a definite step away from the concept of self-regulation by the exchanges. Compared to Cohen's final version, however, the Stokes-Taylor bill was moderate. See I. N. P. Stokes, Preliminary Draft for a Bill to Regulate Security Exchanges, January 10, 1934; Stokes and Taylor, Draft of Exchange Regulation, February 1, 1934; both *SEC,* II, JMLPH.

should be clearly defined and circumscribed in order to make precise the relationship between members and clients and in order to force the exchanges to fulfill their primary obligation as a public marketplace; (3) trading by directors, officers, and principal stockholders of listed corporations should be subject to public scrutiny and legal redress; (4) the financial affairs of listed corporations should be a matter of public record. Cohen's bill gave the Federal Trade Commission almost plenary control over the exchanges. The FTC would register exchanges when they filed statements to comply with and enforce all provisions and amendments to the statute and to abide by all subsequent rules and regulations. Sections 6, 7, 8, 10, and 15 contained the most important provisions.[8]

Section 6, detailing margin requirements, had been written with Riefler's assistance. Brokers were forbidden to extend or maintain credit on any securities not registered upon a national securities exchange. They were further forbidden to extend or maintain credit in an amount exceeding "which ever is the higher of (1) 80 per centum of the lowest price at which such security has sold during the preceding three years; or (2) 40 per centum of the current market place." The Federal Trade Commission was empowered to set higher requirements. It could not, however, fix lower ratios. Through this section, the bill's draftsmen hoped to reduce the volume of trading by restricting collateral to listed securities and by discouraging small investors from entering the market. High margins, they believed, would prevent precipitous liquidation. In addition, the provisions favored as collateral those securities which had demonstrated three years of relative price stability. "From the sheer unmoral standpoint of public policy," Corcoran said, "it is probably more important to protect the business system . . . than it is to protect the lamb." Margin requirements, he added, must have statutory definition: "Any Government com-

8. Senate Banking and Currency Committee, *Stock Exchange Practices* (73d Cong., 2d sess., 1934), p. 15, pp. 6493–94. A typewritten copy of the Cohen bill may be found in *SEC*, II, JMLPH. The bill is also printed in full in House, *Stock Exchange Regulation*, pp. 1–15.

mission that is put down here with complete discretion is going to be under terrific pressure all the time to push these margins to the limit. The placing of a bright line beyond which discretion cannot go assures you . . . of the . . . policy you are trying to effect." Section 7 of the bill placed further restraints upon exchange credit. Brokers could not borrow funds except from a member bank of the Federal Reserve System, and their aggregate indebtedness was limited to ten times their current assets. Here again, the draftsmen had opted for stability. "This is a provision," Corcoran said, "to make certain that brokers do not operate on a shoestring and that there is a capital cushion for their customers.[9]

Section 8 prohibited by statute numerous deceptive and manipulative techniques used by exchange members and corporation insiders to unsettle and exploit the market. Wash sales, matched orders, and joint trading accounts, "for the purpose of raising or depressing the price of . . . securities or for the purpose of creating . . . a false or misleading appearance of active trading," were declared illegal. Trading for the purpose of "pegging, fixing, or stabilizing the price" of a security was forbidden without prior notification to the exchange and to the Federal Trade Commission. Finally, all transactions were forbidden in securities "whereby any party . . . acquires any put, call, straddle, or other option or privilege."[10]

Section 10 contained the boldest innovations. Brokers could not function as dealers or underwriters "whether or not registered on any national securities exchange." Floor trading by members for their own account was thus abolished. Moreover, specialists were forbidden to trade for their own account and could not effect transactions "except on fixed price orders." By design, then, section 10 limited exchange membership to commission brokers who executed orders for the public. Section 10 elevated the outside investor by eliminating the inside gambler.[11]

9. Senate Banking and Currency Committee, *Stock Exchange Practices,* p. 6494; House, *Stock Exchange Regulation,* pp. 1–15.
10. House, *Stock Exchange Regulation,* pp. 11–12.
11. Ibid.

Section 10 had occasioned prolonged debate among the bill's draftsmen. Flynn, financial critic for the *New Republic* and soon to be Senator Nye's alter ego during a munitions investigation, was the most vocal proponent of complete, statutory segregation for brokers and dealers. He possessed a quick but conspiratorial mind, and few men could match his hatred of the New York financial community. In Flynn's opinion, floor traders and specialists who bought and sold securities for their own account were immoral and parasitical. Recently slighted by Richard Whitney during Fletcher's inquiry, he nursed deep, personal resentments against the leadership of the New York Stock Exchange. This leadership was composed almost entirely of floor traders and specialists. Despite the skepticism of Cohen and others, Flynn's attitude prevailed on section 10. They thought the provisions were too radical to withstand congressional scrutiny. Nonetheless, Corcoran made a spirited defense of the section before both House and Senate committees. He noted that four major Wall Street firms had collapsed recently because their underwriting business had been connected with brokerage accounts. Underwriters, committed to a successful flotation, could not respond as impartial investment counselors. He deplored firms "combining all these functions," and brushed aside the possibility that many underwriters and brokers might be forced out of business as a result of segregation. Corcoran reserved his strongest condemnation for floor traders: "There is no reason why anyone trading for himself should have a jump on the rest of the buying public by being on the floor and knowing what is going on whereas the rest of the public has to buy strictly from the ticker outside. . . . They [floor traders] simply follow the market the way sea birds follow a ship. . . . They serve no purpose . . . to make the market any better for the investor on the outside."[12]

Under section 15, the FTC's jurisdiction reached exchange

12. Senate, *Stock Exchange Practices,* pp. 6520–27; House, *Stock Exchange Regulation,* pp. 116–24; interview with Benjamin V. Cohen, August 21, 1967. On Flynn see Schlesinger, *Coming of the New Deal,* p. 461, and Flynn's own writings: *Investment Trusts Gone Wrong,* passim, and *Graft in Business,* passim.

trading by directors, officers, and principal stockholders of listed corporations. Directors, officers, and beneficial owners of 5 percent "of any class of securities of any issuer . . . registered on a national securities exchange" were required to inform the commission of their holdings and to report monthly all changes in their portfolios. They were forbidden to purchase the securities of their corporations with the intention or expectation of selling within six months. All profits made on such transactions, extending over a period of less than six months, would be recoverable by the corporation, irrespective of the "intention or expectation" of the director, officer, or beneficial owners.[13]

13. Senate, *Stock Exchange Practices*, pp. 6466–67. Cohen's bill, of course, contained other vital provisions. Section 9, for instance, prohibited all short-selling or the execution of stop-loss orders, "except in accordance with such rules and regulations as the Commission may prescribe." Sections 11 and 12 enumerated the information required from corporations. Here, Cohen followed closely the disclosure provisions of the Securities Act. In addition, the FTC could demand quarterly balance sheets, income statements, and monthly reports, including a statement of sales or gross income. Section 13 subjected all proxy solicitations to detailed statutory requirements and the rules and regulations of the commission. Section 18, considered by Cohen the most important, defined the commission's special rule-making authority. An administrative tribunal without flexible powers, Corcoran said, "would be like advising that one put a baby into a cage with a tiger to regulate the tiger." The Federal Trade Commission must have such powers, he warned, "or the stock exchanges and the forces allied with the stock exchanges will actually regulate the regulators." The FTC, through rules and regulations, could prescribe the form of listing requirements, "the methods to be followed in the preparation of accounts, in the appraisal or valuation of assets and liabilities, [and] in the determination of depreciation and depletion." The commission could also define accounting, technical, and trade terms used in the statute. In addition, the FTC was given authority to promulgate rules and regulations for the exchanges, including the classification of members, uniform rates of commissions, minimum units of trading, the expulsion or disciplining of members, and suspension of trading in any registered security for a period of ninety days. Through Section 14, the commission received a broad mandate to draft rules and regulations for the vast over-the-counter market.

Frankfurter was delighted with the bill. "That," he wrote FDR from England, "is an astonishingly careful and acute piece of draftsmanship. . . . A fine blend has been achieved between fixity and flexibility, between the things that specifically should be enumerated by legislation . . . and the things as to which necessary discretionary power must be left to the Federal Trade Commission." Ominously, he alerted the President to the dangers ahead and to the strategy of the exchanges: "Their game, plainly enough, is like . . . that of the utilities . . . namely, to have the 'right' kind of regulatory body . . . devoid of the necessary courage and resourcefulness for making the legislation effective. They would like . . . what might be called the [Tom] Prendergast type of administration." Frankfurter correctly diagnosed the broad strategy of some opponents. But even he would have been surprised by the numerous interest groups about to descend upon the measure.[14]

From the standpoint of greater economic stability and improved business morals, the first Rayburn-Fletcher bill was, as Frankfurter observed, brilliantly conceived and expertly drawn. But from the standpoint of political possibilities in the fourth year of depression, it was doomed to revision. Seldom has one measure antagonized so many different constituencies. It promised an organizational revolution on the exchanges, including the abolition of existing, lucrative functions such as those of odd-lot dealers and floor traders. And while increasing the influence of brokers and commission houses, it promised to reduce their volume of business through high margin requirements. The Federal Reserve Board could only feel threatened by the introduction of the Federal Trade Commission into a major area of national credit supervision. The board, in a hasty memorandum to Senator Glass, argued that control over margin accounts should not be vested "in a completely separate administrative authority like the Federal Trade Commission, whose policies may well be at variance with the policies adopted

14. Felix Frankfurter to FDR, February 22, 1934, FFPLC, Box 34. Tom Prendergast was the Democratic party's power broker in Kansas City.

by the Federal Reserve Board." Under section 7, banks outside the Federal Reserve System were deprived of all participation in brokers' loans. These state-chartered institutions, long hostile to central banking ideas, viewed such a provision as detrimental to their own business and as another attempt to force them into the tentacles of the Federal Reserve. A dedicated congressional battalion stood with the state banks on this issue. Businessmen, big and small, looked askance at the disclosure sections which presaged further upgrading of corporate accounting and reporting. Paul V. Shields, an influential New York commission broker and long an opponent of Whitney's regime, expressed the sentiment of Wall Street moderates: "These smart young birds, commonly referred to as the Frankfurter fellows, are going way too far." Reform sentiment within the business and financial community, always a fleeting commodity, vanished suddenly. Robert E. Wood, the testy Sears and Roebuck president who supported much of the early New Deal and who "shed no tears over any beating given to the New York Stock Exchange," feared that the measure would place "every corporation in the land under the supervision of the Federal Trade Commission, loading it with reports and subjecting it to . . . bureaucratic control." Raising the income of farmers was one thing; probing Sears and Roebuck was another. John Biggers, president of Libbey-Owens-Ford, and other businessmen agreed.[15]

The bill's sponsors, as Corcoran's testimony revealed, hoped to rationalize the exchanges by carefully segregating major functions. Using the New York Stock Exchange as a model, they failed to evaluate the peculiar economic situation of small-

15. Federal Reserve Board, memorandum on S. 2693, Box 316, CGP; Paul V. Shields to James A. Farley, March 22, 1934, OF 34, FDRP, Box 2; Robert E. Wood to FDR, February 28, 1934, CGP, Box 316; John Biggers to Carter Glass, February 28, 1934, CGP, Box 316. Secretary of Commerce Roper, usually a barometer of business opinion, objected violently to the "numerous very detailed provisions going outside the field of strict stock exchange regulation . . . to regulate various corporate practices" (Daniel C. Roper, memorandum, February 20, 1934, OF 34, FDRP, Box 2).

er, regional exchanges. They also failed to calculate the immense political leverage of these institutions and their members. Regional exchange members commonly combined the activities of dealers and brokers. In addition to executing odd-lot orders in securities listed on the New York Stock Exchange, they participated as dealers in national underwriting syndicates, purchased the offerings of local enterprises for their own accounts, and acted as brokers for local securities when traded on the regional exchanges. As dealers they helped to finance local public works projects. Segregation would restrict the activities of regional exchange members by forcing them to become brokers and exchange members or dealers without exchange membership. Either choice threatened to reduce their income during lean years. The governing committees of regional exchanges were loath to see membership decline further. Local businessmen and political leaders, moreover, disliked the thought of any reduction in the number of informal underwriting sources provided by the smaller firms which traditionally combined dealer and broker functions. Regional exchanges could play upon all of these anxieties, real and imagined, to convince congressmen that section 10 meant economic stagnation for local enterprise, public and private. On the issue of segregation, the New York Stock Exchange had a valuable ally in its tiny, often destitute rivals.[16]

For three weeks, the patriarchs of investment banking and the exchanges sat grimly before the Rayburn and Fletcher committees. They condemned the proposed legislation as unnecessary, unworkable, and un-American. Whitney and Redmond led the assault, but representatives from the regional exchanges were particularly effective when forecasting the imminent economic doom of their home areas. "I do not believe any administrative body could have the information, or experience, as compared with what members of the governing committee [of the exchanges] have in order to take such action

16. For a perceptive inquiry into the economic difficulties of the regional exchanges see Frank P. Smith, "The Future of Small Securities Exchanges," *Harvard Business Review* 14 (Spring 1936): 360–70.

with the promptness that such action warrants," Whitney said. Any attempt to regulate the exchanges by statute, he told the Senate committee, "is impossible of accomplishment." He advocated regulation by a "new board of seven members," including two exchange members, the secretary of the treasury, and the secretary of commerce. Above all, regulation should be "flexible and mobile," in the areas of margin requirements, segregation, and corporate reporting. E. Burd Grubb, president of the New York Curb Exchange, endorsed Whitney's plea for a new regulatory agency. Such an institution (he said, "would be confined to exchange problems only and would not be one of the many problems which the regulatory body was considering . . . the commission would not be bound by congressional limitations." Segregation of broker-dealer functions, said Robert Christie of the Investment Bankers Association, would destroy the efficient marketing of state and municipal securities as well as encourage concentration of financial power in New York by eliminating the smaller firms. Representatives from the Cincinnati and Baltimore exchanges were of the same opinion. "Corporations," said W. W. Gradison of Cincinnati, "should not be at the mercy of any one city . . . local capital markets should be encouraged rather than destroyed."[17]

The original draftsmen, smothered by an avalanche of abuse, lacking positive support from any segment of business or finance, and criticized by cabinet members, retreated from the first Rayburn-Fletcher bill. They, too, split apart on the issue of administrative discretion. Flynn and Cohen continued to insist upon explicit statutory prohibitions and requirements, above all in the areas of margin and segregation. Landis and Stokes, on the other hand, preached more administration and less legislation. "The problem is very complex," Landis said, "very delicate, very technical. . . . Flexibility and the opportunity to move rapidly, to experiment, as the exchange itself experiments . . . is imperative in legislation of this type." To individuals like Whitney, discretion and flexibility meant little

17. House, *Stock Exchange Regulation*, pp. 196, 273, 368, 593–94; Senate, *Stock Exchange Practices*, pp. 6582–85, 6734.

more than yawning statutory crevices where one could place enough legal dynamite to demolish a regulatory structure. Landis's plea sprang, in part, from genuine uncertainty about effective regulatory techniques and from an unwillingness to limit administrative resources. But Landis and others also recognized the desirability of compromise. The bill needed new political allies and they could be recruited only by real concessions.[18]

In order to gain friends for a revised bill, Landis, Cohen, and Corcoran broadened their drafting efforts to include representatives from the Federal Reserve Board, the Treasury Department, and New York brokerage houses. Eight days and nights of bargaining in the Federal Reserve building resulted on March 19 in a modified bill. That bill appeased the Federal Reserve by giving the board jurisdiction over margin requirements. The provisions, however, remained complex, and the board's discretion was limited. The new section drew a distinction between an initial extension of credit by brokers and the maintenance of credit. In order to soften the impact, existing margin accounts would not be affected by the requirements until January 1939. Brokers were forbidden to extend credit on listed securities exceeding 40 percent of the current market price, "or if such security has been traded in on a national exchange for a period not less than thirty-six months, 100 percent of the lowest price at which such security has sold during the preceding thirty-six months, but not more than 75 percent of the current market price. If such security has been traded in for a period less than thirty-six months, such amount, but not more than 75 percent of the current market price." Brokers were further forbidden to maintain credit on listed

18. The original bill drew tepid support from large institutional investors, including a few insurance companies and some mutual-fund managers. While welcoming improved investor information, they were not prepared to endorse the entire measure. House, *Stock Exchange Regulation,* pp. 20, 44–46, 674; I. N. P. Stokes, memorandum on Stock Exchange Bill, March 8, 1934, *SEC,* II. JMLPH; interview with Benjamin V. Cohen, August 21, 1967.

securities exceeding 60 percent of the current market price, "or if such security has been traded in for a period of not less than thirty-six months, 100 percent of the lowest price. If such security has been traded in for a period of less than thirty-six months . . . not more than 85 percent of the current market price." The board could increase the ratios "as it may deem necessary or appropriate in the public interest." The board could not reduce the ratios as easily. The bill provided that the statutory figures should "be strictly adhered to . . . as the considered policy of Congress." They could not be changed "except in extraordinary circumstances" and lower ratios could only be set when "vitally essential to the accommodation of commerce and industry."[19]

Cohen, for one, had opposed the administrative shift. The board, in his opinion, was a captive of current financial folklore and too respectful of Wall Street sentiment. He favored unified administration under the Federal Trade Commission and hoped to limit all margin revisions to "a finding of grave national emergency." Cohen's views did not prevail, but with the help of Corcoran, Riefler, and Herman Oliphant of the Treasury, the revisions did include rigid margin guidelines. In addition to circumscribing the board's discretion, the new section provided a unique method for computing margins prepared by Oliphant and Riefler. Although opposed to the distinction between extension and maintenance of credit, Oliphant was nonetheless anxious to provide a margin formula that did not rest entirely on the current market value of securities. A majority of the enlarged drafting team accepted his innovation. "Instead of calculating brokers loans on the basis of the current market," Riefler said, "the lending value . . . should be based upon their [securities] investment record. . . . The most important thing which this bill does is to attempt to set up a new formula . . . which takes into account the history of the security, its general investment value and prevents the security from rapidly increasing its lending value just because it has

19. The revised bill may be found in *SEC,* IV, JMLPH, or House, *Stock Exchange Regulation,* pp. 625–45.

had a speculative rise in price." The new bill also attempted to mollify the numerous, vocal banking institutions that were not members of the Federal Reserve System. They would be permitted to make brokers' loans subject to the rules and regulations of the Federal Reserve Board "where there are no member banks, or to meet emergency needs."[20]

Exchange members were a more difficult constituency to satisfy. The new bill attempted to maintain the principle of segregated functions while allowing the Federal Trade Commission ample administrative flexibility. Cohen, true to the first bill, wished to limit exchange membership to brokers and to prevent members from trading for their own accounts except in the case of odd-lot dealers and specialists. They would be subject to the commission's rules and regulations. The revised bill, however, went further. Subject to FTC regulations, exchanges could permit the registration of members as dealers. Such members were forbidden to trade for their own accounts "while on the trading premises" of the exchange, or "while on the trading premises . . . as a broker to give an order to another member to be executed for his own account." This language seemed to provide for segregation, but an additional provision gave the commission power to permit members "to effect transactions . . . for their own account . . . where, because of the limited volume of transactions effected on an exchange, it is, in the judgment of the Commission impracticable and not in the public interest to deny access to the trading premises . . . to a member . . . for the purpose of effecting . . . any transaction . . . for his own account." The revised section, heavily in-

20. Benjamin V. Cohen, typewritten revision of bill, March 4, 1934, *SEC,* II, JMLPH; Herman Oliphant to James M. Landis, March 8, 1934, JMLPLC, Box 149; House, *Stock Exchange Regulation,* pp. 788–89. An attempt to fragment further the administration of margin requirements had been rejected during the eight-day drafting period. This proposal, drawn by Raoul Desvernine, counsel for the commission brokers, would have given each district Federal Reserve Bank "absolute control over the amount that can be borrowed by [exchange members] in respect to securities" (Raoul Desvernine, memorandum, *SEC,* II, JMLPH).

fluenced by Oliphant's solicitous regard for the smaller exchanges, promised them some relief. At the same time, it sought to curtail excessive, speculative floor trading in New York. Dealers who functioned as brokers were still forbidden to extend or maintain credit on any security "offered to the public by him as a dealer or distributor within six months prior to such transaction," unless the dealer disclosed this participation to customers. It also remained unlawful for specialists registered as brokers, to act as dealers or for specialists, registered as dealers, to act as brokers.[21]

The sections on manipulative devices, corporate reports, listing requirements, proxies, and trading by directors underwent no substantive revision. Other sections, however, were modified in the direction of administrative discretion and self-regulation by the exchanges. Transactions in puts, calls, and options were not prohibited by statute, but subject to the rules and regulations of the FTC. Under a new section 18, exchanges were encouraged to police their members, subject to the commission's review. But the drafting compromises did not include major revisions advocated by Raoul Desvernine, representing the New York brokerage houses. Desvernine, who participated in some sessions, urged the creation of a Securities Exchange Commission composed of three members appointed by the President. At least one commissioner, Desvernine urged, should be experienced in stock exchange practice. In addition, he had suggested the elimination of sections relating to trading by directors, over-the-counter markets, and corporate reports. They were not, he said, "pertinent to exchange regulation."[22]

Roosevelt, while taking a strong position on the second

21. Cohen, typewritten revision of bill, March 4, 1934, *SEC,* II, JMLPH; Oliphant to Landis, March 8, 1934, JMLPLC, Box 149.

22. Raoul Desvernine, memorandum, *SEC,* II, JMLPH; Desvernine to FDR, March 20, 1934, OF 34, FDRP, Box 2. Regulation of directors' transactions was especially offensive to businessmen. Alexander Sachs of the Lehman Corporation accused Landis, Cohen, and Corcoran of attempting to convert management "into a mere salariat and bureaucracy which cannot . . . share in entrepreneurial profits through selling out when occasion arises" (Sachs to Landis, March 9, 1934, *SEC,* VIII, JMLPH).

Rayburn-Fletcher bill, restricted the issue of regulation to margin requirements. While other supporters of the bill tended to emphasize the greater importance of broker-dealer segregation, FDR saw credit as the key to reform. "Speculative trading must be very greatly curtailed," he told Henry Morgenthau, Jr., "[and] that means . . . a much smaller volume of trading on the . . . exchanges; it means also of necessity the requirement of very large margins and sufficient flexibility in some agency of government to increase margin requirements if the minimum amount provided in the bill itself does not in practice greatly curtail speculative trading." He endorsed the entire package, however, four days later in a public letter to Senator Fletcher. "I do not see how any of us," he said, "could afford to have it [the new bill] weakened in any shape, manner or form."[23]

Nonetheless, business and financial spokesmen gave the revised bill a chilly reception. Compromise weakened the bill. It had not produced many new friends. In an attempt to sever the New York commission houses from Whitney's influence, the brokers received a voice in the redrafting sessions. But rejection of Desvernine's major suggestions left the commission houses more antagonistic than before. Shields, speaking for them, said the measure had been written with the intent "to punish all people dealing in securities. They [the bill's draftsmen] do not recognize that there are honest, decent people in this business, and that such people should not be destroyed." The section on margins, he noted, flippantly, was "too involved" and "a bad compromise." The second bill, Fred Kent, a prominent financial columnist, complained to Roosevelt, "is just as unfortunate as the first and will be just as harmful to this country if it is passed. It has a positive tendency to separate men in Government and men out of Government into two opposing camps, which is most unfortunate for a people."[24]

23. Henry Morgenthau, memorandum on conversation with FDR, March 22, 1934; FDR to Duncan Fletcher, March 26, 1934, both OF 34, FDRP, Box 2.
24. Paul V. Shields to Sam Rayburn, March 22, 1934, OF 34, FDRP, Box 1; Fred I Kent to FDR, March 23, 1934, PPF 744, FDRP.

Predictably, Richard Whitney and the governing cabal of the New York Stock Exchange found little to praise in the fresh proposals. "The New York Stock Exchange is opposed," he told Rayburn's committee, "for the same reasons it was opposed to the [first] bill." Whitney wanted the margin section altered to give the Federal Reserve Board "full power to fix such margin requirements as it may deem necessary in view of economic conditions." All statutory prohibitions on floor trading should be removed. The FTC, according to Whitney, could settle this issue through rules and regulations. "Instead of having a fixed rule of law," he said, "we advocate the power being put in a commission to make these rules and regulations, which, if they are wrong, they can immediately change." Rayburn, angered by Whitney's recommendations, said that many members of the New York Stock Exchange urged complete broker-dealer segregation and the abolition of all floor trading. "They are a little tenderfooted about coming down here and saying so in public," he quipped, "but they say so to me." Rayburn, Whitney retorted, had been listening to a few commission brokers who had "a special interest" and who did not "look at the whole point of view." With considerably less aplomb, Whitney returned to New York where, in a desperate effort to unite his constituency, he began to circulate the idea that the legislation had been written "by a bunch of Jews out to get [J. P.] Morgan."[25]

Representatives from regional exchanges remained equally dissatisfied. They wanted explicit statutory assurances that members could function both as brokers and dealers. Floor traders on the New York Stock Exchange were vehement about their exclusion. Specialists lamented the bill's restrictions and predicted that the liquidity of the market would be destroyed. Herbert Lehman, New York's Democratic governor and a Wall Street intimate, warned Roosevelt that the revised bill would reduce the state's revenue by $40 million

25. *House, Stock Exchange Regulation*, pp. 723–26; William B. Harris to James M. Landis, April 24, 1940, JMLPLC, Box 23.

annually in stock transfer taxes. But it remained for James H. Rand, Jr., of Remington Rand Company, and Dr. William A. Wirt, superintendent of schools in Gary, Indiana, to turn the final round of House hearings into *opéra bouffe*. They alleged that the legislation had been written by "brain trusters" who hoped to move the country "along the road from Democracy to Communism." Wirt was certain that the bill formed part of "the whole communistic plot." Instead of dismissing these preposterous accusations, Rayburn's colleagues demanded and secured a special House investigation. The legislative process was thus interrupted for weeks while members of a select committee meditated upon Wirt's muddled discourse. During this frivolous exercise, however, legislation to regulate the exchanges became subject to new influences and underwent further modification. Public debate was only a prelude to a longer, more confused struggle.[26]

The Seventy-third Congress was not inclined to radicalism. While Roosevelt went fishing for seventeen days in the Caribbean, the revised bill encountered major difficulties in both House and Senate committees. Rayburn, who hated friction within his committee, expected a rebellion on the revised bill. Taken as a whole, the Interstate Commerce Committee of seventeen Democrats and seven Republicans was distinguished by its mediocrity: one tobacco farmer, one dairy farmer, one automobile dealer, one independent oil producer, one railroad engineer, four small manufacturers, two real estate promoters, and a few local lawyer-politicians. Eleven members had served in the Congress for fourteen years or more. Like most House committees in 1934, it was Southern in leadership, pedestrian in temperament, and provincial in allegiance. With the exception of Democrats Rayburn, Clarence Lea, and Alfred Bulwinkle, and Republicans Carl Mapes, Schuyler Merritt, and Carrol Reece, members of the committee were not intellec-

26. House, *Stock Exchange Regulation*, pp. 740–49, 763–65, 914–15; Herbert Lehman to FDR, March 24, 1934, and FDR to Lehman, March 27, 1934, both OF 34, FDRP, Box 1; Schlesinger, *Coming of the New Deal*, pp. 457–61.

tually equipped to evaluate the details of exchange legislation.[27] They were capable, however, of accepting at face value the anguished cries of exchange presidents, brokers, dealers, floor traders, specialists, and businessmen who predicted increased unemployment and financial chaos if the revised bill became law. Sensitive to these pressures and to the limitations of his fellows, Rayburn, between March 24 and April 2, ordered revisions made in the bill that would anticipate objections and avoid a committee imbroglio. These defensive alterations further weakened the measure.

The margin section was changed by removing all reference to the considered policy of Congress. The Federal Reserve Board was instructed simply "to prescribe the amount of credit that may be initially extended and subsequently maintained . . . based on the following standards." The ratios designed by Oliphant remained intact. The segregation section was totally rewritten in an attempt to appease further the smaller exchanges. Membership was no longer even theoretically limited to brokers, nor was floor trading prohibited. The FTC was instructed to prescribe rules and regulations "to prevent floor trading by members . . . for their own account and . . . to prevent such excessive trading on the exchange, but off the floor by members . . . for their own account, as the Commission may deem detrimental to the maintenance of a fair and orderly market." In addition, the commission could exempt exchanges and members from all rules and regulations governing floor trading "if because of the limited volume of transactions . . . it is . . . impracticable and not in the public interest . . . to apply any of the foregoing provisions." Even these concessions did not satisfy the full House committee. Members denounced the margin ratios as excessive. After two hours of bitter debate on April 3, Rayburn accepted a motion to refer the controversy to a subcommittee including Lea, George Huddleston, Mapes, and John Cooper, an Ohio Republican. "There will be a statutory formula for margins," Rayburn said after the meet-

27. *Biographical Directory of the American Congress, 1774–1961* and *Congressional Directory,* passim.

ing, "but it is not fixed yet." He denied, rather sheepishly, that there was a conspiracy at work to mutilate the legislation: "That," he said, "is just so much tommyrot."[28]

A storm of equal magnitude buffeted the measure in the Senate. On April 2, Senator Glass let it be known that, in his opinion, the Federal Reserve Board "should not be charged with the responsibility for the fixing of margins, but should keep out of the market." Members of the board, he said, did not know and were not expected to know "very much about transactions on the Stock Exchange." These were portentous words from an individual who viewed the Federal Reserve System as his personal legislative fiefdom. On April 7, Fletcher hinted that the committee might give the Federal Reserve Board complete discretion on margin requirements, but retain for the Federal Trade Commission "all other powers." Two days later, however, by a two-vote margin, Fletcher's committee adopted a Glass amendment that abolished the jurisdiction of both the Federal Reserve Board and the Federal Trade Commission and created a three-man Securities Exchange Commission appointed by the President. The committee delayed a vote on the issue of whether or not the new commission would have total discretion to set margins.[29]

Glass's maneuvers were rooted in a peculiar combination of political and personal attitudes. On the one hand, he hoped to preserve an Olympian independence for the Federal Reserve Board. On the other hand, he wished to satisfy a diverse group of businessmen who feared stock exchange supervision

28. Confidential Committee Print, April 3, 1934, and I. N. P. Stokes, memorandum of amendments for April 3 Committee Print, both *SEC*, III, JMLPH; *New York Times*, April 4, 5, 1934. Stokes, who helped to write the new segregation section, justified the changes on the basis of economic insight rather than political expediency: "It seems unwise to abolish floor trading by statute. The floor trader may serve a very useful function . . . by virtue of the potential competition which he furnishes."

29. *New York Times*, April 3, 4, 1934; Confidential Senate Committee Print, April 4, 1934, *SEC*, V, JMLPH; *New York Times*, April 4, 8, 1934.

by the Federal Trade Commission. A separate regulatory commission had been advocated by the exchanges since the introduction of legislation. As late as April 3, Lathrop Withington, president of the Boston Stock Exchange, had urged the two committees to place control in the hands of a separate, five-man agency. Whitney also favored a new commission. These proposals assumed, however, that the Federal Reserve Board would retain jurisdiction over margin requirements. Yet Glass's amendment removed the board entirely, which made his handiwork no more palatable to the exchanges than the original bill. "My idea," he explained, "was to prevent the Federal Reserve Board from being mixed up with stock gambling." Glass was not an uncritical admirer of the exchanges. Consistently, he advocated a federal stock transfer tax on securities held less than sixty days. Such a proposal, he said, would tax "these gamblers who periodically destroy the business of this country." He also endorsed the elimination of *all* brokers' loans. Glass was a profoundly conservative man who did not want the Federal Reserve Board involved in regulatory functions that he had not personally authorized. The board, he believed, should concentrate on banking problems, and Carter Glass defined banking problems very narrowly. In addition, he had been deluged with complaints from exchange members and businessmen who distrusted the Federal Trade Commission. W. Bowen Fairfax of Hornblower and Weeks told the senator that the men who ran the FTC "are certainly not . . . of wide experience in financial matters." Landis, he said, "is absolutely incapable of handling practical matters." Somewhat naïvely, Glass saw his amendment as one way to maintain the pristine duties of the Federal Reserve Board while at the same time assuaging FTC critics.[30]

Glass's stratagem alarmed the Federal Reserve Board, particularly Governor Eugene Black, who had cooperated origi-

30. *New York Times*, April 10, 1934. W. Bowen Fairfax to Carter Glass, March 27, 1934; George Farney to Glass, March 29, 1934; Mason F. Ball to Glass, April 2, 1934, all in CGP, Box 329; *Congressional Record*, 73d Cong., 2d sess., 78, pp. 8392–96.

nally with the Landis-Cohen group in order to wrest control over margins away from the Federal Trade Commission. Black attempted to wring the same concessions from Senator Glass. He achieved limited success. On April 11, without a record vote, the Banking and Currency Committee adopted an awkward compromise written by Glass and Black. The new regulatory commission would fix margin requirements with respect to the amount of credit that brokers could extend to customers. The Federal Reserve Board, however, would prescribe margin requirements with respect to the amount of credit granted by member banks to brokers. The committee then voted to eliminate all statutory guidelines for margin. The Glass-Black compromise succeeded in technically isolating the Federal Reserve Board from contamination by the stock market, but it also promised divided responsibility and administrative confusion. By deleting all margin ratios, moreover, it left both agencies prey to intense pressure.[31]

The Virginian's amendments created considerable division within the financial community. The governing committees of twenty-five exchanges, including the New York Stock Exchange, endorsed the proposals. Brokerage firms, on the other hand, split over the issue of margin requirements. Many large houses wanted national ratios fixed by statute. The Glass amendments, while eliminating guidelines, also permitted the new commission to adjust brokers' margin requirements on a local or regional basis. "It stands to reason," one New York broker said, "that if people are going to be obliged to put up a fixed margin required by law, they are going to deal with those houses that have the greatest capital, have been in the business the longest time and have offices scattered around the country. The granting of more liberal margins was one of the methods by which small brokerage firms formerly competed with the larger houses." In addition, many investment bankers who had functioned for one year under the jurisdiction of the

31. Confidential Senate Committee Print no. 2, April 14, 1934, *SEC*, V, JMLPH; *Wall Street Journal*, April 11, 1934; *New York Times*, April 12, 1934.

Federal Trade Commission were not pleased by the idea of having to cultivate new relationships with another commission. Robert Christie, IBA president, expressed this sentiment. "I have had a pleasant relationship with Commissioners Landis and [George] Mathews," he told Roosevelt, "and I have a very high regard for them." Finally, many exchange members, investment bankers, and businessmen who disliked the FTC were equally alarmed by the idea of a new commission with substantially the same powers. From their point of view, all administrative tribunals were suspect.[32]

Roosevelt, faced with Glass's amendments, acted cautiously. Conflicting rumors circulated that he favored the new commission and that he opposed the innovation. On April 17, Senator James Byrnes, a reputed spokesman for the White House, introduced an amendment in committee to increase the membership of the new commission from three to five. The amendment passed without objection from Senator Glass. The Senate committee adopted three additional modifications. Administration of the Securities Act was transferred to the new commission. Section 23, dealing with court review of commission orders, was changed to provide that the findings of the commission as to facts would be conclusive, if supported by "substantial evidence." Monthly reports of trading by directors, and principal stockholders would be required only of those owning 10 percent of a corporation's equity securities instead of 5 percent.[33]

The new Senate bill faced two major challenges during floor debate. Robert Bulkley, Ohio's erratic liberal Democrat, introduced an amendment to prohibit brokers' loans entirely. Bulkley's proposal, supported by Southern and Western sen-

32. *New York Times,* April 11, 14, 21, 1934; Robert Christie to FDR, April 18, 1934, OF 242, FDRP, Box 2.

33. Confidential Senate Committee Print no. 2, April 14, 1934; Committee Print no. 3, April 18, 1934; Committee Print no. 4, April 18, 1934, all *SEC,* V, JMLPH; *New York Times,* April 18, 1934; *Federal Securities Exchange Act of 1934* (Senate Rept. 792, 73d Cong., 2d sess., 1934), pp. 1–23.

ators, was beaten 48 to 30. Colorado's Edward Costigan then attempted to return administration of the measure to the Federal Trade Commission. His motion was defeated, 51 to 29. "Progressive sentiment," Costigan bluntly told FDR, "strongly prefers the Federal Trade Commission. . . . It was the combination of the conservatives on both sides of the aisle which gave undue emphasis to the result. . . . The impression prevailed . . . that you desired a new commission. . . . Had that not been so, the result would have been as decisive the other way." Costigan was mistaken. The strength of "progressive sentiment" was demonstrated on Bulkley's amendment. Costigan managed to attract twenty-nine votes only through the addition of five conservative Republicans, some of whom favored the FTC for reasons of economy. Two of them, Warren Austin and Fred Steiwer, hoped to delay the bill by sowing more confusion among the Democrats. Austin, a Vermont Republican, voted against the entire bill. Steiwer, in tandem with his Republican colleague John Townsend of Delaware, attempted to riddle the measure with crippling amendments. Steiwer and Townsend wished to scale down the penalties incurred for violating rules and regulations; remove the new commission's power to require financial statements in addition to those specified by statute; prevent the commission from setting accounting standards; and permit specialists to execute both discretionary and stop-loss orders without reference to the commission's rules and regulations. All of these amendments failed. The Senate bill, complete with a new five-man commission and Senator Glass's cumbersome margin provisions, went to conference with the House.[34]

In the House, Rayburn's special subcommittee had rewritten important sections of the bill between April 3 and April 17. Oliphant's margin formula was the first casualty. In addition, the distinction between initial extension of credit

34. *Congressional Record,* 73d Cong., 2d sess., 78, pp. 8295–98, 8386–96, 8398–8404, 8500–03; Edward P. Costigan to FDR, May 15, 1934, OF 34, FDRP, Box 2. See also Comparative Print of House and Senate bills, *SEC,* VI, JMLPH.

and maintenance of credit disappeared. Statutory guidelines remained, but the ratios were greatly reduced. For an initial extension of credit, brokers could lend 55 percent of the current market value of securities or 100 percent of the lowest market price during the previous thirty-six months, but not more than 75 percent of the current market price. The maintenance of credit fell entirely to the rules and regulations of the Federal Reserve Board. Moreover, the board was instructed simply to fix higher or lower requirements "as it deems necessary to accommodate commerce and industry." Congressman Cooper, speaking for the nation's second largest steel-producing community, pushed through two revisions which weakened the FTC's control over corporate reports and proxy solicitations. The commission was instructed to prescribe the form of reports by corporations "in accordance with accepted principles of accounting." Corporations with listed securities would file reports with the exchanges; duplicate reports would be sent to the FTC, but only if the commission made a specific request. The same procedure was provided for the monthly trading reports of directors, officers, and principal stockholders. All statutory requirements governing the solicitation of proxies were eliminated. This matter was left entirely to the FTC's rules and regulations. Even these revisions did not satisfy the full House committee. Before Rayburn could file a favorable report, the full committee voted to delete the provision in section 15 which enabled stockholders to institute civil suits against directors, officers, and principal stockholders who profited from transactions in a corporation's securities within a six-month period.[35]

Final debate and voting on the House bill was perfunctory. Democrats spoke endlessly on the perfidity of stock exchanges

35. House Subcommittee Print, April 13, 1934, and April 17, 1934, both *SEC,* IV, JMLPH. Comparison of April 17 print with *Securities Exchange Bill of 1934* (House Rept. 1385, 73d Cong., 2d sess., 1934), pp. 24–25; *New York Times,* April 25, 1934; *Congressional Record,* 73d Cong., 2d sess., 78, p. 7929.

and Wall Street. Republican members, led by the reactionary Fred Britten of Illinois, showered vitriol upon Rayburn, Cohen, Corcoran, and Landis who, they said, were attempting to Russianize the American economy. But Rayburn, now commanding a sizable majority, rolled back further attempts to weaken the measure and quashed all innovations from the floor before the House passed the measure on May 4, 281 to 84.[36]

At this juncture, Rayburn, like the President, was more concerned with margin requirements than with a specific administrative structure. Representative Bulwinkle accused Rayburn of wanting the Federal Trade Commission only for trading purposes: "In the end you will come back here from the conference . . . and vote for a different commission." The chairman, feigning injury, replied: "I shall never agree to it unless I have to, in order to get a bill or have to give up something I think is more important." On May 16, before the conference, Roosevelt dealt the Texan a strong hand. "I am telling the conferees," he informed Costigan, "that I kept my hands off while [the bill] was in the Senate but that my personal preference is the Federal Trade Commission." Roosevelt reaffirmed

36. An amendment allowing mutual savings banks to participate in brokers' loans, without submitting to the rules and regulations of the Federal Reserve Board, did not attract a majority. Representative Samuel Pettengill of Indiana sought to eliminate monthly trading reports by those owning 5 percent of a corporation's securities. Republican John Hollister attempted to place all orders of the Federal Trade Commission under the possibility of immediate court injunction. Republican Hamilton Fish disliked all rules and regulations. He wanted the FTC to issue only formal orders, thus opening up another avenue for litigation. Representative Jed Johnson of Oklahoma favored a federal stock transfer tax on "white-collared parasites." He hoped in this way to "tax the damnable stock exchanges out of business." Alfred Bulwinkle and Merritt proposed a new three-man commission "to control stock exchange activity, and not business management and business practices." All of these amendments failed. See *Congressional Record,* 73d Cong., 2d sess., 78, pp. 7698, 7700, 7861–68, 7935–39, 8020–38, 8090–99, 8102–16.

his attitude at a press conference on the following day, but emphasized that he was "speaking personally."[37]

The President's remarks, when combined with the cavalier tactics of Fletcher, provoked great resentment in the Senate. Fletcher, ignoring the seniority of Glass, Robert Wagner, and Townsend, all supporters of the new commission, chose Alben Barkley, Byrnes, and James Couzens as the Senate's conferees. Byrnes and Couzens had voted with Fletcher in committee against the Glass proposals. Moreover, Couzens had voted on the floor of the Senate for Costigan's FTC amendment. Calling these selections "a gross affront," Glass resigned from the Banking and Currency Committee and denounced the President for breaking an alleged promise to support the new commission. Barkley offered to step down from the conference committee. He, too, accused the President of bad faith. Roosevelt, as usual, had given encouragement to many but promises to few. The President, according to Arthur Krock, told Glass "he did not object to the new agency." This, of course, did not preclude a preference for the FTC or the tender of bargaining support to Rayburn. Majority Leader Robinson refused to accept the theatrical resignations, but Barkley vowed he would never accept the Federal Trade Commission "because . . . the bill touches 50,000,000 people . . . who have investments and whose interests should be protected by an agency . . . not . . . too busy with other matters."[38]

The Landis-Cohen group threw their support behind Rayburn. They, too, hoped to increase the leverage of House conferees on the margin requirements by providing a strong argument for the retention of the Federal Trade Commission. Entrusting administration to the FTC, they said, "would obviate the necessity for setting up an entirely new governmental agen-

37. *Wall Street Journal,* April 13, 17, 1934; *Congressional Record,* 73d Cong., 2d sess., 78, pp. 8108–09; FDR, memorandum for Marvin McIntyre, May 16, 1934, OF 34, FDRP, Box 2; *New York Times,* May 20, 1934.

38. *Wall Street Journal,* May 16, 1934; *New York Times,* May 16, 17, 1934.

cy with the attendant delay and organizational difficulties." A separate commission would require new personnel, including secretaries, lawyers, economists, statisticians, and a complete field organization. They estimated that the government would save $500,000 annually through administration by a division of the Federal Trade Commission, rather than by a separate agency. More dramatically, they noted that public utility companies were planning to sell "hundreds of millions" of refunding issues during the next year. These companies hoped "to have the registration of . . . offerings in other hands than the Federal Trade Commission, with its voluminous records of the financial practices of power companies and its staff of experts intimately informed on these matters."[39]

Federal Reserve spokesmen also rallied to the House bill because it gave the board complete control over both bank loans to brokers and brokers' loans to customers. They pointed out the absurdity of Glass's attempt to divide these duties: "to divorce the regulation of one . . . from the regulation of the other, or to place . . . the regulation of either in the hands of two distinct governmental agencies, is utterly impracticable and will defeat the purposes of this legislation." Unified control of stock exchange credit, the board concluded, could best be achieved by adopting the major provisions of the House bill.[40]

When the bargaining began in the conference committee, Rayburn quickly accepted a separate five-man commission to administer both the exchange legislation and the Securities Act. The Senate conferees, in turn, agreed to the margin ratios contained in the House bill and gave complete control over this section to the Federal Reserve Board. Reluctantly, Glass swallowed the compromise. "I regret," he said, "that they bring the Federal Reserve Board into the picture in a rather dangerous way." The Senate prevailed in two other major areas. The Securities and Exchange Commission could pre-

39. James M. Landis and Benjamin V. Cohen, memorandum, May 1934, CGP, Box 316.
40. Federal Reserve Board, memorandum, May 1934, CGP, Box 316.

scribe the form and methods to be followed in the registration statements of corporations without regard to "accepted principles of accounting." Directors, officers, and principal stockholders remained liable for the recovery of trading profits within a six-month period, but the section fell only upon holders of 10 percent of a corporation's securities.[41]

The stock exchange bill, which Roosevelt signed into law on June 6, 1934, provided the first real confrontation between his administration and important segments of the business community on the issues of domestic financial reform and stability. Political circumstances had delayed the test until 1934. Congress, racked by a general economic crisis in 1933, played a more independent role a year later. The exchanges, alert to the imminence of legislation, wielded considerable influence. Because of its greater complexity, the 1934 legislation touched a wider spectrum of public and private groups. It thus incurred more enemies. But above all, the original conception of the exchange legislation had been revolutionary. Unlike the Securities Act, the first and second Rayburn-Fletcher bills of 1934 proposed drastic organizational changes for the financial community as a whole and entirely new methods of transacting business on the exchanges. Congress, however, vetoed all major innovations for computing margin requirements and only instructed the new commission to study the feasibility of broker-dealer segregation.

The fact that Congress rejected one radical proposal and deferred another accounted, in part, for the guarded enthusiasm with which members of the financial community received the final bill. But many also welcomed the measure because it promised to remedy the most flagrant exchange abuses and, hopefully, restore the public's faith in those institutions. "The trend in the brokerage business," said Jesse Halstead of the Chicago Stock Exchange, "will be more and more toward a

41. First Preliminary Conference Print, May 25, 1934, *SEC*, VI, JMLPH; *Conference Report on Securities Exchange Act of 1934* (House Rept. 1838, 73d Cong., 2d sess., 1934), pp. 1–42; *New York Times,* May 27, 1934.

professional relationship between broker and customer. . . . The Act marks a new period in this business." Raoul Desvernine said the final bill "corrects most of the original objections. . . . [It] should prove practicable and might readily result in revived confidence in the stock exchanges."[42]

Numerous, substantive issues remained unresolved. Congress, unwilling to offend powerful, entrenched economic interests and reluctant to impose statutory solutions, had given the new commission extensive rule-making authority. The legislature avoided clear decisions in such areas as floor trading, options, proxies, short-selling, and over-the-counter markets. Administration of the act would play a major role in the future of regulation. Those who hailed the legislation and those who initially opposed it recognized the importance of administration, but they emphasized contrasting qualities of the administrative process. Frankfurter, writing to Roosevelt, stressed the importance of the more combative aspects of administration. "The extent and effectiveness of the powers conferred by the legislation will depend largely upon the understanding of the possibilities under the statute by those charged with its administration. . . . And so, plainly, you need administrators who are equipped to meet the best legal brains whom Wall Street always has at its disposal, who have the stamina and do not weary of the fight, who are moved neither by blandishments nor fears, who, in a word, unite public zeal with unusual capacity." Raoul Desvernine, on the other hand, emphasized the cooperative aspects of administration and the importance of encouraging financial stability. The "success, effectiveness and practicability of the Act," he told Landis, would depend upon "the formation of the initial Rules and Regulations. . . . Theoretical knowledge alone will not suffice, but practical experience is required to perfect, not impair, the mechanics of the Exchange and to assure the liquidity and mobility of credit, and to avoid unintentional and unnecessary impairment of security values." Frankfurter and Desvernine had raised important

42. *Wall Street Journal,* June 2, 7, 1934. See also Richard Whitney to FDR, May 20, 1934, OF 1060, FDRP, Box 1.

questions for the future. To what extent could the new commission promote further reform through administration? To what extent could it share regulatory power with private groups? These were issues which the SEC would face when administering both the Securities Act and the Securities Exchange Act. Before it began to grapple with these problems, however, Roosevelt's commitment to securities regulation presented the commission with an additional burden.[43]

43. Felix Frankfurter to FDR, May 23, 1934, FFPLC, Box 34; Raoul Desvernine, memorandum for James Landis, June, 1934, *SEC,* VIII. JMLPH.

6

Broadening the Mandate

"Have you heard anything," David Lilienthal asked Frankfurter in 1933, "about the possibility of early formulation and
enactment of a Federal utilities regulation program? It strikes
me that it will be a serious thing if this matter should be put
over . . . for another year. In the meantime, the concentration
of control of utilities proceeds at an almost incredible pace and
the power of resistance to anything effective gathers strength."
Almost two years elapsed before Lilienthal's question received
an affirmative response from the Roosevelt administration.
That response, in the form of a comprehensive proposal for
federal regulation of the nation's power resources, precipitated
the most bitter legislative battle of Roosevelt's first term. Although the Public Utility Act of 1935 provided less than the
administration desired, it nonetheless completed Roosevelt's
program for national regulation of corporate securities and
gave the new Securities and Exchange Commission an enlarged role to play in that regulation.[1]

Previous developments in the electric utility industry presented a formidable barrier to orderly and efficient utilization of
power resources and to economic stability. Like railroads of an
earlier era, electric utilities grew within an economic and political culture that placed a premium upon rapid private expansion
and limited public planning or supervision. The industry's
flourishing technology, financial cunning, and legal imagination
(not necessarily in that order) overwhelmed rudimentary gov-

1. David Lilienthal to Felix Frankfurter, April 3, 1933, FFPLC,
Box 70.

ernmental structures, both state and federal, hastily erected for their control in the three decades after 1900. Supervision, such as it was, fell ultimately to New York bankers, and they endeavored only to stabilize existing investments and to prevent excessive financial bloodshed.

Between 1900 and 1930 improved generating equipment and other engineering advances permitted interstate electric transmission over hundreds of miles. As a consequence, an industry once local became regional. Interstate transmission accounted for only 17 percent of the nation's private electric production by 1935, yet state variations were immense. Whereas Vermont and Maryland exported over 72 percent of the electricity generated within their borders, Mississippi and Arkansas imported almost 100 percent of their power needs. Financially and legally, the industry assumed national proportions through abundant use of the interstate holding company.[2]

General Electric, faced with a fluctuating demand for new, sophisticated generating equipment and the penurious condition of small operating companies, pioneered during 1905 in the application of a holding company device to electric utilities. Electric Bond and Share, organized by General Electric with a state charter to hold the securities of other corporations, financed the purchase of generators in return for an equity interest in operating plants. The activities of Electric Bond and Share assumed larger dimensions over the next two decades. Ultimately, operating companies under its control represented 13.3 percent of the total generating capacity in the United States; 13 percent of the industry's annual revenues; and over $3 billion in assets. Through eight intermediate holding companies, Electric Bond and Share directed operating

2. Federal Power Commission, *Eleventh Annual Report* (Washington, 1931), pp. 1–7, and *Twelfth Annual Report* (Washington, 1932), pp. 10–11; *Utility Corporations,* Summary Report of the Federal Trade Commission on Holding and Operating Companies of Electric and Gas Utilities (Senate Doc. 92, pt. 73-A, 70th Cong., 1st sess., 1935), pp. 1–58, 167–82.

utilities in twelve states, Mexico, Cuba, and Latin America. Its interests were not restricted to holding stock. As a vast managerial organization, Electric Bond and Share provided its operating companies with financial, sales, engineering, and construction service.

Where Electric Bond and Share led, many corporations followed. The engineering firm of Stone and Webster, confronted with dwindling business as a result of acquisitions by other corporations, adopted the holding company device to control its own chain of operating utilities. Some promoters were lured by the attraction of fabulous bonanzas to be made through the issuance of securities. Among the more sagacious in this regard were Samuel Insull and the organizers of Associated Gas and Electric. A holding company with a small investment in the voting securities of other holding companies or operating companies frequently gained more than control over these subsidiaries. Engineering, construction, and financial companies were often included within one system. Income flowed to the top holding company both from dividends paid on the securities of operating companies and from management fees, usually a fixed percentage of gross income, assessed against subsidiaries. Moreover, the small initial investment in the common stock of operating companies could constitute the sole foundation for public distribution of holding company securities, including preferred stocks and bonds. These funds became a fresh source of largesse which permitted holding companies to enlarge their operations, not by development of existing properties but by the acquisition of new operating companies.

The more fortunate operating companies maintained some financial autonomy. Commonly, however, operating companies within one system serviced both their own securities and those imposed from above. The financial chain that bound operating utilities to holding companies, including fixed management fees and extortionate interest rates, prevented the maintenance of adequate reserves, reduced depreciation charges, and curtailed improved service. Above the level of operating properties, a holding company's financial structure was limited only by the fecund imagination of its promoters, the resourcefulness of lawyers, and the permissiveness of state incorporation laws.[3]

By 1932, for example, the Associated Gas and Electric system contained 264 corporate entities; forty were pure holding companies. At the apex rested Associated Gas and Electric Properties, a Massachusetts voluntary trust with two certificates of one-half beneficial interest owned by J. I. Mange and H. C. Hopson. The Massachusetts trust owned the voting stock of Associated Securities Corporation, which in turn held the class B voting common stock of Associated Gas and Electric Company. This intermediate holding company had distributed thirty-five separate classes of securities, including one bond issue with a maturity date of 2875. The assets of Associated Gas and Electric Company were limited to the bonds and voting stock of Associated Gas and Electric Corporation (Delaware). The Delaware holding company had its own complement of securities based largely upon voting stock in additional holding companies. "It is like the Hanging Gardens of Babylon," one critic commented, "a pyramidal structure, built in weird design, worthy of a Nebuchadnezzar. The luxurious vegetation in this ethereal garden, the many and varied types of securities that have germinated there, has grown with rare rapidity."[4]

3. James C. Bonbright and Gardiner C. Means, *The Holding Company,* pp. 91–222; *Report of the National Power Policy Committee* (House Doc. 137, 74th Cong., 1st sess., 1935), pp. 4–7; Merwin H. Waterman, "The Financial Policies of Public Utility Holding Companies," *Michigan Business Studies* 5 (1932): 1–168; *Utility Corporations* (Commonwealth and Southern Corporation and Southern Utilities Company), letter from the chairman of the Federal Trade Commission (Senate Doc. 92, pt. 78, 70th Cong., 1st sess., 1935), pp. 74–162, 206–301; *Utility Corporations* (Cities Service Power and Light Company), letter from the chairman of the Federal Trade Commission (Senate Doc. 92, pt. 73, 70th Cong., 1st sess., 1935), pp. 119–281.

4. N. R. Danielian, "Gas, A Study in Expansion: The Case of Associated Gas," *Atlantic Monthly,* July 1933, pp. 481–97.

Consolidation of independent operating companies proceeded rapidly during the 1920s. Whereas eighty-five systems controlled two-thirds of the nation's private electric power output in 1914, sixteen holding company groups controlled 92 percent by 1929. Due in part to this integration, the average price per kilowatt-hour for residential service declined from 7.52 cents to 5.91 cents between 1921 and 1930. Unfortunately, holding companies did not demonstrate a corresponding concern for reducing corporate complexities or reallocating properties to achieve even greater economies. The furious scramble for operating companies produced a national holding company map more irregular than many legislative gerrymanders. Even Electric Bond and Share, a veteran of the holding company wars, found its major subsidiaries directing widely scattered operations. American Power and Light ran properties in Florida and Oregon while Electric Power and Light managed separate Oregon companies in addition to Arkansas properties. Operating companies in Texas but adjacent to Arkansas remained under the jurisdiction of American Power and Light. Compared to other systems, however, Electric Bond and Share was a model of geographic and managerial integration.[5]

Private efforts to avoid costly battles among holding company groups came late in 1929. But this endeavor, engineered by J. P. Morgan's United Corporation, was limited in geographic scope and economic intention to perpetuating existing holding company relationships in the East. United Corporation, in a share-for-share exchange, acquired substantial voting interest in strategic systems: Public Service Corporation of New Jersey, United Gas Improvement, Commonwealth and Southern, Niagara-Hudson Power, Columbia Gas and Electric, American Water Works and Electric, and Consolidated Edison of New York. United, a financial success for its promoters, promised little in terms of long-range development. It formed a loose community of interests, but contributed nothing to the

5. *Utility Corporations,* Summary Report of the Federal Trade Commission, pp. 3–6.

utilities' pressing need for actual reorganization and integration.[6]

The stock market crash and three years of depression in large measure arrested holding company growth and on a limited scale promoted corporate reorganization. The more grotesque systems, burdened with overvalued assets, excessive capitalization, and mountainous debts, were thrown into receivership. Other empires survived only through the ability of captive operating companies to meet the obligations of holding companies. Organizational and financial relationships between major holding companies and their subsidiaries changed little between 1929 and 1935. "The general course of the . . . readjustment," one expert noted, "has demonstrated the rigidity of their financial structures. . . . These readjustments . . . reflect a policy of patching up the corporate structure sufficient to weather the current difficulties." Many holding company promoters, however, realized that the buccaneering days would never return. Harold Stuart, the powerful Chicago banker, was not alone when he expressed concern over the declining value of utility stocks and sagging investor confidence in holding companies. The utilities, he told Milo Maltbie, chairman of New York's Public Service Commission, "had better realize it and do their part in helping to cure these abuses. . . . Because the public [will] have no more of their securities, and [because] the day when the holding company could exploit the operating companies for the holding company's benefit [is] past."[7]

The industry's technological and financial growth had created obvious regulatory problems. "The geographic relations," according to the Federal Power Commission, "are those de-

6. "High Finance in the 'Twenties: The United Corporation," *Columbia Law Review* 37 (May 1937): 785–816, and (June 1937): 936–80.

7. William H. Taylor, *Financial Readjustment of Utility Corporations since 1929*, pp. 3–16; minutes of conference among Milo R. Maltbie, H. L. Stuart, and Bernard Flexner, December 9, 1932, FFPLC, Box 66.

termined by distance rather than by State boundaries, and the result is economic rather than political units." Nonetheless, state-by-state regulatory efforts had constituted the single bulwark since 1900 against tumultuous and potentially destructive national development. Although twenty-eight states permitted incorporation of holding companies within their borders, twenty-five of the twenty-eight provided no supervision after incorporation. Local operating companies escaped regulation in states without utility commissions. Even states with commissions provided very different levels of regulation. In no state jurisdiction could a commission control the security issues of interstate holding companies or obtain relevant information prior to the acquisition of local operating companies. The authority of state commissions to approve the issuance of operating company securities varied widely, as did the authority to review or set local utility rates. Nine states required corporate reports only for tax purposes; fourteen states made no provision for a uniform system of accounting by operating companies.[8]

Federal concern for the industry's development had been equally narrow and complacent. Under the Water Power Act of 1920 Congress created a federal power commission to encourage and supervise hydroelectric facilities on the nation's navigable rivers and public lands. Composed of three overburdened cabinet officers until 1930, handicapped by meager appropriations, inadequate personnel, and statutory limita-

8. *Utility Corporations,* Summary Report of the Federal Trade Commission, pp. 3–6. David Lilienthal to James M. Landis, January 27, 1933; Landis to Lilienthal, March 15, 1933, both JMLPLC, Box 6. In the landmark case of *Public Utilities Commission of Rhode Island v. Attleboro Steam and Electric Co.,* 273 U.S. 83 (1926), the United States Supreme Court upheld the decision of Rhode Island courts that the state could not regulate the rates charged by a Rhode Island generating and transmission company for electricity sold to distributing companies in Massachusetts. See Felix Frankfurter, "Mr. Hoover on Power Control," *New Republic,* (October 17, 1928), p. 242.

tions, the Federal Power Commission offered encouragement to developers but very little supervision.

The FPC's authority extended to the issuance of licenses for hydroelectric installations and to surveillance over such projects. Even these limited duties were hampered by the reluctance of the War, Interior, and Agriculture departments to provide manpower. The commission noted in 1928 that it "had no staff of its own; and neither sufficient time nor qualified employees . . . available for inquiring into the financial arrangements of applicants, the cost of construction of their projects, or the items which they were entering into the fixed capital accounts of their projects. . . . The Commission has proceeded with the issuance of licenses in the annual expectation that it would be given the means to exercise adequate supervision over them." In addition, the FPC could regulate the rates, service, and securities of its own licensees only in states without utility commissions. Although President Hoover and the Congress created a full-time Federal Power Commission of five non-cabinet members in 1930, they did nothing to enlarge its mandate. That task fell to the new commission and, above all, to the next President who realized the necessity for a comprehensive national power program and who possessed intimate knowledge of its many complexities.[9]

Roosevelt's gubernatorial years in New York had produced many skirmishes between the executive branch and the utilities. In terms of substantive change, Roosevelt achieved little. A regulatory program, shaped by decades of executive apathy and legislative hostility, could not be modified at once through superb appointments to the Public Service Commission or the creation of a Power Authority to plan state hydroelectric developments. Of far greater importance was Roosevelt's zest for personal education in the nuances of regulation and his success in recruiting men who were experts in public utility finance, valuation, rate-making, and law. In addition to Frankfurter,

9. Federal Power Commission, *Eight Annual Report* (Washington, 1928), pp. 1–12; *Eleventh Annual Report* (Washington, 1931), pp. 1–14.

his official and unofficial advisers included Maltbie, Morris L. Cooke, Leland Olds, and James C. Bonbright. In no other area of public policy was the President's experience so rich or his commitment so complete.[10]

Until early 1935, however, the administration's utility policy remained scattered among commissions, departments, presidential committees, and the Congress. Different objectives characterized these fragmented endeavors. The Federal Trade Commission and the House Interstate Commerce Committee had conducted exhaustive investigations into the utility industry. Their studies, directed by Robert E. Healy and Walter M. W. Splawn, came to focus upon the holding company with the assumption that federal efforts should commence with legislation to simplify, regulate, or abolish these structures. The Treasury Department, for reasons of reform and revenue, also singled out public utility holding companies as important objects for tax legislation. The emphasis of the Federal Power Commission conflicted somewhat with these other tentative goals. Commissioner Frank R. McNinch, a Hoover appointee, and Basil Manly, a Roosevelt addition, were both eager to upgrade the FPC's prestige and influence. Part of their program included an electric rate survey followed by negotiations with holding companies in an effort to reduce and standardize national rates. McNinch and Manly were also anxious to amend the Water Power Act in order to bring within the commission's jurisdiction problems of interstate generation, transmission, rates, and service. The FPC, in short, had become more interested in coordinating existing facilities than in revising the nation's private power map. Roosevelt, attempting to reconcile viewpoints, created a National Power Policy Committee in the summer of 1934. Harold Ickes, secretary of the interior, served

10. Frank Freidel, *Franklin D. Roosevelt,* pp. 100–19. See also Felix Frankfurter to FDR, January 5, April 19, June 27, September 17, 1929, FFPH, Roll 11; James C. Bonbright to Frankfurter, March 13, 1930, FFPLC, Box 5; Bonbright to Frankfurter, January 21, 1931; Frankfurter to Bonbright, January 25, 1931, and FDR to Frankfurter, January 28, 1931, all FFPH, Roll 11.

as chairman and Ben Cohen as counsel. The committee, including McNinch, Healy, Cooke, and Lilienthal, made holding company regulation the first order of business.[11]

In November 1934 at Warm Springs, Roosevelt informed members of the Power Policy Committee that he opposed any legislation that did not have as its primary purpose the abolition of holding companies. "The President's thesis," Lilienthal wrote, "was that you can't regulate holding companies so the only thing that can be done is to eliminate them entirely." Investment companies which held the securities of utilities could be tolerated, Roosevelt added, "and an argument could be made for management services by a holding company on a cost basis." But a holding company that existed for the control of operating companies was "against the public interest, and since it couldn't be regulated, should be abolished." He suggested taxation as one means of eliminating holding companies of this kind. McNinch, at whose request the meeting had been called, "got gloomier and gloomier," Lilienthal noted. "[He] looked at his plate very solemnly, and tried to get it perfectly clear that what the President wanted was not some form of regulation of holding companies, and that, I think is what McNinch would have preferred." Cohen, then in the process of preparing a rough draft of possible legislation for the National Power Policy Committee, was surprised by Roosevelt's radical posture. "McNinch," in Cohen's opinion, was "not a strong man and on one or two occasions indicated that he was somewhat embarrassed by the decision to abolish or limit the use of the holding company instead of regulating it." One explanation for

11. *Relation of Holding Companies to Operating Companies in Power and Gas Affecting Control* (House Rept. 827, 73d Cong., 2d sess., 1934), passim; *Utility Corporations,* Summary Report of the Federal Trade Commission, pp. 65–76; John M. Blum, *From the Morgenthau Diaries: Years of Crisis, 1928–1938,* pp. 298–99; Frank R. McNinch and Basil Manly to Marvin McIntyre, November 14, 1934, OF 284, FDRP, Box 1; Federal Power Commission, *Fourteenth Annual Report* (Washington, 1934), pp. 4–13; Benjamin V. Cohen to James C. Bonbright, December 7, 1934; Bonbright to Cohen, December 8, 1934, Cohen File, NPPCR, Box 10.

the President's blunt attitude, Cohen told Frankfurter, was that Roosevelt distrusted McNinch's conferences on standardized rates and "wanted to put a stop to the idea that as a result of such conferences the holding companies would be given a new lease on life."[12]

Chastened by Roosevelt's remarks, McNinch told holding company executives two months later that "there should be, and probably would be legislative measures directed toward radical simplification of corporate structures." Intermediate holding companies "should be eliminated," McNinch said, while top holding companies "might possibly be permitted to continue . . . but under a transformation . . . making them practically investment trusts." He still hoped the FPC and the utilities could work out a rate program within a reasonable time and that agreement could be reached among the companies, TVA, and the Public Works Administration on the matter of government financing for municipal generating plants and transmission lines. Roosevelt was even more frank. He told the same executives, including Wendell Willkie of Commonwealth and Southern, that any effort on their part to avoid "the breaking up" of holding companies was futile.[13]

Roosevelt's stern dicta did not, of course, constitute a precise legislative formula for the elimination of holding companies. Reform through taxation appealed to many, including Frankfurter. "I think it's the most powerful way of getting at these things," he told Henry Morgenthau. "I don't think there's any doubt but that [a tax on intercorporate dividends] is the most effective way of dealing with the problem. . . . [Although] there are many matters which have nothing to do with taxation at all." Frankfurter, having accepted Bernard Flexner's argument that it was desirable to outlaw many holding company practices but not the holding company device itself, urged the taxation remedy upon Roosevelt. "They [holding companies]

12. David E. Lilienthal, *Journals: TVA Years,* pp. 42–43; Benjamin V. Cohen to Felix Frankfurter, February 5, 1936, FFPLC, Box 53.
13. Frank R. McNinch, memorandum, January 29, 1935, OF 234, FDRP, Box 1; Lilienthal, *Journals,* p. 47.

cannot be eliminated over night," he cautioned, "and therefore the policy would seem to be temporary stiff regulation and taxation, with the defined objective of elimination." Adolph A. Berle tendered parallel advice to Cohen. "A simple method of providing for elimination," he said, "would be a progressive increase in taxation upwards in case you do not feel like brutally cutting off the existence of the holding company." The Federal Trade Commission, upon the basis of its long inquiry, also favored this method.[14]

Cohen, aware of Roosevelt's strong prejudice, proceeded nonetheless to draw a bill which "does not outlaw the holding company but regulates and restricts the use of the holding company form and provides a mechanism through which, over a period of time, existing holding company structures may be simplified, and their field limited to a sphere where their economic advantages may be demonstrable." He was caught, Cohen told Ickes, between FDR's sentiments and Healy, who "is not quite prepared to recommend the abolition of the holding company." Cohen's bill, prepared with Corcoran's aid, compelled registration by interstate holding companies with the Securities and Exchange Commission. Registered companies would file information comparable to the data required of other corporations under the Securities Exchange Act.[15]

The SEC was given power to approve future financing, in-

14. Henry Morgenthau, Diary, December 19, 1934, 2: 332, FDRP; Bernard Flexner to Felix Frankfurter, November 29, 1932, FFPLC, Box 65; Frankfurter to FDR, January 24, 1935, FFPH, Roll 2; Adolph A. Berle to Benjamin V. Cohen, December 8, 1934, Cohen File, NPPCR, Box 10. "I have seen for too long powerful interests playing ducks and drakes with regulatory schemes," Frankfurter told William O. Douglas. "Tax 'em, my boy, tax 'em, and otherwise reduce the opportunities for bludgeoning that interrelation and concentration of money interests make possible" (Frankfurter to Douglas, January 16, 1934, FFPLC, Box 10).

15. Benjamin V. Cohen to Robert E. Healy, November 23, 1934, and January 9, 1935; Cohen to Harold Ickes, February 8, 1935, all Cohen File, NPPCR, Box 10. In order to placate Healy, the final report of the National Power Policy Committee did not recommend a specific legislative solution to the holding company problem.

cluding the acquisition of capital assets and securities. Holding companies would be removed from the business of service, management, and construction through the creation of mutual or cooperative service companies subject to the commission's scrutiny. Upstream loans were forbidden as well as commissions on intercorporate security transactions. The SEC, Cohen said, could compel the simplification of holding company structures if they were "unnecessarily complicated" and require the divestment of subsidiaries if they had "no economic relation to the other companies in the system." In addition, "necessary incentives," were provided to induce holding companies to adjust their activity voluntarily. Cohen's bill proposed an amendment to the pending Revenue Act limiting to 80 percent the deduction allowed public utility companies on dividends received from other corporations. This inducement, Cohen hoped, would force holding companies to eliminate a number of intermediate firms and limit their investment in operating companies to those "which are so closely related that the economies . . . effected by common control easily compensate for the slightly increased tax burden."[16]

No rigid ideology regarding the virtues of small versus big business dominated the Cohen-Corcoran draft. Other potential supporters of holding company legislation saw the issue in those terms. "A utility is essentially a local institution," said Senator Burton K. Wheeler of Montana, Chairman of the Senate Committee on Interstate Commerce. "It should be locally controlled and locally owned." Cohen and Corcoran were guided by different considerations. As in their earlier efforts to secure securities and stock exchange regulation, they stressed efficient and orderly economic development. Their approach included careful delineation of the many functions involved in one economic endeavor and the modification of those functions which, because of private convenience, inadvertence, or avarice, had become detrimental to the long-range growth and stability of the entire economy. Corporate

16. Cohen to Ickes, February 8, 1935, Cohen File, NPPCR, Box 10.

size, per se, was of secondary importance. This attitude they shared with Frankfurter. "Neither you nor I," he told Raymond Moley, "are doctrinaires either about the curse of bigness or the blessings of littleness. Like most things that matter in this world, it's a question of more or less, of degree, of when is big too big, and when is little too little. In any event, what we most need is luminous and authentic experience." The bill Cohen and Corcoran took to a White House meeting on January 22, 1935, emphasized a flexible approach to the holding company and, above all, "time . . . for the making of necessary adjustments."[17]

They clashed with Roosevelt on both issues. The President wanted a definite statutory timetable in order to hasten the simplification of holding company systems. In addition, Roosevelt wished to abolish all public utility holding companies with the exception of those meeting two rigorous requirements. To Cohen's chagrin, the President's position received fervent support from some men who had urged restraint in the past, including McNinch, Healy, and Splawn. A committee, headed by Attorney General Homer Cummings, revised the Cohen-Corcoran bill to meet Roosevelt's specifications, deleted the tax provisions, and added a second title written by the Federal Power Commission. Rayburn and Senator Wheeler, included in all White House sessions, introduced the legislation in early February.[18]

Roosevelt's revisions instructed the SEC at the end of three years to order every registered public utility holding company and its subsidiaries to dispose of securities and capital assets "not necessary or appropriate to the operation of a geographically and economically integrated . . . system." At the end of three years the commission was further instructed to compel

17. Cohen to Healy, November 23, 1934, Cohen File NPPCR, Box 10; *Congressional Record,* 74th Cong., 1st sess., 79, pp. 8387; Felix Frankfurter to Raymond Moley, November 16, 1935, FFPH, Roll 4.

18. FDR to Marvin McIntyre, January 17, 1935, OF 293, FDRP, Box 1; Homer Cummings to FDR, February 6, 1935, OF 10, FDRP, Box 4; interview with Benjamin V. Cohen, August 21, 1967.

the reorganization or dissolution of holding companies and subsidiaries whenever the corporate structure "unduly or unnecessarily complicates the structure of the public utility system." The SEC could defer action under these two provisions for two additional years. Immediately after January 1, 1940, however, the SEC should require every registered holding company "to dispose of securities or to be reorganized or dissolved insofar as may be necessary to make such company cease to be a holding company." Holding companies could survive this provision if (1) they secured a certificate from the Federal Power Commission stating their existence to be "necessary for the operation of a geographically and economically integrated . . system serving an economic district extending into two or more contiguous States," *and* (2) the merger or consolidation "of such . . . holding company with its subsidiary company or companies is impossible under the applicable State . . . law." The SEC would act as sole trustee under federal courts during the process of reorganization or dissolution. In a private meeting with FDR, Frankfurter spoke against the harsh formula but, he told Henry Stimson, "I got rapped for it." Roosevelt did accept the remainder of the bill as drawn by Cohen and Corcoran, including mandatory creation of mutual service companies, separation of electric and gas retail properties, and SEC control over securities, acquisitions, and reports.[19]

The administration's omnibus public utility bill also embraced proposals increasing the responsibilities of the Federal Power Commission. Whereas the SEC would manage the reorganization of holding companies, the FPC would regroup the properties into a comprehensive national system. The Federal Power Commission was given jurisdiction, including rate-making power, over the production, transmission, and

19. Cummings to FDR, February 6, 1935, OF 10, FDRP, Box 4; see H. R. 5423 or S. 1725 in Senate Committee on Interstate Commerce, *Public Utility Holding Company Act of 1935* (74th Cong., 1st sess., 1935), pp. 9–32, and House Interstate Commerce Committee, *Public Utility Holding Companies* (74th Cong., 1st sess., 1935), pp. 1–24; Henry L. Stimson, Diary, February 10, June 30, 1935, HLSP.

sale of electric energy in interstate commerce. Public utilities engaged in interstate commerce were made common carriers and required "to furnish energy to, exchange energy with, and transmit energy for any person upon reasonable request." The FPC could compel electric utilities to make necessary additions, extensions, or improvements in generation or service and to establish physical interconnection with other utilities. The commission would form regional power districts and issue certificates of public convenience as a method of controlling new private power developments. In addition to rate-making, the FPC was instructed to prescribe uniform methods of accounting and to fix "proper and adequate rates of depreciation" for all electric utilities engaged in interstate production, transmission, and sale of energy.[20]

The bill Rayburn introduced in the House contained yet a third title, drafted by members of the Federal Trade Commission with his encouragement. This proposal gave the FTC substantially the same powers over interstate transmission and sale of natural gas as those given to the Federal Power Commission over electric energy. Interstate pipelines were made common carriers, and distributors were required to furnish, exchange, and transmit natural gas for all producers upon reasonable request. Like the FPC, the Federal Trade Commission would fix interstate rates, issue certificates of public convenience, compel extensions, additions, and improvements in interstate pipelines, and regulate the accounting practices of distributors, including rates of depreciation. The FTC's legislative recommendations were designed to provide comparable federal supervision over the electric utilities' newest competitor. Support for this section of the bill could be expected from the independent natural gas-oil producers and their congressional allies, among them Rayburn, who favored governmental controls rather than private dictatorship by large natural gas pipeline companies like Standard Oil. At the same time, Rayburn was actively en-

20. House, *Public Utility Holding Companies,* pp. 24–43; Senate, *Public Utility Holding Company Act,* pp. 32–49.

gaged in efforts to secure PWA funds for the construction of an "independent" natural gas pipeline from the Gulf of Mexico into the Midwest.

Unfortunately, Title III heightened the initial antagonism of some legislators to the entire public utility package. Many congressmen, North and South, represented regions with highly developed private electric utility systems. As they saw it, stringent holding company legislation threatened the industrial growth of their regions. Moreover, they viewed holding company legislation as part of a larger program to encourage cheap federal power in less industrialized areas of the South and Northwest. Federally sponsored power projects in those regions could not benefit their constituents. Some Northern congressmen, in addition, spoke for economically distressed coal areas. Federal natural gas regulation appeared to be a further effort to promote the resources of less industrialized regions at the expense of older energy sources like coal. Even the most naïve congressman could not miss the fact that vigorous proponents of holding company legislation, including Rayburn, John Rankin of Mississippi, and Huey Long of Louisiana, were also zealous supporters of rural electrification, federal hydroelectric projects, and natural gas regulation.[21]

Cohen and Corcoran did not view the legislation as either radical or injurious to the utilities. Economic and geographic integration, they argued, would be financially beneficial. "That is an ideal," Corcoran told Wheeler's committee, "many of the best . . . holding companies . . . have been trying to realize for a long period of years." Cohen told Wendell Willkie, president of Commonwealth and Southern, that "if we want to avoid the sort of regulation which we both abhor, we have got to simplify the rules of the game. I for one am not interested in regulation which absorbs the energy of the industry in debating the rules of the game. We need that energy . . . in operating and developing the industry." The more progressive holding com-

21. On the natural gas provisions see House, *Public Utility Holding Companies*, pp. 43–49, and the acerbic criticism of Illinois's coal-minded Congressman Everett Dirksen, pp. 1908–10.

panies, including North American, Commonwealth and Southern, United Gas Improvement, and Niagara-Hudson, had undertaken programs since 1930 which moved in the direction of the administration's proposals. Superfluous, intermediate holding companies had been phased out. Management and service contracts had been placed in some instances upon a cost basis. Operating properties had been regrouped by regions, although even the more consolidated companies, like Commonwealth and Southern, continued to manage two or more separate regions in the Midwest and South. The industry's less benighted chieftans, among them Willkie, recognized the many benefits in the proposed bill and they supported important provisions of the legislation, including democratic allocation of voting power among shareholders; prohibition of upstream loans; regulation of service contracts; SEC approval of future financing; and SEC control over the acquisition of capital assets and securities "to prevent," as Willkie said, "the race for property."[22]

These same companies rejected, however, the proposition that their systems should be restricted to one geographically contiguous region. They rebelled also against mandatory mutual service companies. "Stop it [the holding company] where it is," Willkie said, "and permit no growth, and permit no change without the consent of your Commission. . . . [Then] you do not go through the dismemberment process." Holding companies which still received lucrative management and construction fees from operating subsidiaries were loath to abandon these functions. S. R. Inch, president of Electric Bond and Share, predicted immediate bankruptcy and receivership for subsidiaries without the "initiative and money" provided by his company. Splawn supplied a more plausible hypothesis: "The service company has been tremendously profitable; and

22. Senate, *Public Utility Holding Company Act,* pp. 202, 563, 597–610; Benjamin V. Cohen to Wendell Willkie, March 21, 1935, Cohen File, NPPCR, Box 10. On the holding companies' internal reform see Bernard Flexner to Felix Frankfurter, November 29, 1932, FFPLC, Box 65.

I think that is the explanation of the struggle to get so many properties. It is only to sell services to these operating companies." Despite reforms in this important area, Cohen was convinced Electric Bond and Share did not have "any more religion than it has to have." Inch's organization, Cohen noted, "still claimed the right to make profit from service fees . . . and they played politics to the extent of even getting those companies that have already substituted service at cost . . . to draw a misleading distinction between a service fee involving a profit when they [Electric Bond and Share] own all of the common stock of the subsidiaries and when they own only a part."[23]

Title I thus became the focus for conflict among the administration, the Congress, and the holding companies. But Title II also alarmed utility executives because of the common carrier provisions and the extensive powers granted to the Federal Power Commission. Their position seemed restrained, however, when compared to the vituperative remarks of state utility commissioners. "There could be no more dangerous extension of centralization in the Federal Government," said H. Lester Hooker, chairman of the legislative committee for the National Association of Railroad and Utilities Commissioners. Hooker and most state commissioners opposed giving the SEC jurisdiction over the financing of holding company subsidiaries. And under Title II, Hooker complained, the authority of state commissions would be "substantially emasculated and devastated." The FPC would disrupt the relationships between state commissions and operating companies engaged in interstate generation and transmission. A distant federal power commission, Hooker said, had no business dictating local service requirements, improvements, extensions, accounting standards, or rates of depreciation. Once the Federal Power Commission began to set interstate rates it would soon meddle with local retail rates. In addition, Hooker noted, many states distrusted the FPC for "retarding developments"

23. Senate, *Public Utility Holding Company Act,* pp. 84, 609; House, *Public Utility Holding Companies,* pp. 1124–34; Benjamin V. Cohen to Felix Frankfurter, April 5, 1935, FFPLC, Box 9.

on navigable rivers through restrictive license requirements. Titles I and II, Hooker said, should be completely revised in order to preserve the autonomy of state commissions. On the issue of national versus state responsibility, the holding companies and their subsidiaries found outspoken, powerful friends among many state commissioners.[24]

Hearings before Rayburn's committee consumed ten weeks. Wheeler's committee did not take up the measure until April 16. During this period the utilities mounted a well-organized propaganda offensive. Congress and the White House were deluged with genuine and bogus correspondence from security holders and consumers who condemned the bill as "wicked," "vicious," and "rankly socialistic." These efforts to arouse fear often strained credulity; some verged upon the ridiculous. The Massachusetts Society for the Prevention of Cruelty to Animals solemnly informed Roosevelt that its investment portfolio would be destroyed and its benign activities curtailed if the legislation passed Congress. "Even the Congressman representing the Muscle Shoals district has been terrified," Lilienthal reported. "He has received six thousand [hostile] letters . . . in a district in which we [TVA] have four thousand men employed and have aided . . . the economic condition . . . of 50,000 people."[25]

Not even Presidential pressure could hasten congressional action. Early in March Roosevelt sent both Houses a special message urging quick passage of the bill. At Rayburn's request it was restricted to holding companies. The Texan had decided that Titles II and III "are not at all Must Legislation." Rayburn's sudden caution arose from a growing suspicion that he could not control the House committee. The hearings revealed that only Rayburn, Clarence Lea, and freshman Edward

24. House, *Public Utility Holding Companies,* pp. 504, 727–45.

25. For a sample of the correspondence see Leonard Fox to Burton K. Wheeler, February 20, 1935; Irene Engard to Wheeler, February 29, 1935; Edith Davidson to Wheeler, April 2, 1935, all SCR, Box 26; Francis H. Rowley to FDR, March 20, 1935, OF 293, FDRP, Box 2; David Lilienthal to Felix Frankfurter, June 10, 1935, FFPLC, Box 70.

Eicher of Iowa supported the administration's omnibus bill with any enthusiasm. The committee's eight Republicans, led by John Cooper but including the usually sympathetic Carl Mapes, were antagonistic. Still more ominous was the hectoring of friendly administration witnesses by Alabama's George Huddleston and the complete indifference of the committee's eight other Democrats.[26]

Rayburn sought a secret compromise. Without consulting Roosevelt, he accepted the suggestion of Winthrop Aldrich, president of the Chase National Bank, that quiet negotiations without Cohen or Corcoran could produce a new bill acceptable to the committee and to the utilities. Aldrich himself offered to serve as "a disinterested intermediary." Rayburn met with Aldrich, Willkie, and two other holding company executives at the conclusion of House hearings. He included Splawn in these clandestine meetings, which lasted over a week and produced a tentative agreement. The Aldrich-Rayburn compromise did not disappoint the utilities. Under its generous terms, regional operating systems would remain virtually intact. Intermediate and top holding companies would be exempt "from all taxes . . . incident to any exchange or issue of securities or transfer of assets . . . it being the intent to encourage the elimination of all intermediate holding companies." A holding company was liberally defined as any company that owned 50 percent or more of the voting stock of operating companies or intermediate holding companies. This language excluded automatically the largest companies from all coverage. Furthermore, a single holding company would be permitted to control at least *four* regional systems. The SEC would retain jurisdiction over security issues and accounting practices; all shareholders would be given voting rights within one year. Title II was eliminated. Rayburn and Aldrich, in brief, had produced a document that promised to spare most companies, including Electric Bond and Share, from the agony of major

---

26. Felix Frankfurter, memorandum, March 5, 1935, FFPH, Roll 3; House, *Public Utility Holding Companies,* passim.

reorganization. FDR's mandatory "death sentence" had become only a gentle reprimand. Cohen, Corcoran, and Wheeler did not learn of the negotiations, Cohen said, "until Rayburn and Splawn got into hot water." Roosevelt, apprised of "the embarrassing and equivocal position into which Sam and Walter were maneuvered by the utilities," demanded that they insist upon the administration bill "substantially without modification." Rayburn terminated negotiations with Aldrich abruptly and prepared to face his uncertain committee.[27]

In the Senate events moved more normally. Wheeler's committee reported a bill on May 13, two weeks after hearings ended. Although the committee made only minor alterations in Roosevelt's formula for eliminating holding companies, it capitulated to the demands of state commissions. Under Title II, the jurisdiction of the Federal Power Commission was rigidly curtailed.

Unlike the original House bill, the Senate version did not propose broad regulation of the natural gas industry. Further, Wheeler's committee restricted the definition of a gas utility company under Title I to corporations engaged in retail distribution. Producers and interstate pipeline companies were thus excluded. The balance of Title I underwent slight modification. The length of time provided for the elimination of holding companies under section 11 was extended two years beyond 1940. During this period, holding companies could voluntarily become investment trusts or rearrange their holdings "so that each holding company will control the management of only a single system of operating companies . . . either . . . predominantly intrastate, or . . . geographically and economically integrated in contiguous States, the laws of which will not permit merger into a single operating system." Vol-

27. On the Aldrich-Rayburn episode see George Roberts to Felix Frankfurter, February 27, 1936; Frankfurter, memorandum, April 19, 1935, both FFPLC, Box 53; Frankfurter, undated memorandum on Public Utility Holding Company Act, FFPLC, Box 66; Benjamin V. Cohen to Frankfurter, March 9, 1936, FFPLC, Box 53; Cohen to Frankfurter, March 31, 1936, FFPH, Roll 22.

untary plans were subject to approval by the Securities and Exchange Commission. After 1940 the SEC could compel simplification and reorganization. The committee vote on section 11 was overwhelming, 11 to 3. SEC control over financing and acquisitions by holding companies and their subsidiaries remained unchanged. Under section 7 the commission could contest a security issue "not reasonably adapted to the security structure of the declarant and other companies in the same holding company system . . . not necessary or appropriate to the economical and efficient operation of . . . business," or if the terms and conditions of sale were "detrimental to the public interest or the interests of investors or consumers." Through section 10 the SEC could oppose the acquisition of securities and capital assets which unduly complicated the capital structure of the holding company systems. Certification was also required from the Federal Power Commission that all acquisitions "serve the public interest by tending toward the economical and efficient development of a geographically and economically integrated public-utility system." The creation of mutual service companies remained mandatory under section 13. Their regulation, however, was shifted to the Federal Power Commission.[28]

Wheeler's committee effectively torpedoed Title II. Little remained of the bold plan for national electric power development and coordination. The Federal Power Commission could create regional districts, but within districts and between districts the commission was forced to secure interconnection and coordination "by voluntary action as far as practicable." The commission could compel interconnection or sale and exchange of energy only after complaint by a state commission or utility subject to the act. While the FPC retained authority to set interstate wholesale rates, it lost all power to issue certificates of public convenience.[29]

28. Burton K. Wheeler to Felix Frankfurter, May 8, 1935, FFPLC, Box 41; *Public Utility Act of 1935* (Senate Rept. 621, 74th Cong., 1st sess., 1936), pp. 1–53.
29. *Public Utility Act of 1935*, pp. 40–53.

The entire Senate filled fourteen days with turgid debate before passing the measure on June 11, 1935. Excluding the quiet, reasoned discourse of Senator George Norris, few members focused upon the bill's economic implications. Democrat William Dieterich of Illinois and Republican Daniel Hastings of Delaware provided a dreary, two-day exegesis on why the measure violated the Constitution. Dieterich buttressed his vacuous contentions by reading portions of Washington's Farewell Address. Rhetorically, administration leaders tried to camouflage the measure's radicalism. "The bill does not eliminate all holding companies," Senator Barkley said. "It does not eliminate holding companies which have stock in or even control utilities operating in two or more States, if it is an integrated territory. . . . There are many of them which it does not eliminate." Senator Long thought this was too bad, since "a holding company is not a thing on God's earth but a scheme set up in order that frauds . . . may be practiced with convenience."[30]

Dieterich manufactured the first substantive threat on June 11 when he introduced an amendment to eliminate section 11 and substitute his own vague reorganization formula. After 1938, under the Dieterich plan, the SEC could require the corporate structure of each registered holding company "to be simplified to the extent that such corporate structures contain unnecessary complexities which are detrimental to the interests of investors, consumers, and the general public." Senator Long seized the floor at once. "What," he asked, "does that mean? It does not mean anything." Wheeler and Barkley, too, warned that Dieterich's amendment would render the bill

---

30. *Congressional Record,* 74th Cong., 1st sess., 79, pp. 8491–8532, 8614–17, 8671–82, 9050–51. Wheeler and administration strategists concentrated their fire on the most vulnerable companies, many of which were held in disrepute by the entire power industry. "I hope Burt will not forget to deal with the Associated Gas . . . on the floor," Frankfurter told Cohen, "and that he will have that big chart about the company as suggested by F.D.R." (Felix Frankfurter to Benjamin V. Cohen, May 21, 1935, FFPLC, Box 9).

harmless by removing all precise statutory guidelines. Rising to new heights of sarcasm, the Kingfish denounced "this Mother Hubbard amendment . . . which covers everything but touches nothing." On a roll-call vote, Dieterich's amendment lost by only one vote, 45 to 44. Twenty-eight Democrats, including such administration stalwarts as John Bankhead, Robert Bulkley, and James Byrnes, followed the Illinois senator.[31]

Democrat Augustine Lonergan of Connecticut led a second assault against section 11. His amendment sought to forestall all proceedings until the SEC received a specific complaint. Wheeler's forces repulsed Lonergan, but only by two votes, 45 to 43. The virulence of Senate opposition to section 11 surprised many; individual votes provoked great indignation. "[Senator Robert] Reynolds," Josephus Daniels fumed, "made his campaign denouncing his opponent because . . . he was a stockholder in the Duke Power Company. And now he [Reynolds] votes, along with [Senator Josiah] Bailey, to cut the heart out of the measure. . . . The power companies have dug their roots deep and are free spenders, and the money from the Duke company to colleges, hospitals . . . and other good causes has seduced many to stand by them."[32]

Narrowly focused amendments fared better. Senator Kenneth McKellar of Tennessee succeeded in eliminating the provision that required federal courts to appoint the SEC sole trustee under section 11 proceedings. Sherman Minton temporarily saved the Indiana water properties of American Water Works and Electric Company by pushing an amendment that permitted electric utilities to retain water works "if not detrimental to the proper functioning of a single . . . system." Long and Champ Clark of Missouri broadened the definition of gas utility to include producers as well as pipeline companies. Long was determined that "this bunch of thieves and criminals

31. *Congressional Record,* 74th Cong., 1st sess., 79, pp. 9050–51, 9063.
32. Josephus Daniels to FDR, July 5, 1935, PPF 86, FDRP.

who have robbed the country" should not escape from Title I.
The Senate then sent the bill to the House.[33]

"There is no question that a number of the members of the
[House] Committee are critical and a few definitely hostile,"
Cohen told James Bonbright, "but . . . I think the Administration's point of view is acceptable to a majority of the committee. Sentiment on the floor is likely to be much more favorable to the bill." Cohen and other administration strategists
gravely misjudged the mood of Rayburn's committee and the
entire House. This became obvious one day after Senate passage when Mississippi's John Rankin informed Roosevelt that
an acceptable bill might pass the House if the Senate version
could be voted upon directly without passing through the Committee on Interstate and Foreign Commerce. A majority of
Rayburn's committee, however, vehemently objected to this
procedure. The Senate-approved bill went instead to the
House committee and returned to the full House on July 24,
badly damaged.[34]

A majority of the utility executives, convinced they could
not secure Aldrich's four-system package, were now prepared
to accept a "death sentence" clause if it permitted them to
retain *two* systems in geographically separate regions. A few
holding companies, among them Electric Bond and Share,
would not survive this "compromise," but important two-system companies, including J. P. Morgan's principal interests,
United Gas Improvement and Commonwealth and Southern,
would remain intact. The utilities received a favorable response
from the House committee where Rayburn had lost considerable influence. Huddleston, Cooper, and Mapes held the winning hand. The Alabama Democrat, reactionary beyond his
years, detested TVA and all PWA-financed power projects.
He hoped to save the Alabama properties of Commonwealth

33. *Congressional Record,* 74th Cong., 1st sess., 79, pp. 8850, 8935,
9058.

34. Benjamin V. Cohen to James C. Bonbright, April 10, 1935,
Cohen File, NPPCR, Box 10; John Rankin, memorandum for FDR,
June 12, 1935, OF 293, FDRP, Box 2.

and Southern from David Lilienthal, TVA, and the SEC. Cooper and Mapes wished to protect the same company's Ohio and Michigan operations. Mandatorily, under the terms of the Senate bill, holding companies like Commonwealth and Southern would have to abandon one system or the other. Five Republicans voted with Cooper and Mapes; five Northern Democrats joined Huddleston. "Compared with the bill as originally introduced, or as passed [by] the Senate," Mapes said, "it [the committee's new bill] is as different as day from night." Harry Sauthoff, a freshman Progressive from Wisconsin, agreed. He thought it resembled "the bastard brat of the Power Trust." Huddleston and his twelve allies were not content with dismantling section 11. They looked askance at mutual service companies and also hoped to restrict in every possible way the control of the SEC and the Federal Power Commission over interstate utility operations. Rayburn could not even salvage natural gas regulation under Title III. "Probably no bill in recent years," the committee majority said, "has so recognized the responsibilities of State regulatory commissions as does . . . this bill."[35]

The House measure eliminated all reference to a "geographically and economically integrated public-utility system," and substituted "integrated public-utility system." This it defined as one or more generating plants, transmission lines, and distribution facilities "physically interconnected or capable of physical interconnection and which under normal conditions may be operated as a single interconnected and coordinated system confined in its operations to a single area or region, in one or more States, not so large as to impair . . . the advantages of localized management and efficient operation." The Senate's deliberate emphasis upon "contiguous states" was ignored. The door was thus open for retention of two scattered systems. In

35. *Congressional Record,* 74th Cong., 1st sess., 79, pp. 10356, 10417, 14010; *Public Utility Act of 1935* (House Rept. 1318, 74th Cong., 1st sess., 1935), p. 8. On the utilities' strategy, after the collapse of Aldrich's plan, see Felix Frankfurter, undated memorandum on Public Utility Holding Company Act, FFPLC, Box 66.

addition, the SEC's power to compel simplification became subject to new limitations. After 1938, the commission was instructed to require each holding company system to confine its operations "to one integrated public utility system." The commission, however, if it found that "such limitation is not necessary in the public interest," could permit each holding company system to control "such number of integrated public utility systems as it finds may be included in the holding company system consistently [sic] with the public interest." The SEC could not compel divestment of nonutility properties without first proving that their retention "would be inconsistent with the public interest."[36]

Ironically, the House committee's munificence may have exceeded the wishes of some holding company executives. "If a law is passed," Willkie told Cohen, "which gives wide discretionary powers to some commission as to the continuation of utility holding companies or their operations . . . the 'boodlers,' the 'fixers,' the 'smoothers,' and the 'political harpies' will be on our neck in a week. . . . Whatever you do, establish the rules so that those of us who live up to the rules have absolute rights and will not be compelled to live by the favor of any man." The House bill provided few definite rules. The committee's revision of section 11 was bad law and invited worse regulation. "Insofar as there is any standard provided," said Congressman Eicher, "it is couched in such a form as to make its effective application by the Commission impossible because of the pressure it invites against its application. The enforcement of such provision truly lies within the whim of the Commission and is . . . of doubtful constitutionality."[37]

Under a new section 13, mutual service companies were made voluntary. Holding companies were forbidden to perform

36. *Public Utility Act of 1935* (House Rept. 1318), pp. 4, 6, 16–17.
37. Wendell Willkie to Benjamin V. Cohen, March 20, 1935, Cohen File, NPPCR, Box 10; *Public Utility Act of 1935* (House Rept. 1318), p. 47. See also Edward Eicher to FDR, July 22, 1935, PPF 2681, FDRP.

service, sales, or construction contracts. Their subsidiaries, however, could perform these activities subject to the rules and regulations of the SEC. Operating subsidiaries, subject to state regulation, were exempt from all SEC rules and regulations regarding security issues, acquisitions, and accounting.[38]

The House committee further narrowed the jurisdiction of the Federal Power Commission under Title II. The Senate bill included both interstate transmission and generation for interstate transmission as legitimate objects of federal concern. Huddleston's majority eliminated all reference to generation. They accepted the Senate's judgment on voluntary interconnection and coordination, but made absolutely certain that it would be voluntary. Following complaint by a state commission or utility, the FPC could compel interconnection "only if the Commission finds that no undue burden will be placed upon the interstate public utility . . . and if no enlargement of generating facilities will be required." Even the FPC's authority to compel proper service and equipment for interstate transmission was limited to complaint by state commissions "and . . . only when it appears that such requirement will not call for the enlargement of generating facilities."[39]

Neither gibes nor votes could alter the efforts of Huddleston, Cooper, and Mapes. An irate Knute Hill read into the record Huddleston's old 1917 speeches attacking power monopolies. "I cannot turn Communist," the Alabaman drawled, "merely to please the gentleman from Washington. So long as the President stands by the doctrines of the Democratic Party of Thomas Jefferson . . . I will go with him to the end." Rayburn, ousted from leadership and completely demoralized, allowed Eicher and Rankin to lead the opposition to the revised and weakened bill. On July 1, Eicher presented amendments to substitute sections 11 and 13 of the Senate bill. Both amendments were beaten on teller votes, 216 to 146 and 163 to 101.

38. *Public Utility Act of 1935* (House Rept. 1318), pp. 5, 12, 15–16.
39. Ibid., pp. 26–29.

The House then passed its own measure in lieu of the Senate version.[40]

Wheeler's thin Senate majority rejected the House substitute, thus forcing a two-month conference period enlivened by House and Senate investigations into the lobbying activities of Tom Corcoran and the utilities and by Huddleston's successful efforts to exclude Cohen and Corcoran from the conference sessions. "The atmosphere was super-charged," Cohen recalled, "with charges that the Congressmen were being used as rubber stamps [and] . . . that no one knew or understood anything about the bill but a couple of young men—hot heads —with no political or practical experience. Every effort was . . . put forth to sow the seeds of suspicion and distrust between the Senate and the House. Tales were carried back and forth to make the leader of each committee feel that the leader of the other was trying to double cross him, every petty jealousy was played upon."[41]

Rayburn attempted to break the conference deadlock on August 1 with a motion that the House substitute again section 11 of the Senate bill. Huddleston's forces denounced the motion, the Senate bill, and Cohen and Corcoran with equal venom. "Some of us were here," declared the pompous Alfred Bulwinkle, "when both [Cohen and Corcoran] were yet in short pants." Huddleston contemptuously referred to Corcoran as "our ambassador to Passamaquoddy." He warned the House not to retreat on section 11: "The difference is between orderly execution of a criminal and mob murder. . . . The gentleman from Texas [Rayburn] champions the lynching bee." Rayburn lost on a roll-call vote, 209 to 155. The defeat revealed a deep split within the New Deal ranks. Democrats from industrialized sections of the North and upper South deserted Rayburn. The future power needs of their regions depended in many instances

40. *Congressional Record,* 74th Cong., 1st sess., 79, pp. 10360–62, 10419, 10555–62, 10637, 10845, 10916–17, 11095.

41. Arthur Schlesinger, Jr., *The Politics of Upheaval,* pp. 316–23; Benjamin V. Cohen to Felix Frankfurter, March 31, 1936, FFPH, Roll 22.

upon continued private development. Massive federal hydro-electric projects could not succeed in states like Pennsylvania, Illinois, or Ohio because of inadequate water resources and entrenched private utility systems. In the opinion of many congressmen from these areas, unfettered private development, regardless of economic cost, seemed not only preferable but the only real alternative to government largess. Representative Samuel Pettengill of Indiana told Roosevelt that he and other Northern Democrats "do not believe in the efficacy of the geographical integration principle." Application of that principle would encourage "local monopolies and a system of rotten boroughs." Holding companies should be permitted to manage operating properties in Michigan, the South, and New England because "this encourages some competition for service." Pettengill and others greatly exaggerated the benefits of competitive private development. Nonetheless, no legislation could pass the House which did not recognize their anxieties and attempt in some manner to remove them.[42]

Frankfurter and Senator Barkley drafted an opaque compromise on section 11 which Roosevelt and a majority of the House finally accepted at the end of August. The House definition of an "integrated public-utility system" remained, but under section 11 the Securities and Exchange Commission could compel each holding company to limit its operations "to a single integrated public-utility system." Holding companies might control one or more additional integrated systems subject to three determinations by the commission: (1) each additional system "cannot be operated as an independent system without the loss of substantial economies"; (2) all additional systems "are located in one State or in adjoining States"; and (3) the continued combination of additional systems under the control of one holding company "is not so large . . . as to impair the advantages of localized management, efficient operation, or the effectiveness of regulation." Holding companies beyond

42. *Congressional Record,* 74th Cong., 1st sess., 79, pp. 10354, 12273, 12271; Samuel Pettengill to FDR, August 17, 1935, OF 293, FDRP, Box 3.

the second degree would be eliminated from all systems. Voluntary reorganizations were encouraged. Compulsory proceedings would commence in 1938, followed by a two-year compliance period.[43]

The House won a partial triumph on section 13. The formation of mutual service companies remained voluntary. Holding company subsidiaries could perform service, sales, and construction activities, but under rules and regulations the SEC would insure that contracts were executed "economically and efficiently for the benefit of . . . associate companies at cost, fairly and equitably allocated among such companies." The conference committee followed the Senate bill on the matter of SEC approval for the issuance and sale of securities by holding companies and their subsidiaries. Subsidiaries subject to state regulation were not accorded an automatic exemption and the SEC retained ample jurisdiction over their acquisition of securities and capital assets. Statutory guidelines were provided to enable the commission to impose terms and conditions before approval. These provisions reflected the greater precision of the Senate bill. Natural gas producers and pipeline companies were excluded under the definition of gas utility in conformity with the House bill. The conferees, in addition, left the Federal Power Commission enfeebled under Title II since all vital issues of interconnection, coordination, and service were left to the initiative of state commissions or the voluntary action of the utilities.[44]

The Frankfurter-Barkley words in section 11, Roosevelt believed, were too generous. Firebrands in the House, however, looked upon the same section as a dangerous snare, composed

43. Raymond Moley, *After Seven Years,* p. 316, n.; Thomas G. Corcoran, memorandum, August 21, 1935, OF 293, FDRP, Box 3; *Congressional Record,* 74th Cong., 1st sess., 79, pp. 14162–71; *Public Utility Act of 1935* (House Rept. 1903, 74th Cong., 1st sess., 1935), pp. 8, 19–22, 70.

44. *Public Utility Act of 1935* (House Rept. 1903), pp. 14–19, 47–50. State utility commissioners remained dissatisfied with both Title I and Title II. See National Association of Railroad and Utility Commissioners, *Proceedings* (1935), pp. 82–96.

by a crafty presidential adviser and designed to achieve Roosevelt's purpose. "The authors of the original decree to eliminate holding companies," Congressman Cooper said, "have rewritten that decree in new language, but the sentence of death remains. . . . Do not think anyone will be deceived by this different shroud of language in which death has been newly wrapped." Whether or not it was a deception, the new language permitted many Northern Democrats to change their votes.[45]

The legislative struggle over the Public Utility Act, particularly Title I, demonstrated again the precarious position of administration measures that seriously threatened entrenched economic power and that lacked support from politically articulate social or economic constituencies. The Securities Act, the Exchange Act, and the Public Utility Act succeeded through compromise, Roosevelt's personal commitment, and the dedication of a small band of reformers. Few organized, politically muscular interest groups lobbied *for* financial regulation. A similar situation doomed the administration's efforts to secure extensive, permanent tax reform. Other measures of Roosevelt's first term found greater private support and congressional favor. Social security, agricultural assistance, rural electrification, regional development, even additional banking legislation did not provoke as much congressional opposition as Title I of the Public Utility Act. One vote saved a strong section 11 in the Senate. The same section was overwhelmed twice in the House. Northern Democrats, who could vote for a revolutionary Wagner Act, supported by organized labor, rejected section 11 until it contained the promise of possible relief for the largest two-system holding companies.

Title I of the Public Utility Act gave the Securities and Exchange Commission an important new mandate. The commission was instructed to do more than inspire "truth-telling" in the underwriting and distribution of securities. It received posi-

45. Thomas G. Corcoran, memorandum, August 21, 1935, OF 293, FDRP, Box 3; *Congressional Record,* 74th Cong., 1st sess., 79, p. 14165. Northern Democrats either switched their votes, or, like Pettengill, abstained.

tive, statutory commands to compel the reorganization of important business institutions. Yet the 1935 act, following the pattern set by earlier statutes, delegated many problems to administrators. Under section 11, for example, administrative interpretations would determine initially whether Congressman Cooper's suspicions were more accurate than the President's doubts. Moreover, the Securities Act and the Securities Exchange Act had not provoked retaliatory litigation. Even before Roosevelt signed the 1935 legislation, however, public utility holding companies and their lawyers prepared for prolonged legal warfare. Constitutional disputation would delay substantive administrative action.

7

The Politics of Administration, I

Between 1934 and 1940, Franklin Roosevelt appointed thirteen men to the Securities and Exchange Commission. In outlook and training they ranged from the self-taught Vermont lawyer, Robert E. Healy, to men with Harvard law degrees like Edmund Burke, Jr., and Ganson Purcell. They included James D. Ross, formerly a director of Seattle's municipal power system, and George C. Mathews, past president of Middle West Utilities; Ferdinand Pecora, the financial community's tenacious interrogator, and John W. Hanes, a senior partner in the brokerage firm of Charles D. Barney and Company. Regardless of background, these men shared one assumption: the commission's basic goals were the perpetuation and the disciplining of American capitalism. Members of the commission engaged in conflicts over methods; seldom over ultimate ends.

"We of the S.E.C.," chairman Joseph P. Kennedy said in 1934, "do not regard ourselves as coroners sitting on the corpse of financial enterprise. On the contrary, we think of ourselves as the means of bringing new life into the body of the security [sic] business." In 1939, Hugh Johnson, the jaded ex-New Dealer turned newspaper columnist, accused the commission's fourth chairman, Jerome Frank, of harboring "a revolutionary purpose to lay the ground for a Nazi or Fascist federal control of almost every activity of American life." Frank, greatly offended, informed Johnson that he was "far more reluctant to use governmental powers extensively than you were when you ran NRA." Furthermore, Frank said, "I think America will go to hell in a hack if there is a drive away from the essentials of our profit system." The SEC existed, Frank told Adolph Berle, "primarily to preserve the capitalist form." Kennedy, a former pool operator on the New York Stock Exchange, and Frank, a scholarly lawyer with a reputation for radicalism, held almost identical views on the desirability of capitalism and the role of the SEC.[1]

This view of the commission's function stressed the breakdown of self-regulation and the failure of private groups to maintain a level of financial stability required for the future existence and growth of capitalism. The Securities and Exchange Commission, through an administrative process, would encourage rational organization within private groups and between private groups in order to achieve that stability. In addition, the commission would eliminate or curtail the most vulgar entrepreneurial practices which, if allowed to continue, threatened to undermine popular belief in the nation's economic and governmental institutions. The commission was both policeman and promoter; a vehicle for reform and a shield against more violent change. The SEC had the responsibility, Kennedy said, "of giving all the aid of which Government is capable to the better organization of the mechanism through which the savings of the people find their way into securities. . . . Domestic tranquility is as essential to business as it is to our political system." James Landis, the commission's second chairman, told the Investment Bankers Association that cooperation with the SEC was imperative, because "if we [the SEC]

1. Joseph P. Kennedy, "Securities and Exchange Commission," *Certified Public Accountant* 14 (August 1934): 454; Jerome Frank to Hugh Johnson, June 19, August 29, 1939, Series 1, Box 7, JFP; Adolph A. Berle to Frank, February 8, 1938, JFP, Series 1, Box 2. "The Securities and Exchange Commission," Chairman William O. Douglas said, "is one of the outposts of capitalism. . . . That outpost is concerned with the preservation of capitalism" (William O. Douglas, address before the Foundation for the Advancement of the Social Sciences, June 22, 1938, JFP, Series 1, Box 26).

fail, others will take charge; their sanctions, their mechanisms, will be different."[2]

Landis and William O. Douglas, who served as chairman from 1937 to 1939, were the major architects of the SEC's administrative and regulatory ideology. The commission's long-tenured members, Healy and Mathews, echoed much of that doctrine. The Landis-Douglas ideology emphasized the common purpose of those charged with regulation and those subject to regulation. Administrative agencies like the SEC were but a higher form of business management. "Once broad national policies have been embodied in statutory law," Douglas said, "the business-government relationship moves out of the realm of controversy and debate. It ceases to be an issue of politics and moves into the province of the technicians. The problems must be worked out, under the law, but in business terms. They are to be worked out not on the political but on the technical level." His agency was equipped, Douglas added, "to meet business on business terms." The commission's future development "will in large part be molded by business," and through joint action, the SEC could become "an efficient business force." The problems of managing a private industry, Landis argued, resembled those entailed by its regulation, and therefore, the policies of an administrative tribunal had to be correct "from an industrial standpoint [in order to] promote the economic soundness of the industry."[3]

Raising an industry's ethical standards, according to Landis and Douglas, was only one task facing administrative agencies. They should provide technical assistance designed to improve

2. Kennedy, "Securities and Exchange Commission," p. 454; IBA, *Proceedings* (1936), p. 193. See also the remarks of Baldwin Bane, the first administrator of the Securities Act under the Federal Trade Commission, in National Association of Securities Commissioners, *Proceedings* (1933), p. 94.

3. William O. Douglas, address before the National Association of Accredited Publicity Directors, November 21, 1938, JFP, Series 1, Box 26; James M. Landis, *The Administrative Process*, pp. 10–16, 70, 99.

the operations of individual constituents and resolve amicably conflicts between constituents. In all of these areas, legislation was sporadic and politically motivated. Courts were cumbersome. Neither provided the continuous and flexible supervision demanded by modern methods of business and finance. The administrative process surpassed legislation and litigation because it could remain informal. "It is easier to plot a way through a labyrinth of detail when it is done in the comparative quiet of a conference room," Landis said, "than when it is attempted amid the turmoil of a legislative chamber or committee room." Ideally, a commission's rules and regulations should evolve out of dialogue and rational discussion with those affected. Self-enforcement and voluntary compliance by private bodies were preferable to formal decrees and courtroom forensics. "Legal mandate," Douglas believed, "is an inferior method of getting the work of the world done. Furthermore, government without the support of business and finance . . . is constantly under the compelling necessity of intruding more and more into the details of business, so that . . . it becomes . . . a bureaucratic blight."[4]

The SEC's activities did not, of course, always correspond to the principles formulated by its leading administrators. The commission and regulated groups might share identical goals and still remain divided over how to achieve those goals. "Technical issues" usually touched economic interests and required political solutions. Dialogue and discussion often proved fruitless. Informal decision making could provoke angry conflicts, even among commissioners. Nonetheless, the SEC's official ideology was no more misleading than the assessment of its activities by others.

4. James M. Landis, "The Place of Administrative Law," *Connecticut Bar Journal* 13 (April 1939): 71–81; William O. Douglas, address before the Foundation for the Advancement of the Social Sciences, June 22, 1938, JFP, Series 1, Box 26. See also Landis, "Shifting Postulates in Modern Legal Development," *Proceedings and Reports of the Associated Harvard Clubs* (April 14–16, 1939), pp. 76–81, and Landis, "Symposium on Administrative Law," *American Law School Review* 9 (April 1939): 181–84.

"I remember one time a few years ago," Ohio governor John W. Bricker told the Investment Bankers Association in 1940, "going into the SEC offices in New York and leaving my name so that I might have forwarded to me the rulings and regulations of that commission. . . . We had difficulty in finding space to pile them." For Governor Bricker, this volume count of rules and regulations bore a precise relationship to the "autocratic and arbitrary authority" of the Securities and Exchange Commission. On the other hand, reform purists, expecting the commission to refashion completely America's financial and business institutions, were frequently bitter and disillusioned. "The truth . . . is," John Flynn wrote in 1940, "that the SEC . . . has erred upon the side of amicability in its dealings. . . . It has been polite, gentle [and] considerate to the point of weakness."[5]

At first glance, a survey of the commission's functions between 1934 and 1941 would appear to confirm Governor Bricker's contention that the SEC was "an autocratic and bureaucratic board." The personnel of the Securities and Exchange Commission expanded from 696 to 1,678. Its annual budget rose from $1.5 million to $5.3 million. Regional offices operated in ten cities from Boston to San Francisco. In addition to the Securities Act, the Securities Exchange Act, and the Public Utility Holding Company Act, the commission's concern extended to general corporate reorganizations, trust indentures, and investment companies.

By 1939 the commission's jurisdiction included twenty stock exchanges and 4,000 listed securities. It maintained continuous surveillance over trading activities in 3,000 listed securities. Registration statements under the Securities Act averaged 450 per year, many involving prolonged investigation. Nearly 7,000 brokers and dealers, engaged in over-the-counter business, functioned under the commission's scrutiny. Over 90,000 securities were traded in this market. Fifty-one public utility

5. IBA, *Proceedings* (1940), p. 66; *New Republic,* April 1, 1940, pp. 441. See Flynn's earlier remarks in *New Republic,* June 10, 1936, pp. 151–52.

holding company systems, complying with the 1935 statute, had registered with the SEC. These included 1,542 separate holding, subholding, and operating companies. A commission inquiry into margin transactions during 1936 entailed the systematic examination of 62,876 customers' accounts. During five years the Securities and Exchange Commission instituted 312 suits in federal courts, secured 657 permanent injunctions, and referred 158 cases to the Justice Department for criminal prosecution.[6]

The scope and magnitude of this administrative burden, however, when weighed against the SEC's limited resources, actually prevented "autocratic and arbitrary authority." Members of the commission constantly complained about personnel deficiencies and financial hardships. On the eve of a major suit against the holding companies, Landis pleaded for staff assistance from the Justice Department because "our budget is small and our General Counsel has a hard time living within the amounts allocated to the legal staff." It is not surprising that the commission's conception of business-government relations resembled more the indictment of John Flynn than the verdict of Governor Bricker. Nor is it surprising that this conception emphasized cooperation and self-enforcement by private organizations. "Government regulation at its best should be residual," Douglas said. "We should not have to be in a position of watching the details of operation. Those are for the [stock] exchanges themselves. If we carried regulation to [that] extent . . . we would be an enormous burden on the national treasury." Mathews, a member of the Federal Trade Commission and the SEC from 1933 to 1940, frequently called upon investment bankers for assistance in combatting "elementary violations of the law." The commission hoped to avoid, he said, "expansion in our organization . . . multiplication of

6. Securities and Exchange Commission, *First Annual Report* (Washington, 1935), p. 69; *Third Annual Report* (Washington, 1937), p. 69; *Fifth Annual Report* (Washington, 1939), pp. 1–2; *Seventh Annual Report* (1941), p. 243.

branch offices . . . the evils of bureaucracy . . . and . . . a large increase in the expenditure of public funds."[7]

During its formative years, however, the SEC's perspective and accomplishments were not products of a simple equation embracing administrative ideology, manpower and budgets. Policy and achievement were also influenced by the ability of separate interest groups to maintain varying degrees of autonomy while formally under the commission's jurisdiction. In numerous and subtle ways, these influences helped to shape early administration of the Securities Act, the Securities Exchange Act, and the Public Utility Holding Company Act. Like other exercises in controlling the economic activities of men, administration often rested upon compromise, involved acceptance of the status quo, progressed by indirection, resulted in stalemate, and produced a few dead ends.

The heavy smoke of ideological warfare, produced by radicals like Flynn and conservatives like Bricker, often obscured regulatory problems. The SEC confronted many issues that had neither "liberal" nor "conservative" solutions. These issues, among them further stock exchange reform, trading in unlisted securities, and over-the-counter markets, involved at most a redistribution of power and economic rewards among existing groups. "In these days of social and economic confusion," the commission's general counsel noted, "it has become the fashion to 'peg' the persons who serve in the public interest. . . . In the minds of many critics the pendulum never stops in the middle. One is either a wild pop-eyed radical committed to a program of revolution or a cringing, timid, spineless slavey to the Wall Street money barons. There is no gray in their color scheme." Attacks from the left upon the SEC

7. James M. Landis to Clarence M. Updegraff, July 12, 1937, JMLPLC, Box 14; William O. Douglas, address before the Seattle Junior Chamber of Commerce, June 15, 1938, JFP, Series 1, Box 26; George C. Mathews, "Your Interest—Our Needs," *Investment Banking* 8 (November 20, 1937): 34–35. See also the comments of Commissioner Healy, "Advantages of Self-Regulation," *Investment Banking* 9 (April 1939): 21.

proved particularly frustrating for Landis. "I sit here every day, taking it on the chin," he told Frankfurter, "from the groups that hate every effort at general reform . . . and to find those who may really be more liberal . . . and perhaps be right in being so—weakening the strength that needs . . . to be built up, is an extraordinary bit of irony." He urged Frankfurter to educate his radical friends "to make them appreciate the things that are significant, and discard those that have no fundamental merit, since nobody can have a batting average of 100 per cent." Kennedy, in a very unsentimental moment, may have best summarized the SEC's basic commitment: "There is no Right or Left in the processes of the Securities and Exchange Commission," he said, "all we are trying to do is to go forward."[8]

Going forward entailed, among other matters, the encouragement of private investment. Pursuit of this policy produced concessions to investment bankers in 1934 and became a continuing problem for the Securities and Exchange Commission throughout the New Deal years. The problem arose because the President and many New Dealers adhered to a theory of recovery that emphasized the preponderant influence of private investment in an automatically self-correcting economy. Not until 1938 did the Roosevelt administration look upon government spending as other than pump-priming or a humanitarian necessity. Conservative critics of the administration effectively attacked programs that appeared to prevent recovery by retarding private investment. Securities legislation and the SEC were obvious targets for that opposition. Because the New Deal failed to evolve an alternative theory of public investment until 1938, securities regulation underwent amendment in order to conform to the economic assumptions of both New Dealers and their opponents. Modifying the Securities

8. John J. Burns, "The Securities and Exchange Commission—Some of Its Problems," *Investment Banking* 6 (November 12, 1935): 35; James M. Landis to Felix Frankfurter, June 6, 1936, JMLPLC, Box 10; Joseph P. Kennedy, "Securities and Exchange Commission," *Certified Public Accountant 14* (December 1934): 723.

Act became, like the administration's futile gold-purchase program, one panacea for securing instant recovery.[9]

Director of the Budget Lewis Douglas and O. M. W. Sprague, former adviser to the Bank of England, Harvard professor, and Treasury consultant, became the center of early opposition to the Securities Act within the administration. Douglas and Sprague, according to Tom Corcoran, were "instinctively hostile" to the legislation. Douglas could also rely for support upon Henry Bruere, former president of the Bowery Savings Bank, executive assistant to William Woodin in the Treasury, and FDR's credit coodinator. These were men with ideological and personal roots in the Eastern banking community. As their technical adviser on the Securities Act they turned to Paul Mazur, an economist for Lehman Brothers, a New York investment house with a Wall Street reputation for liberalism. At a cabinet meeting in early September 1933, Douglas submitted a memorandum written by Mazur which criticized the Securities Act for preventing "needed long-term financing." The key to recovery, Douglas argued, lay in the stimulation of heavy industry through new private investment. The Securities Act, filled with awesome liabilities and onerous registration requirements, prevented recovery. Henry Wallace for one was impressed by Mazur's memorandum. Wallace told FDR that he believed Mazur "about the necessity for amending the securities bill." He could support the Securities Act in its present form if the situation were 1927 or 1929, the secretary of agriculture said, "but I am really fearful of its influence at the present time."[10]

Besides Mazur, other men with considerable Wall Street influence predicted rapid recovery if the Securities Act were

9. John M. Blum, *From the Morgenthau Diaries: Years of Crisis, 1928–1938,* pp. 380–451; Marriner Eccles, *Beckoning Frontiers,* pp. 310–11.

10. Thomas G. Corcoran to Felix Frankfurter, September 8, 1933, FFPH, Roll 10; Henry Wallace to FDR, September 2, 1933, OF 396, FDRP, Box 1. On Douglas and Sprague see Arthur M. Schlesinger, Jr., *Coming of the New Deal,* pp. 8–9, 95, 98, 209, 244–45, 289–92.

revised. Sidney J. Weinberg of Goldman, Sachs and Company, said the act was "impractical in many respects and unworkable in practice." The President's recovery program could only succeed if the market for capital issues were revived and "this . . . cannot take place as long as the present law is in effect." Recovery could not be assured, J. P. Morgan's partner Russell Leffingwell said, until long-term capital for new enterprises and for funding floating debts was readily available. Certain "doctrinaire provisions" of the Securities Act, he held, made that capital unavailable. The arguments of those supporting revision seemed to be confirmed by the investment trend in September 1933, usually a month of substantial corporate financing. New offerings consisted exclusively of seven brewery issues. "It is . . . evident," IBA president Frank Gordon said, "that the unusual liabilities of the law constitute hazards which officers and directors of corporations decline to assume." Arthur Dean of Sullivan and Cromwell, and Allan M. Pope, former IBA president, agreed. Both predicted a wave of defaults and bankruptcies unless the Securities Act were modified.[11]

Mazur's memorandum and the opposition of administration leaders such as Douglas moved Roosevelt to reassess the Securities Act. In late September the President casually told Yale economist James Harvey Rogers, "I think I have the Securities Bill difficulties straightened out." Rogers was delighted "as the lack of securities issues is . . . one of the chief obstacles to recovery." Roosevelt, after deciding to reevaluate the measure, gave the same task to two different groups, who soon expanded to three. He told Henry Bruere "to get working on the problem of possible revision." The President wanted Bruere to form a committee to include Federal Trade Commissioners Landis and Mathews and IBA counsel William

11. Sidney J. Weinberg to Louis M. Howe, September 11, 1933, OF 242, FDRP, Box 1; Russell C. Leffingwell to FDR, October 2, 1933, PPF 866, FDRP; *New York Times,* October 16, 1933; *Financial Age,* September 16, 1933, pp. 226–27; September 23, 1933, p. 256; *Fortune,* August 1933, pp. 50, 99–106.

Breed. "This should be done quietly," Bruere said, "and without indicating that he [FDR] was taking up revision of the Act. He [FDR] wished to take his position after further consideration of matured recommendations from this committee." Roosevelt also asked Secretary of Commerce Roper to form a committee to study the Securities Act. Roper's committee included Landis, Dean, Berle, Assistant Secretary Dickinson, and Henry Richardson. Roper proceeded to create a third committee within the Business Advisory Council. This committee included Walter Gifford of American Telephone and Telegraph and two investment bankers, Averill Harriman and Weinberg.[12]

While encouraging the formation of these committees, the President began to collect evidence for use against those resisting the Securities Act. Typically, Roosevelt moved in many directions simultaneously without committing himself to one course of action. He gave increasing attention to the assertions of those who interpreted the hiatus in private investment as a bankers' conspiracy "deliberately fostered . . . to create . . . an argument against the Act." The Pennsylvania Railroad could not find underwriters for an $85-million bond issue to carry out new electrification programs. A $40-million bond offer by the Port of New York Authority did not gain private backing, nor did bond issues by San Francisco and Dallas, two cities with impeccable financial reputations. All of these offerings were totally exempt from the Securities Act. "I am personally convinced," Harry Hopkins said, "the bankers agreed amongst themselves not to bid on these bonds." He urged FDR to take action against Wall Street because "the bankers through collusion are refusing to buy good public securities." Roosevelt sent a terse note to Governor Black of the Federal Reserve Board demanding an explanation. Black

12. James H. Rogers, memorandum on conversation with President Roosevelt, September 26, 1933, James H. Rogers Papers, Box 92, Yale University; Henry Bruere, memorandum, October 29, 1933, OF 21, FDRP, Box 1; Daniel C. Roper to FDR, November 25, 1933, OF 242, FDRP, Box 1.

dismissed the idea of collusion and assured the President that "other factors" had been involved. He included as evidence a confused document prepared by governors Calkins and McKinney of the San Francisco and Dallas Reserve Banks. "I do not think the gentlemen [Calkins and McKinney] . . . have made out a case," FDR concluded. "I am still from the revered state of Missouri."[13]

Berle gave Roosevelt additional reason to doubt Wall Street's good faith. After a frank conversation with Lewis Strauss, a member of Kuhn, Loeb and Company, Berle told FDR: "there has been a tacit understanding among security houses that no issues would be floated for the time being, pending revision of the Securities Act." If the bankers' attitude persisted, said Berle, "I see no escape from giving the Reconstruction Finance Corporation the right to go into the investment banking business." Jesse Jones, the RFC's ebullient entrepreneur, thought Berle's suggestion excellent, but the proposal was far too radical for the President.[14]

Frankfurter and his followers were less inclined to blame investment bankers for the shortage of private investment. Corcoran was convinced that the "trained seal" opinions of New York law firms had terrified the bankers. "This is a deliberate lawyers' rather than a bankers' strike," he said, "and . . . the bankers are all being flabbergasted by the shortsighted, microscopic attitude of the lawyers." The "real culprits" in the drive against the Securities Act, Frankfurter said, "are some of the leading law firms who make such a fat killing out of the abuses which brought the Securities Act into existence. They really want to do business at the old stand." These same law firms, he told Henry Stimson angrily, "have come out of their

13. Bernard Flexner, "The Fight on the Securities Act," *Atlantic* 153 (February 1934): 234–35. Harry Hopkins, memorandum, December 5, 1933; Eugene R. Black to FDR, December 13, 1933; FDR to Black (undated memorandum), all OF 90, FDRP, Box 1.
14. Adolph A. Berle to FDR, December 9, 1933, OF 242, FDRP, Box 1; Jesse Jones to FDR, December 22, 1933, PPF 1820, FDRP. Box 1.

storm cellar of fear—not to improve but to chloroform the Act." The argument that the Securities Act stopped capital issues, Frankfurter told William O. Douglas, "is just rubbish." Landis communicated these sentiments to Roosevelt in a brilliant, caustic memorandum. Revising the statute, Landis argued, would not bring forth the promised capital financing. "The pressure of this damned-up capital," he said, "is doubtful." The Securities Act had not acted as a brake on new flotations or prevented refundings. Most of the issues in need of refunding were selling far below par and, under these conditions, refunding was difficult, if not impossible, even without the new law. As proof, he noted that the Federal Trade Commission was willing to relax registration requirements on refunding issues, but no companies had accepted the offer. The strike, Landis concluded, was a deliberate attempt to emasculate a system of regulation which had not been tested adequately. This crude power play by the bankers and their lawyers had to be resisted or the administration would be subjected to additional strikes "until further modifications again take place."[15]

Frankfurter's resourceful protégés were not content with verbal fencing. They enlisted the assistance of sympathetic New York bankers and lawyers in a daring attempt to break Wall Street's resistance. Corcoran persuaded the investment house of Fuller, Rodney and Company to underwrite a large issue of distillery stocks. If similar flotations proved profitable, Corcoran said, "the rest of the strikers will come along in five minutes rather than see somebody else making money. The Street will strike together only so long as somebody doesn't

15. Thomas G. Corcoran to Felix Frankfurter, September 8, 1933, FFPH, Roll 10; Frankfurter to Louis M. Howe, September 13, 1933, FFPLC, Box 49; Frankfurter to Henry L. Stimson, December 19, 1933, HLSP, Box 322; James M. Landis to FDR, December 4, 1933, JMLPLC, Box 94. See also Stimson to Frankfurter, December 5, 1933, HLSP, Box 322; Stimson to Frankfurter, January 26, 1934, HLSP, Box 323; Frankfurter to Stimson, February 20, 1934, and Stimson to Frankfurter, May 1, 1934, HLSP, Box 326; Frankfurter to William O. Douglas, January 16, 1934, FFPLC, Box 10.

scab and scalp profits on them." Corcoran also advocated a vigorous publicity campaign to discredit the bankers and their legal advisers. "Farmers like to hate lawyers," he said, "and a frontal attack on Cravath Henderson, White and Case, et al., would give the Progressives something more than the New York bankers to shoot at and put the fear of God into the New York offices." Corcoran's strategy failed to move Wall Street, to generate wide support for the existing legislation, or to prevent revision. The financing of distillery and mining ventures in 1933 and 1934 only helped to confirm the arguments of those opposing the Securities Act: well-established enterprises, vital to economic recovery, could not raise needed funds because of severe liabilities and complex registration requirements. The legislation favored speculative, fly-by-night promotions. Corcoran's propaganda offensive against New York investment bankers and legal firms was also ineffective. Inexorably, the committees sanctioned by FDR moved toward specific modifications of the legislation. Roosevelt had been convinced to proceed with revision by a few powerful men wielding specious arguments.[16]

Henry Bruere and Lewis Douglas formulated detailed amendments by the middle of November. Civil liabilities "should be limited to damages reasonably attributable to the untrue statement or omission." Liability should be further "limited to instances where the purchaser has relied on the registration statement," and liability "should be apportioned among the underwriters [and] . . . limited to participation in the issue." These amendments, Bruere said, would restore business confidence, increase the flow of private capital, and aid employment. Douglas was more concerned with refunding maturing obligations. In a memorandum supporting Bruere's amendments, Douglas explained how new funds would be spent. He analyzed fifty-one companies and found only ten which anticipated using funds for capital expansion. The other

16. Thomas G. Corcoran to Felix Frankfurter, September 8, 1933, FFPH, Roll 10.

companies, all of them utilities, needed money to refund old obligations or to meet bank loans. Douglas, nonetheless, maintained that Bruere's amendments would revitalize the economy by encouraging capital expansion. "We do not want conflicts," Bruere concluded, "we want cooperation, understanding and confidence in the reliance which the administration places in the capacity of the business community to think for itself, to act for itself and to cooperate."[17]

Roper's committee urged substantially the same amendments. In addition, this committee recommended that the standard of reasonable care "be clarified by providing that the reasonable care and reasonable ground of belief required of persons made liable for the registration statement . . . be that of a reasonably prudent man in the conduct of his own affairs." The Roper committee also suggested that defeated parties in civil suits bear all court costs plus an added penalty of $500 "and thus discourage possible strike suits." Landis and Arthur Dean did not endorse the recommendations. Berle, for his part, filed a blistering dissent and endorsed the existing legislation. He objected to the new definition of reasonable care. He opposed the attempt to limit damages to the amount of the loss caused by the untrue statement or omission. "I am not able to convince myself," Berle said, "that it is practicable under American [investment] procedure to limit the measure of damage to the drop in value 'caused' by the false statement or material omission. False statements as such do not 'cause' a drop in value nor a measurable item of damage. They act as an element tending to induce a buyer to purchase; and the result to him is the loss of a part of his money."[18]

17. Henry Bruere, memorandum, November 2, 1933; Bruere, memorandum of interview with FDR, November 16, 1933; Bruere, memorandum on Federal Securities Act, November 18, 1933, all OF 21, FDRP, Box 1; Bruere to FDR, December 8, 1933, PPF 862, FDRP.

18. Daniel C. Roper, memorandum to FDR, February 2, 1934; Adolph A. Berle, memorandum to FDR, January 30, 1934, both OF 34, FDRP, Box 2. Landis also objected to the "cause" amendment. He noted that the gathering of sufficient proof would usually exceed

The Bruere and Roper amendments were not inconsequential. They sought to alter substantially the legal relationships between investors and sellers contained in the original legislation. Nonetheless, the Bruere and Roper modifications were moderate when compared with the demands of others. The American Bar Association drafted similar amendments, but coupled them to major revisions in the schedule of information required for registration. The Bar Association said the schedule could be simplified by eliminating: the names of underwriters; the names of persons holding 10 percent of the capital stock; the amount of securities held by officers and directors; the proceeds from previous issues; payments to promoters; and material contracts not made in the ordinary course of business. The Bar Association found these provisions either "immaterial and vague," or "of little value to the investor." Its recommended amendments were incorporated verbatim into a bill introduced by Senator Hastings of Delaware on April 5, 1934.[19]

By the spring of 1934, business and financial groups were effectively mobilized in favor of amending the securities legislation. Some, such as eleven major life insurance executives, endorsed the specific Hastings bill. Others, including the United States Chamber of Commerce, the NRA's Durable Goods Industries Committee, and the Investment Bankers Association, adopted either the recommendations of the Roper committee or supported the general idea of amendment. "A revision of the Securities Act," according to the Durable Goods Industries Committee, "would go a long way toward . . . stimulation of the durable goods industries and the opening up of many new opportunities for employment of men now being supported

---

the means of small purchasers involved in civil suits against large corporations (James M. Landis to FDR, December 4, 1933, JMLPLC, Box 94).

19. American Bar Association, *Report of Fifty-Seventh Annual Meeting* (Baltimore, 1934), pp. 567–69, 574–85; *New York Times,* April 2, 6, 1934.

by direct government relief or artificial work created by government expenditures." The flow of investment capital would begin "first in driblets and then in streams, and then in rivers," Leffingwell said, "if the door were opened," by adopting the Roper amendments.[20]

Roosevelt kept a tight rein on the final amending process. Bruere and Roper were excluded from strategy meetings in January and March 1934. The President turned instead to Landis, Cohen, Rayburn, Fletcher, Morgenthau, and Oliphant. They decided to submit amendments to the Securities Act as a rider to the pending Securities Exchange bill. Landis and Oliphant prepared the finished draft which FDR approved.

The Landis-Oliphant amendments made concessions to opponents of the original statute. What the bankers lost in 1933 they partially regained in 1934. The time limit on civil suits was reduced from two and ten years to one and three years. The element of causality was introduced into the civil liability section by providing that "if the defendant proves that any portion or all of such damages represents other than the depreciation in value of such security resulting from such part of the registration statement . . . not being true or omitting to state a material fact . . . such portion or all such damages shall not be recoverable." The definition of reasonable care was also altered. As originally drawn, a director was responsible for the reports of experts unless he could show that he "had reasonable ground to believe and did believe . . . that the statements therein were true." The new language provided that a director was liable unless he "had no reasonable ground to believe . . . that the statement therein were untrue." Moreover, the definition of reasonable care was changed to "that required of a prudent man in the management of his own property," instead of "that required of a person occupying a fiduciary relationship." The liability of underwriters was limited to the extent of their

20. *New York Times,* April 13, 23, 26, May 5, 1934; American Bankers Association, *Journal* 26 (December 1933): 57; 26 (February 1934): 33; Russell C. Leffingwell to FDR, January 4, 1934, PPF 866, FDRP.

total dollar participation, and courts were instructed to assess full cost against parties presenting "unmeritorious claims or unmeritorious defenses." Fortunately, the Landis-Oliphant amendments did not concede to the demand that purchasers prove reliance upon the registration statement. Amendments reducing the statutory requirements for financial data were also ignored. Administration leaders in Congress defeated the Hastings-American Bar Association bill and other amendments supported by the Durable Goods Industries Committee. The administration's amendments passed with the Exchange legislation. Against unremitting pressure, reluctant compromisers like Landis, Oliphant, and Cohen salvaged as much of the original bill as possible.[21]

"These amendments," Landis told Roosevelt, "do not hurt the main objectives of the Act in any way but at the same time redress such balances as may, perhaps, have militated too strongly against [new investment]." According to Rayburn, the revisions were only "psychological and clarifying," and designed "to offset fear." Yet the amendments, despite attempts to deprecate their substantive content, were constructed to cement an informal agreement between the Roosevelt administration and the investment banking community. In return for some liberalizing provisions, the bankers promised new financing to spur the recovery program. Landis outlined the nature of the compromise that had emerged from his discussions with M. M. Freeman and Robert Christie of the Investment Bankers Association, Averell Harriman and Robert Lovett of Brown Brothers Harriman, and Henry Harriman of the Chamber of Commerce. "These amendments," Landis said,

21. Henry M. Kannee, memorandum to Marvin McIntyre, January 15, 1934, OF 21, FDRP, Box 2; James M. Landis, memorandum to FDR, March 9, 1934, OF 242, FDRP, Box 2; Benjamin V. Cohen to James M. Landis, March 20, 1934, FDRP, Box 2; Herman Oliphant, memorandum, April 17, 1934, both JMLPLC, Box 149; *Wall Street Journal*, May 18, 1934; Henry L. Stimson, Diary, May 17, 1934. For an incisive analysis of the 1934 amendments see George E. Barnett, "The Securities Act of 1933 and the British Companies Act," *Harvard Business Review* 13 (October 1934): 6–14.

"accord, in the main, with the suggestions of Mr. Freeman acting for Mr. Christie, on the basis of what Mr. Freeman deems as absolutely minimum demands." Christie expressed satisfaction with the changes. "The more unworkable provisions," he said, "have been modified." Other financial spokesmen praised the amendments and predicted a resurgence of private financial activity as a result of the modifications. "A year ago," said George W. Bovenizer of Kuhn, Loeb and Company, "the Securities Act . . . was an unworkable law. . . . Today, through its amendments, the Securities Act has become a much more workable instrument, more equitable toward honest enterprise." Eustace Seligman said the amendments removed "four-fifths of the . . . objections to the original act. . . . The brake on long-term financing existing under the original act will be removed by at least 80 per cent."[22]

Though the amendments appeared to satisfy some members of the financial community, they did not unleash a torrent of new private investment. As early as August 1934, one observer noted that the amendments had little impact upon the flow of investments. The market absorbed $373 million of new securities in July, but of this total, $227 million represented federal and state financing. Corporate issues accounted for $145 million, but $100 million were railroad bonds not subject to the Securities Act. Of the remaining $45 million, less than half was devoted to capital expansion and $25 million involved the refunding of old obligations. The failure of private investment to promote sustained recovery continued through the remaining years of the New Deal. Once the stimulus of modest federal deficit-spending had been removed, the temporary upturn of 1936–37 turned into a bewildering recession during 1937–38. The American economy, without the federal government as

---

22. James M. Landis, memorandum to FDR, March 9, 1934, OF 242, FDRP, Box 2; Henry I. Harriman to Landis, April 27, 1934, JMLPLC, Box 149; *Wall Street Journal,* May 15, 1934; *New York Times,* June 14, October 30, 1934; *Literary Digest,* June 16, 1934, p. 41.

chief underwriter, seemed unable to generate its own growth.[23]

Not surprisingly, the recession of 1937–38 encouraged fresh attempts by the business and financial community to liberalize both the Securities Act and the Securities Exchange Act. Once again, the proponents of revision found members of the administration who shared their opinion that regulation of the securities market prevented recovery. Paul Gourrich, head of the SEC's research division, blamed the recession upon the undistributed earnings tax and "impediments to the capital market." Gourrich's memoranda to SEC Commissioner Jerome Frank echoed Chamber of Commerce tracts by stressing "fears and lack of confidence on the part of those possessed of capital." Like Gourrich, spokesmen for Wall Street blamed the recession upon the Securities Act and "over-regulation of the stock market." The SEC could encourage recovery, New York economic consultant Elisha Friedman told Frank, if the commission would relax its rules for exchange trading by directors, officers, specialists, and floor traders. This opinion was even shared by Carl E. Parry, head of the Federal Reserve Board's security loan division, and by the board's research division. Parry said the SEC should increase the opportunities for professional trading in securities: "Restrictions upon professional trading . . . should be lifted and should be removed in very great part if not in whole." Fortunately, attempts to modify the Exchange Act in 1938 encountered firm opposition from SEC commissioners and Federal Reserve Governor Marriner Eccles. The clamor for amendments, Frank said, "is an indication of intellectual bankruptcy. . . . The solution is to be found not in increasing professional trading on the stock exchange,

---

23. The Roosevelt recession has provoked great debate among historians and economists. Businessmen at the time, however, emphasized only the vindictiveness of government policies. Recent studies have focused upon the deficit and other factors. See Kenneth D. Roose, "The Recession of 1937–1938," *Journal of Political Economy* 56 (June 1948): 239–48; Cary E. Brown, "Fiscal Policy in the 'Thirties: A Reappraisal," *American Economic Review* (1956): 857–79; Blum, *From the Morgenthau Diaries*, pp. 380–451.

but . . . in bringing about a larger volume of long term investment." Eccles concurred in this judgment.[24]

Suggestions to alter the Securities Act received greater consideration than did suggestions to revise the Exchange Act.
Commissioner John Hanes actively promoted the former.
Hanes went so far as to prepare a bill that contained additional
amendments to the 1933 statute. He wished to reduce or abolish the twenty-day waiting period; allow solicitation of orders
from the date of registration; and eliminate the requirement
that dealers deliver a prospectus with every sale. Hanes worked
feverishly to enlist the support of other commissioners and to
have the bill introduced in Congress during 1938. The amendments, he told Frank, "have nothing to do with the philosophy
of the statute, but . . . would make the mechanics of underwriting and distributing far more simple than it is at the present
time." The recession had frightened Hanes as it had frightened
other members of the administration. His modifications of the
Securities Act, Hanes believed, would help the President by
promoting recovery. "I do not believe we can go to the well
again after this trip," he said. "The [regulatory] machinery
must be well oiled in order to bring forward a continuous flow
of private capital . . . to start business forward again." But
Hanes could not sway a majority of the SEC, and his amendments were not sent to Congress.[25]

The Securities Act and the Exchange Act emerged from the
recession unscathed, yet the continued emphasis upon amending these laws to encourage recovery indicated the confusion
about recovery that characterized the business community, the
Roosevelt administration, and certain members of the Securities and Exchange Commission. It also indicated one way in

24. Paul Gourrich to Jerome Frank, May 11, July 20, 1938; Frank
to Gourrich, July 2, August 1, 1938, all JFP, Series 1, Box 5; Frank
to Elisha Friedman, May 4, 1938; Frank to Marriner Eccles, April 25,
May 3, 1938; Eccles to Frank, April 27, May 26, 1938, all JFP,
Series 1, Box 4.

25. John W. Hanes, memorandum to Jerome Frank, April 15, 1938,
JFP, Series 1, Box 6.

which larger political pressures complicated the commission's regulatory activities.

"I was up the night before and talked to some accountants," Landis told Frankfurter in 1935. They were, he noted, "a very strange class of people whom I suppose by the very nature of their profession are without any humor." Occupational stress may have increased the accountant's seriousness, but they were concerned primarily with the demands which the SEC might make upon their profession under the Securities Act and the Securities Exchange Act.[26]

Financial disclosure constituted the heart of both statutes. Accounting requirements, therefore, became an explosive administrative issue. Although both the Securities Act and the Securities Exchange Act enumerated specific categories of data for disclosure, the commission could define accounting terms; prescribe the form of reports, including the items to be shown in balance sheets and income statements; and set forth the methods to be followed in the preparation of accounts and the valuation of assets and liabilities. These were sweeping powers. The commission, however, did not invoke the mandate. Instead, the SEC hastily delegated these powers to individual accountants and to the American Institute of Accountants. Few professional groups came to enjoy similar independence and influence under the Securities and Exchange Commission. At times, this relationship proved frustrating to the commission because autonomy for the accounting profession also meant substantial autonomy for corporations filing financial statements.

Both the Federal Trade Commission and the SEC inherited a regulatory problem shaped by years of professional neglect, financial expediency, ad hoc court decisions, and feeble state incorporation laws. "Accountancy lacks definitions," one journal editor wrote in 1929. "Unlike the law, it has no high court. . . . Textbooks have mostly shunned the responsibility of for-

---

26. James M. Landis to Felix Frankfurter, January 19, 1935, FFPLC, Box 21.

mulating clearly-cut definitions, and the results obtained thus far by professional bodies have been almost nil." Henry R. Hatfield, addressing the American Institute of Accountants, compiled a more devastating critique: "Net earnings, net income, gross profits, profits, net profits? I have tried for years to find the proper term to be used and the exact connotation of each of the terms just quoted. I have appealed to academic writers, both economists and accountants, and I found only confusion. I have turned to the courts and found their decisions a confusion overwhelmingly ludicrous." As one example, Hatfield noted that all accountants could agree that if a machine wore out in ten years, its cost had to be distributed as a charge during those years. But there was no agreement as to the proportion of charges in each year. This was a prerogative of management and individual accountants. "Accountants, with rare impartiality, apply one system to one class of assets, another to other classes. . . . It is somewhat as if one applied the Ptolemaic system to the motion of Mars, but regarded Jupiter as operating according to the Copernican system."²⁷

Organized accountants took few steps to improve this situation. They blamed ignorant and corrupt state legislators for creating incorporation laws that sanctioned dubious practices. They berated immoral officers and directors who forced accountants to accept these practices. At the same time, they opposed legislative interference with the conduct of the profession. Reform, they argued, should come from self-improvement or through cooperation with other private organizations such as the New York Stock Exchange.

27. Eric L. Kohler, editorial in *Accounting Review* 4 (September 1929): 192; Henry R. Hatfield, "What Is the Matter with Accounting?" *Journal of Accountancy* 44 (October 1927): 271–76. Conflicting state incorporation laws and diverse court decisions compounded the profession's own confusion. Accounting principles, in short, were largely determined by what management desired, state legislators permitted, and courts tolerated. See Adolph A. Berle and Frederick S. Fisher. Jr., "Elements of the Law of Business Accounting," *Columbia Law Review* 33 (April 1932): 573–622.

The profession's viewpoint was dramatically revealed on the matter of earned surplus. A special committee of the American Institute reported in 1927, after an examination of state statutes, that the existing laws provided neither uniformity in legal requirements nor exactitude in the definition of sources from which dividends might be paid. Not surprisingly, the committee also found that "there exists a serious lack of uniformity among the members of our own profession as to just what constitutes earned surplus." Faced with this problem, the committee recommended that the institute develop a standard definition and procedure "based on the practice of the principal accounting firms of the country . . . the surest foundation for any action looking to an improvement in the state laws governing corporations." Uniform state legislation could come after "we put our own houses in order." Federal legislation was dangerous and impractical, because "the very character of the practice itself depends upon the local industries and commercial ventures, and the accountant adapts himself to the demands of particular businesses." On the larger issue of requiring corporations to submit to independent audits, most accountants predicted improvement through "public opinion supported by gradual education."[28]

Theoretically, the Securities Act and the Securities Exchange Act altered the accountant's formal role. In addition to requiring independent audits, both statutes made accountants liable for misleading statements or the omission of material facts in the preparation of registration materials. Both laws upgraded financial reporting and accounting practice to the extent of demanding at least a balance sheet and an income statement from corporations whose securities were listed on the stock exchanges or sold interstate. But despite the profession's initial

28. American Institute of Accountants, *Yearbook* (1927), pp. 170–71; *Journal of Accountancy* 43 (January 1927): 35–39; George O. May, *Twenty-Five Years of Accounting Responsibility, 1911–1936,* pp. 42–43, 54–56, 69–70. On the earned surplus debate see *Journal of Accountancy* 47 (March 1929): 214–18; 47 (February 1929): 134–35; 47 (June 1929): 447–48; Henry B. Fernald, "Accountants' Certificates," *Journal of Accountancy* 47 (January 1929): 18–19.

hysteria, neither the statutes nor the commission's rules and regulations significantly changed the accountant's relationship to American corporations or deprived the profession of self-government in the crucial areas of terminology and methodology.

"The accounting officer as well as the independent certified public accountant see their public recognition greatly enhanced," one accountant noted, "but along with this welcome enhancement comes a burden of responsibility that is truly appalling." Leading spokesmen for the profession like Rodney F. Starkey of Price, Waterhouse and Company, paid lip service to the desirability of having a federal statute establish uniform standards of disclosure, but condemned the Federal Trade Commission's initial registration forms as "expensive and tedious," and deplored the tendency of both the Securities Act and the Exchange Act to weaken "the privity of contact between our profession and our immediate clients." Other accountants predicted a sweeping, commission-imposed revision in auditing techniques. Accounts receivable and inventory, usually certified by management, might require detailed examination by accountants. These fears and objections were largely overcome when administration of the laws passed to the new Securities and Exchange Commission. On November 21, 1934, in the *Northern States Power Company* case, the SEC announced that it would not prescribe the methods to be used by accountants. Two months later, in cooperation with members of the accounting profession, the commission promulgated new registration forms to replace the FTC forms and a revised instruction book for accountants. Registration form A-2 became the basis of the commission's administrative relationship with the profession. Form A-2 recognized that the SEC could not remedy at once the accounting errors and abuses of the past. It was also, Chairman Kennedy candidly told Roosevelt, "where we hope to get private capital back into industry."[29]

29. Robert Weidenhasumer, "The Accountant and the Securities Act," *Accounting Review* 8 (December 1933): 272–78; Rodney F. Starkey, "The Special Problems and Responsibilities of the Accountant

Registration form A-2 was designed for what the SEC called "seasoned" corporations, which meant a majority of America's largest industrial enterprises. Formal amendments to the Securities Act had removed some of their objections to the statute by reducing the liabilities of officers and directors. Form A-2 made further concessions both to corporations and to accountants by eliminating extensive historical data originally required by the Federal Trade Commission. Many corporations, for example, had great difficulty meeting the FTC's demand for a balance sheet that included the cost of all major classifications of property, plant, and equipment from the date of organization, "or, if not practicable, beginning January 1, 1922." They encountered equal difficulty when attempting to compute on the same historical basis all intangible assets and the division of corporate surplus. Form A-2 avoided these historical problems. The new registration form required separation of tangible and intangible assets in the balance sheet, but corporations could combine both items, "if in the books of the issuer intangible assets had not been kept separate." The same provision was made for the separation of capital surplus from earned surplus. "To have gone further," Harvard professor and SEC consultant T. H. Sanders said, "would have greatly enhanced the difficulty of preparation of statements." The SEC, Sanders added, "took a practical view of the case," whereas the Federal Trade Commission's earlier requirements had been an "unwarranted burden on business by not considering that account-

---

under the New Act," *American Management Association Bulletin* (1935), pp. 9–10; Rodney F. Starkey, "Practice under the Securities Act of 1933 and the Securities Exchange Act of 1934," *Journal of Accountancy* 57 (December 1934): 432–38; A. I. Henderson, "Practice under the Securities Act," *Journal of Accountancy* 57 (December 1934): 448–58; James Hall, "Problems of Accountants under the Securities Act," *Journal of Accountancy* 56 (December 1933): 452–61; R. C. Hunt to James M. Landis, September 24, 1935, JMLPLC, Box 11; Securities and Exchange Commission, *Securities Act Release No. 254*, November 21, 1934; *New York Times*, January 11, 1935.

ing information is ordinarily classified and accumulated for the company's own purpose."[30]

With the assistance of Professor Sanders and the American Institute, the SEC wrote off much of the past and allowed corporations abundant accounting flexibility in the future. The commission insisted only upon full disclosure. Trade practices, if disclosed, could justify the inclusion of dubious items in current assets and liabilities. Inventories could be classified and valued "as the conditions of the industry and of the company may suggest." Reacquired stock could be treated as a deduction from capital stock, from surplus, or as an asset, provided corporations disclosed the reasons for their choice. "A careful study of the Commission's regulations," Sanders said, "will show that very few rigid rules are to be found in them. . . . A good deal of latitude will be allowed individual companies to deal with the circumstances of their own business." Some dissenters looked upon the new registration form as a hasty abdication by the commission of its accounting powers. "The temper of the present Commission," C. Aubrey Smith said, "is to permit the accountants to draw up for themselves what they shall consider 'accepted accounting principles and practice.' . . . [The new form] fails to incorporate certain requirements for which the better practitioners have been striving during the past fifteen years." But major corporations, including Standard Oil and Swift, greeted the new requirements with more enthusiasm. Both corporations announced refinancing programs which included registration and public distribution of securities aggregating $35 million.[31]

30. Comparison of Federal Trade Commission, *Registration Form A-1* and Securities and Exchange Commission, *Registration Form A-2;* T. H. Sanders, "Accounting Aspects of the Securities Act," *Law and Contemporary Problems* 4 (April 1937): 192–208.

31. Securities and Exchange Commission, *Registration Form A-2* and *Instruction Book for Form A-2* (1935), passim; T. H. Sanders, "Influence of the Securities and Exchange Commission upon Accounting Principles," *Accounting Review* 11 (March 1936): 66–74; C. Aubrey Smith, "Accounting Practices under the Securities and Exchange Commission," *Accounting Review* 10 (December 17, 1935):

After 1935 the SEC continued to expose shoddy accounting practices by threatening stop orders and insisting upon full disclosure. But the commission took no affirmative action to promote uniform accounting terminology or techniques, even in areas where many practitioners believed uniformity was long overdue. Nor did the commission, until 1941, promulgate rules and regulations to govern the scope and content of independent audits. Nothing jarred the SEC's confidence in the accounting profession's ability to evolve more uniform terminology and techniques. Commissioners and staff members merely became impatient.

"I am very much afraid," the commission's chief accountant said in 1937, "it is difficult to name very many principles that are generally accepted. Almost daily, principles that for years I had thought were definitely accepted . . . are violated in a registration statement. . . . Indeed, an examination of hundreds of statements filed . . . almost leads one to the conclusion that aside from the single rules of double entry bookkeeping, there are very few principles of accounting upon which accountants of this country are in agreement." Commissioners themselves echoed these sentiments. They deplored the paucity of viable accounting standards and agonized over the "environmental influences" that perpetuated professional servitude to management. Despite these setbacks, the commission continued to hope "the profession will itself develop greater consistency in many places where uniformity appears essential to avoid confusion in the presentation of financial data."[32]

325–32; *New York Times,* January 17, 1935; *Wall Street Journal,* January 14, 15, 18, 1935. See also editorials in *Journal of Accountancy* 54 (February 1935): 81–82, and *Certified Public Accountant* 15 (February 1935): 107–11.

32. Carmen G. Blough, "The Need for Accounting Principles," *Accounting Review* 7 (March 1937): 30–37; George C. Mathews, "Accounting in the Regulation of Security Sales," *Accounting Review* 8 (September 1938): 225–30. The commission and many academic accountants attacked principally the wildly fluctuating standards that existed in the areas of depreciation, separation of surplus, and the sale or retirement of capital assets.

Even though greater consistency did not develop, the SEC carried self-regulation a step further. In 1938 the commission announced an administrative policy for resolving disputes between registrants and the SEC over proper principles of accounting. The SEC would not insist upon revisions in registration statements if corporations could demonstrate "substantial authoritative support for the practices followed," and if the commission had not already published rules and regulations dealing with these issues. Since the commission had provided few such rules and regulations, this startling administrative decision vested substantial power in professional accounting associations, above all, the American Institute of Accountants. Immediately, the institute formed a special committee on accounting procedure. This group, dominated by practicing certified public accountants, proceeded to publish bulletins which became a prime source for corporations needing "substantial authoritative support" for specific accounting practices. "If anyone outside of the profession is stronger than we are and is able to tell us what to do," Robert H. Montgomery of Price, Waterhouse and Company told the institute, "from that moment the profession will deteriorate. It is not so today."[33]

The SEC's early administrative experience with accountants revealed more than the organized strength of one interest group or its effective resistance to governmentally encouraged change. This experience also revealed the deadening weight of past economic relationships and habits which unhappily, given the crisis of 1933–40, could have been abolished only at the cost of not going forward at all. A minority of the commission, led by Healy, insisted throughout that the wrong road had been chosen as early as the *Northern States Power Company* case. The SEC, Healy said, should have entered the accounting area vigorously by demanding more than full disclosure. At the very

33. Securities and Exchange Commission, *Accounting Series Release No. 4,* April 25, 1938; George O. May, "Uniformity in Accounting," *Harvard Business Review* 17 (Autumn 1938): 1–8; Robert H. Montgomery, "What Have We Done, and How?" in American Institute of Accountants, *Fiftieth Anniversary Celebration* (New York, 1938), p. 205.

least, Healy added, these issues should have been tested in the courts. Landis, for one, held the opposite and majority opinion. "If his [Healy's] viewpoint had carried in several significant instances," Landis told Roosevelt, "the work of administration would have been seriously clogged due to his failure adequately to appreciate the exigency for practical and workable methods of control. Part of that attitude springs . . . from an unwillingness to sacrifice certain ideal qualities and take the chance of making things work." But by 1939, even Landis was forced to admit that the commission's self-improvement emphasis had produced deleterious results. "As long as you have the [George] May leadership in the accounting situation," he despaired, "I have very little hope of seeing them accomplish much." The May leadership, of course, had been made possible by the SEC's early capitulation.[34]

34. Robert E. Healy, "The Next Step in Accounting," *Accounting Review* 13 (March 1938): 1–9; James M. Landis to FDR, May 4, 1936, PSF, FDRP, Box 58; James M. Landis to Donald McCruden, March 9, 1939, JMLPLC, Box 25.

8

The Politics of Administration, II

The conflict between what James Landis distinguished as "ideal qualities" and "making things work" confronted the Securities and Exchange Commission again when it devised administrative programs for stock exchanges and over-the-counter markets. The SEC faced both the recalcitrance of existing institutional arrangements and the absence of organizations that could make regulation possible. It did not, to the despair of critics, pursue a program of immediate and radical reform. Instead, the commission attempted to perpetuate many existing economic relationships and to maintain parity between the two trading markets and among separate exchanges. It relied upon self-regulation and voluntarism; when these techniques failed, the commission employed the threat of direct intervention and ultimately supported factions among the regulated groups that promised acceptable cooperation in the future.

Under section 11 of the Securities and Exchange Act, the commission drafted sixteen trading rules which the exchanges voluntarily adopted. In view of the intense legislative struggle over section 11, the rules were moderate and often vague. Trading by exchange members for their own account was prohibited if "excessive in view of the financial resources of such member . . . or in view of the market for such security." Trading for joint accounts was subject only to prior approval by the exchange and the filing of weekly reports with the commission. Specialists could not trade for their own account, "unless such dealings are reasonably necessary to permit such specialist to maintain a fair and orderly market." Short sales were forbidden only "at a price below the last sale price." Enforcement of these rules, including discipline over members, was left to the exchanges. In January 1935, pursuant to section 19, the SEC reported on the exchanges' internal governments. It found them negligent, archaic, and oligarchical, but opposed legislation as a remedy. In 1936 the commission recommended against mandatory segregation of broker and dealer functions on exchanges or in over-the-counter markets. At the same time, the SEC secured legislative approval for a continuation and expansion of trading in securities not formally listed on exchanges or registered under the 1934 statute.[1]

These decisions, particularly with respect to segregation and unlisted trading, outraged many of the commission's liberal friends. The SEC, they argued had become a passive tool of the exchanges, above all the New York Stock Exchange. Landis was singled out for heavy abuse. "[His] tenure," Max Lowenthal wrote Frankfurter, "however vernal may have been the hope with which it started, faded out in a dismal autumn fashion. . . . It has become increasingly clear that Landis likes the big boys and that the big boys like Landis." A. Wilfred May, a member of the commission's staff, resigned following disputes over segregation and unlisted trading. May took up residence on the *New Republic* where he and John Flynn published venomous articles accusing the SEC of conspiring with the exchanges to destroy the regulatory system.[2]

The accusations of Lowenthal and others were highly exag-

1. Securities and Exchange Commission, *First Annual Report* (Washington, 1935), pp. 40–44; Securities and Exchange Commission, *Report on the Government of Securities Exchanges* (House Doc. 85, 74th Cong., 1st sess., 1935), pp. 1–17; Securities and Exchange Commission, *Report on the Feasibility and Advisability of the Complete Segregation of the Functions of Dealer and Broker* (Washington, 1936), pp. 101–14; Securities and Exchange Commission, *Trading in Unlisted Securities* (Washington, 1936), p. 24; *Congressional Record,* 74th Cong., 2d sess., 80, pp. 6040–43, 7724–25, 7728–30.

2. Max Lowenthal to Felix Frankfurter, January 15, 1937, FFPH, Roll 9; John Flynn in the *New Republic,* June 10, 1936, pp. 151–52; James M. Landis to Felix Frankfurter, June 6, 1936, FFPLC, Box 21.

gerated. The commission's early activities under the Exchange Act revealed greater solicitude for the welfare of "little guys" than sensitivity to the demands and pressure of "big boys." Its willingness to tolerate exchange trading, even in securities not fully listed, resulted from the same considerations and from the belief that trading on exchanges was preferable to increased over-the-counter trading where no regulatory machinery, beyond registration of brokers and dealers, existed.

Unlike many of its critics, the SEC did not view segregation primarily in terms of its impact upon the New York Stock Exchange or upon the larger investment houses. The commission faced the same dilemma that had prevented congressional resolution of the issue. In addition to the New York Stock Exchange, segregation would affect twenty other exchanges and all over-the-counter firms. Was it desirable, economically or politically, to institute a program that, while further protecting investors, held out the possibility of closing many regional exchanges and reducing the number of firms operating as brokers or dealers? The commission's chief economist, Kemper Simpson, and his assistant, Wallis Ballinger, believed in the necessity of complete segregation. Their initial report in 1936, recommending this remedy, was rejected by Landis and a majority of the commission as hastily written and based upon questionable evidence. Instead of revising their report, Simpson and Ballinger leaked the document to reporters; were summarily fired for insubordination; and joined the chorus of SEC critics. When called upon to defend rejection of the first report and the removal of two employees, Landis and the commission argued convincingly that the merits of segregation did not outweigh the dangers of increased financial concentration. "Neither brokerage orders nor trading opportunities on the local exchanges," the commission believed, "are sufficient to enable their members . . . to confine themselves to one type of activity." Regional exchanges, engaged in a fierce competitive struggle with over-the-counter markets, had been unable to attract more listings or to encourage members to effect more transactions on a brokerage basis. Greater profits and greater volume led these members to operate as dealers over the counter. Segregation might accentuate the trend toward over-the-counter trading, cripple the local exchanges, and limit available brokerage business to companies with large resources and nationwide branch offices. Small firms, dependent upon a combined income from broker and dealer business, would bear the brunt of segregation both on the exchanges and over the counter.[3]

"If tomorrow . . . unlisted trading should be abolished," Landis told the Senate Banking and Currency Committee, "the result would be that many small exchanges would be forced to close." Sixteen exchanges, including the New York Curb, permitted trading in unlisted securities. Many, including Boston and Philadelphia, conducted a large odd-lot business in stocks fully listed on the New York Stock Exchange, but not listed locally. All of the regional exchanges fought with local over-the-counter markets for unlisted securities. Under section 12 of the Exchange Act, new securities could not be admitted to unlisted trading; those admitted before September 1934 faced the alternative of full registration or removal from the exchanges in 1936. A continuation of this policy, the SEC argued, would benefit only the odd-lot dealers on the New York Stock Exchange and force additional securities into over-the-counter markets.[4]

3. Securities and Exchange Commission, *Report on Segregation*, passim; James M. Landis to Felix Frankfurter, June 6, 1936, FFPLC, Box 21; William B. Harris to James M. Landis, April 24, 1940, JMLPLC, Box 23; IBA *Proceedings* (1939), pp. 83–87. The New York Stock Exchange, of course, had little interest in the economic health of other exchanges. Robert L. Stott, chairman of the committee on floor procedure, told an SEC staff member "that it was desirable in the national interest that there should be only one market for stocks. . . . Smaller exchanges should be devoted only to financing local industries and . . . dealings in the issues of the large corporations should be concentrated on the national [New York] exchange" (Memorandum of conversation between Walter Louckheim, Jr., and Robert L. Stott, February 12, 1940, Leon Henderson Papers, Box 24, FDRP).
4. Senate Banking and Currency Committee, *Trading in Unlisted Securities upon Exchanges* (74th Cong., 2d sess., 1936), pp. 3–45; House Interstate Commerce Committee, *Unlisted Securities* (74th Cong., 2d sess., 1936), pp. 8–11.

Amendments to section 12, passed in 1936, gave the SEC broad jurisdiction over unlisted securities, including the important determination of where and to what extent unlisted trading would be permitted. Previously, these questions had been resolved by tugs-of-war among management, exchange members, and over-the-counter dealers. The commission now became the arbitrator. Trading in unlisted securities would be tolerated on exchanges after a formal hearing before the commission. The SEC would evaluate each security in terms of distribution, trading activity, and price spreads on exchanges and over the counter. The commission would not approve exchange trading in an unlisted security unless information, substantially equivalent to that required under the Exchange Act, was available to investors.[5]

"We would not be interested in building up trade in Boston purely for the sake of Boston," Landis said in 1936. "Considerations of self-interest would be . . . far removed with us, certainly further removed, than the exchanges themselves." Nonetheless, the SEC could not ignore the chronic economic difficulties of the smaller exchanges. In fact, the commission labored to keep them solvent. The smaller exchanges made extensive use of the 1936 amendments to gain trading privileges in securities previously bought and sold only over the counter and to increase odd-lot trading in securities fully listed on the New York Stock Exchange. In 1937, when approving the application of the Boston Stock Exchange for odd-lot trading in fifteen securities listed on the New York Stock Exchange, the commission noted that "expansion in its unlisted trading is . . . of acute importance to the applicant." The Boston exchange was then operating at a net loss and maintaining itself out of accumulated surplus. The SEC followed a similar policy of encouraging unlisted trading on the other regional exchanges. "Should the Buffalo Stock Exchange fall by the way

5. *Amendments to Securities Exchange Act of 1934* (Senate Rept. 1739, 74th Cong., 2d sess., 1936), pp. 1–4; *Amendments to Securities Exchange Act of 1934* (House Rept. 2601, 74th Cong., 2d sess., 1936), pp. 1–10.

side," its president told Landis, "I know it will be through no fault of mine or yours."[6]

Over-the-counter dealers had opposed the 1936 amendments. They manifested even greater alarm over the commission's treatment of the smaller exchanges than did the New York Stock Exchange. Regional exchanges and the New York Curb threatened to absorb a growing volume of unlisted securities, and the SEC appeared to favor trading on these organized exchanges. Over-the-counter dealers felt impotent. "Stock Exchanges are compact bodies," Orrin G. Wood told the Investment Bankers Association, "well organized, and usually with a reasonable amount of financial resources, and so are able to engage counsel and properly present their case for unlisted trading privileges to the Commission." Over-the-counter dealers, Wood complained, were "an unorganized group . . . widely scattered through the country." The IBA created ad hoc financial and legal machinery to assist over-the-counter members, but they longed for an institutionalized method of representing their interests. This sentiment corresponded with the SEC's desire for more permanent supervision of over-the-counter markets.[7]

The 1938 Maloney Act met the aspirations of over-the-counter brokers and dealers as well as the practical needs of the commission. "The problem of direct Government regulation of the over-the-counter market," Commissioner Mathews said, "is a little like trying to build a structure out of dry sand. There is no cohesive force to hold it together, no organization with which we can build, as authoritatively representing a substantial element in the over-the-counter business." While over 6,000 individual firms had registered with the SEC under section 15 of the Exchange Act, only 1,700 firms were members of the IBA-sponsored Investment Bankers Conference, an off-

6. House, *Unlisted Securities,* p. 8; *New York Times,* July 15, 1937, and April 18, 1938; Lewis S. Castle to James M. Landis, September 25, 1935, JMLPLC, Box 9.

7. Senate, *Trading in Unlisted Securities,* pp. 53–70; IBA, *Proceedings* (1936), pp. 9–10.

spring of the NRA's defunct code group. For their part, the IBA and its affiliate were willing to accept governmental regulation that promised to extend their own control over marginal elements in the industry, permitted decentralized self-regulation, and gave over-the-counter members an institutionalized, national voice in the commission's affairs.[8]

The Maloney legislation permitted the SEC to register voluntary national securities associations, organized regionally, which undertook to prevent fraudulent and manipulative practices in over-the-counter markets. Subject to commission review, the associations could discipline members and adopt rules and regulations to insure "free and open markets." The associations could not engage in activities designed to permit "unfair discrimination between customers, or issuers, or brokers or dealers, nor to fix minimum profits . . . nor impose any schedule of prices, nor fix minimum commissions, allowances, discounts or other charges." In 1939 the Investment Bankers Conference, renamed the National Securities Dealers Association, became the first and only over-the-counter association to register with the SEC. The commission employed Henry H. Egly of Dillon, Read and Company to encourage rapid organization. " To stall along and merely go through the motions of conforming to the Maloney Act," Egly told Cleveland's IBA members, "will result in a weak, meaningless organization which will have little standing before the public, a poor position in Washington, and will be pushed further and further into the background by exchanges." Ineffective self-regulation, Egly added, would encourage more government control, "and when that day comes, I doubt that you will want to be in business any more than I will."[9]

8. Senate Banking and Currency Committee, *Regulation of Over-the-Counter Markets* (75th Cong., 3d sess., 1938), pp. 7–26, 32–69; *Regulating Over-the-Counter Markets* (Senate Rept. 1455, 75th Cong., 3d sess., 1938), pp. 1–11.

9. House Interstate Commerce Committee, *Regulation of Over-the-Counter Markets* (75th Cong., 3d sess., 1938), pp. 5–19, 29; *Regulation of Over-the-Counter Markets* (House Rept. 2307, 75th Cong.,

Ultimately, the National Securities Dealers Association functioned through fourteen district organizations. Extensive police powers, including the initiation of complaints, hearings, and discipline, rested initially with local members and district business-conduct committees. This regulatory structure, Commissioner Healy said, "permits . . . greater flexibility of action and a freedom and informality of procedure which an administrative agency like the SEC does not have. . . . Every effort . . . has been made to give regional autonomy to the various diverse groups in the country." Seldom had federal regulation been less autocratic or arbitrary.[10]

While encouraging self-regulation in over-the-counter markets, the commission also attempted to upgrade self-regulation on the exchanges, particularly on the New York Stock Exchange. The SEC promulgated new rules further restricting short sales and specialists' trading. More importantly, it supported exchange dissidents and outside businessmen in their successful reorganization of the New York Stock Exchange.

By 1937 the commission had reached the conclusion that reorganization provided one answer to the prevention of recurring manipulative practices. Without reasonable vigilance and enforcement by the New York Stock Exchange itself, all of the commission's resources would be drained away in detecting and instituting formal proceedings against such practices. The expulsion of individual members by the SEC, although sometimes spectacular, was also costly and inefficient. Chairman Douglas threatened compulsory reorganization under section 19. Bowing to this pressure, President Charles Gay of the New York Stock Exchange appointed a committee on reorganization headed by Carle Conway, president of the American Can

---

3d sess., 1938), pp. 1–18; *New York Times,* March 11, June 20, 1937; "Scope of Maloney Association." *Investment Banking* 9 (January 15, 1939): 2–3.

10. "Securities Dealers Association," *Investment Banking* 9 (February 1939): 8–9; Robert E. Healy, "Advantages of Self-Regulation," *Investment Banking* 9 (April 1939): 21.

Company, and Kenneth Hogate of the *Wall Street Journal.* Conway was among a growing group of corporate executives who believed "that what so-called 'big business' needs is a good stock exchange reorganization." Both he and Hogate were close, personal friends of Commissioner Hanes. While a Wall Street member, Hanes, E. A. Pierce, and Paul Shields had led the commission brokers in their abortive efforts to wrest a larger share of influence away from specialists and floor traders who dominated the governing board and all major administrative committees of the New York Stock Exchange. The SEC, for its part, viewed the excessive leverage of specialists and floor traders as the principal obstacle to more effective enforcement and self-regulation by the New York Stock Exchange.[11]

The recommendations of Conway's committee, adopted as constitutional amendments by the Exchange membership in early 1938, provided more than increased representation for commission brokers. They modernized the entire administrative structure by creating a salaried, nonmember president and an executive staff to carry out functions formerly conducted by the governors sitting as committee members. The number of standing committees was reduced from seventeen to seven. The new thirty-man governing board included three nonmembers, two bond brokers, five specialists, and twenty commission brokers. "That," said one investment banker, referring to the waning influence of floor traders and specialists, "is a great change from the old days when the government of the Stock

11. Securities and Exchange Commission, *Third Annual Report* (Washington, 1937), pp. 69, 78; *Fourth Annual Report* (Washington, 1938), pp. 20–21; *Fifth Annual Report* (Washington, 1939), p. 44; William O. Douglas to Felix Frankfurter, January 14, 1938; William B. Harris to James M. Landis, April 24, 1940, both JMLPLC, Box 23; Kenneth Hogate to Jerome Frank, March 18, 1938; Wetmore Hodges to Frank, March 24, 1938, both JFP, Series 1, Box 6; H. Terry Morrison to John Hanes, May 4, 1938, JFP, Series 1, Box 10; Carle Conway to Frank, June 25, 1938, JFP, Series 1, Box 3; Frank to Hanes, July 8, 1938; Hanes to Frank, July 11, 1938, both JFP, Series 1, Box 6; Fred Rodell, "Douglas over the Stock Exchange," *Fortune* 17 (February 1938): pp. 118–19, 120–26.

Exchange was largely acquainted only with the technique in the auction market."

On May 16, 1938, the Exchange installed as its nonmember president thirty-two-year-old William McChesney Martin, a former commission broker, cofounder of the *Economic Forum,* and a member of the graduate faculty at the New School for Social Research. St. Louis-born and Yale-educated, the boyish Martin presented a striking contrast to past presidents like Simmons, Whitney, and Gay. He viewed the New York Stock Exchange as a public utility, not as a private club. "The spirit and purpose of the reorganization," Martin said, "has been to provide a simpler, more efficient and more democratic structure, adapted to changing times and conditions." Government intervention into business and finance, he held, "is the trend of the times." The SEC provided rules and regulations "in our interest and in the public interest." Close cooperation between Washington and business "ought to be the rule, not the exception." Members of the commission were as delighted with the organizational and personnel changes as were members of the financial community. "Martin has been working with us," Frank told the attorney general. "He represents a sort of New Deal in the Exchange."[12]

A palace revolution on Wall Street could not solve all problems of exchange regulation any more than creation of a National Securities Dealers Association could resolve all issues arising out of over-the-counter supervision. In many respects, Martin's progressively attired regime proved as reluctant as earlier dynasties to follow suggestions emanating from the commission. It turned down the idea of a brokerage bank to safeguard customers' securities, did not endorse a proposal permitting member firms to separate brokerage and underwriting business, and refused to compel member firms to file annual

12. Securities and Exchange Commission, *Fourth Annual Report* (Washington, 1938), pp. 20–21; IBA, *Proceedings* (1939), p. 69; *Fortune* 17 (August 1938): 38–39, 102–108; *New York Times,* May 17, June 12, December 21, 1938; Jerome Frank to Frank Murphy, March 15, 1939, JFP, Series 1, Box 10.

financial statements. Content with half a loaf, the SEC, more-over, did not push these proposals vigorously. Both on the exchanges and over the counter, reorganization and new orga-nization provided only a framework for future administration based upon negotiations, voluntarism, and self-regulation.[13]

Voluntarism and cooperation proved less successful under the Public Utility Holding Company Act. Difficulties arose not only because the legislation anticipated substantial structural changes in a powerful industry, but also because, as Adolph Berle observed, "the Public Utility Holding Company Act is one of the few cases where the Commission really has a chance to lay down some rules in advance governing corporate organi-zation." When the SEC challenged basic prerogatives of man-agement and began to tamper directly with corporate organiza-tions the active resistance of business and finance increased proportionally.[14]

During Roosevelt's presidency, the commission made pain-fully slow progress toward the simplification and geographical integration of major holding company systems under section 11. In part this was due to a determined minority within the industry, led by Willkie and Thomas N. McCarter, who resisted every application of the statute, even to the point of refusing to register with the SEC without a constitutional test. Many holding company executives, swayed by the arguments of Gerard Swope and others, opposed this strategy and, accord-ing to William Z. Ripley, the utility expert, "were fed up with the litigation and . . . seriously consider[ed] registering under the . . . Act." These companies hoped to refinance maturing obligations or, like Stone and Webster, acquire the construc-tion business made available through new financing. Swope, representing General Electric, also wished to boost construc-tion activity and avoid endless warfare with the Roosevelt ad-

13. Securities and Exchange Commission, *Fifth Annual Report* (Washington, 1939), passim; *Sixth Annual Report* (Washington, 1940), passim.

14. Adolph A. Berle to Jerome Frank, February 8, 1939, JFP, Series 1, Box 2.

ministration. He could not, however, convince the holdouts who were seduced by John Foster Dulles, their chief legal adviser, into believing that they would be vindicated in court and thereby "convince the SEC that the death sentence was unworkable."[15]

Nearly three years were thus consumed by what Ben Cohen aptly called "protracted and relatively futile litigation" before the courts proved Dulles wrong and the largest companies succumbed to formal registration. Eight more years elapsed before the Supreme Court affirmed that such companies were engaged in interstate commerce and that Congress could regulate and reorganize their operations. Even then no formal decision was rendered on the meaning of section 11, although the commission's interpretation of that section had been accepted voluntarily by one company. By 1946 the thirteen largest systems had only reduced their corporate entities from 670 to 446. The total assets of the thirteen systems remained virtually unchanged. Commonwealth and Southern still controlled operating properties in ten states; American Power and Light, the major subsidiary of Electric Bond and Share, functioned in thirteen states; Middle West Corporation in fourteen; North American Company in twelve; Standard Gas and Electric in fifteen.[16]

Progress under section 11, however, did not accurately measure the commission's impact upon the industry or corporate financial practices. The SEC broke important new ground while regulating the partial reorganization and refinancing of many holding companies. Two cases, *Columbia Gas and Electric* and

15. James M. Landis, memorandum of conference with William Z. Ripley, Benjamin V. Cohen, and John J. Burns, January 5, 1939; Landis to Morris L. Cooke, January 6, 1937; John Foster Dulles to Ripley (undated), all JMLPLC, Box 9.

16. Benjamin V. Cohen to Wendell Willkie, September 8, 1937, FFPLC, Box 9; *Electric Bond and Share Co.* v. *SEC,* 303 U.S. 419 (1938); Ranald A. Finlayson, "The Public Utility Holding Company under Federal Regulation," *Journal of Business* (University of Chicago) 19 (July 1946): passim.

North American Company, dramatized the commission's pioneer efforts in areas traditionally reserved for managerial disposition. These episodes also illuminated the divisions within the SEC over the extent of proper intervention, and, for one commissioner at least, raised serious questions about the benefits of informal proceedings.

Both the commission and the registered holding companies recognized the necessity for recapitalization as a prelude to resumption of dividend payments and new financing. Burdened with excessive securities issues from the past, numerous companies labored under swollen capital structures and large arrearages on their preferred stock. These two factors delayed even voluntary efforts to rehabilitate the industry and to comply with section 11. Under the statute the SEC had responsibility for reporting on all reorganization plans. Proxies or consents could not be solicited unless accompanied or preceded by a copy of the commission's report on the plan. Section 7 gave the commission broad powers over any securities issued pursuant to reorganization plans. The commission could not, as Douglas noted, "produce perfect plans. There is no such thing as a perfect plan." Nonetheless, the SEC could strive not to duplicate what staff member Abe Fortas termed "the days when utility reorganizations were effected in a state of anarchy" because of maldistributed voting power, legal chicanery, and the leverage of management.[17]

17. William O. Douglas, "A Cooperative Program," June 3, 1938, JFP, Series 1, Box 23; Abe Fortas, memorandum to Jerome Frank and William O. Douglas, June 2, 1938, JFP, Series 1, Box 4. While recognizing the need for recapitalization and new financing, most holding company executives and investment bankers combined these perceptions with extravagant demands for amending the statute, delaying Section 11 proceedings, curtailing TVA's operations, and reducing PWA's power-related expenditures. They persisted in these attitudes before and after Electric Bond and Share lost the registration suit in March 1938. See Ben Grey to FDR, March 20, 1936; Basil Manly to FDR, June 8, 1936; Alexander Sachs, memorandum on conversation with Russell Leffingwell, George Whitney, and Thomas Lamont, July 24, 1936, all PPF 1983, FDRP; Wendell Willkie

In 1938, Columbia Gas and Electric sought to revalue property accounts by eliminating what its directors euphemistically termed "questionable items" arising from past valuations and intracompany profits. This was a commendable project that promised to make the company's balance sheet a more reliable indicator of financial health. In order to avoid charging these write-downs to earned surplus and thus further diluting dividend payments, the directors wished to create a special capital surplus account of $182 million by reducing the company's common stock from $15 to $1 a share. The write-downs would be charged against this account while releasing current earnings for payment of dividends on preferred, preference, and common stock. Mathews, who negotiated with the directors, accepted their plan without reservation. Frank, although recognizing "that . . . we must be practical and not create undue impediments to corporate activities," demanded safeguards to insure that future activities by the directors would benefit not only their own constituents, the common stockholders, but also the entire corporation. Mathews viewed these safeguards as "an unwarranted reaching out for control of managerial functions." Frank, however, swung a majority of the commission behind his proposals.[18]

The SEC approved Columbia's plan subject to three conditions. The proposed reduction of common capital would have to be approved by majority vote of each class of shareholders, including preferred, who were disenfranchised under the company's Delaware charter. No charge could be made to the special capital surplus account without thirty days prior notice

---

to Benjamin V. Cohen, October 19, 1937, FFPLC, Box 9; memorandum for Chairman Douglas on conversation with Mr. Fogarty (North American) and Mr. Groesbeck (Electric Bond and Share), December 22, 1937, OF 293, FDRP, Box 3; Willkie to FDR, January 1, 1938, OF 3030, FDRP; Frank to Edward S. Greenbaum, March 13, 1938, JFP, Series 1, Box 3.

18. *New York Times,* October 23, 1938; Jerome Frank to George C. Mathews, December 29, 1938, JFP, Series 1, Box 26; *Wall Street Journal,* January 29, 1939.

to the SEC. After a hearing, the commission could still disapprove all charges. In addition, the SEC retained jurisdiction to prevent dividend payments on common stock, unless after the payment of existing dividend requirements on preferred and preference stock, Columbia Gas and Electric retained earned surplus sufficient to pay an additional six quarterly dividends on the preferred and preference shares.[19]

Although the commission did not retreat from Frank's position, it did veto stronger regulations which he, at least, felt necessary to safeguard the refinancing and reorganization of holding companies. North American raised these questions in 1938–39 when it sought commission approval for a $105-million program of limited corporate simplification and refinancing. North American hoped to eliminate one intermediate holding company, North American Edison, by acquiring all of its assets through the sale of new debentures and preferred stock. During negotiations, Douglas suggested three conditions, which North American accepted. The preferred stock would carry voting rights, elect a minority of the board of directors, and, in the event of a stated number of dividend defaults, elect a majority of the board. As long as the preferred stock remained outstanding, no common stock dividends could be paid unless North American's earned surplus equaled at least 15 percent of the par value of the preferred.[20]

Frank, assuming that Douglas's negotiations were, like Mathews's preliminary to more formal discussions, proposed additional restrictions upon North American's management and common shareholders. Consent by a majority of the preferred should be required before the company could increase its debt. Preferred shareholders should have an affirmative voice in the payment of all dividends on common stock and a guar-

19. Securities and Exchange Commission, *Holding Company Act Release No. 1417;* Securities and Exchange Commission, *Fifth Annual Report* (Washington, 1939), pp. 67–68.

20. Jerome Frank to William O. Douglas, January 6, 1939, JFP, Series 1, Box 3; *Wall Street Journal,* January 31, 1939; *New York Times,* January 31, 1939.

antee that all unpaid and accumulated preferred dividends would be paid on the preferred before the common. "The fundamental question," Frank said, "is whether there can be any preferred stock that is really fair. . . . The common gets a big play, because, in a considerable measure, it is using other people's (i.e., the preferred stockholders') money. . . . Unless preferred stock can be made peculiarly safe, there should not be anything but common stock."[21]

To Frank's amazement, Douglas insisted that the commission could not make additional demands upon North American. The informal discussions had become final. Douglas emphasized the need for quick action. North American's stockholders were anxious to ratify the plan; the market was propitious for selling the new securities; it was the largest utility issue in recent memory; and war threatened in Europe. In rebuttal, Frank pointed out that the proxies had not been sent out and that the SEC had spent only two hours in "hasty and sketchy" discussion of the plan "with no opportunity for study by the commission or by the members of the staff." Douglas and the other commissioners remained adamant. They even convinced Frank to delay his formal dissent until after North American's financial operations were successfully completed. "Unless some method can be worked out by which informal discussions will not create estoppels," Frank concluded, "I, for one, will feel strongly inclined to adopt the policy of never joining in any informal comments." Despite Frank's chagrin in this case, the SEC, generally, had succeeded in introducing a modicum of equity into dark areas of corporate reorganization and refinancing usually reserved for the fang and the claw.[22]

The commission continued to urge cooperation on section 11. "Many leaders of the [power] industry," Douglas told

21. Jerome Frank to William O. Douglas, January 12, 1939, JFP, Series 1, Box 3; Frank to Beardsley Ruml, February 8, 1939; Frank to Paul Gourrich, March 15, 1939, JFP, Series 1, Box 5.

22. Frank to Ruml, February 8, 1939; Frank to Gourrich, March 15, 1939, JFP, Series 1, Box 5; Securities and Exchange Commission, *Holding Company Act Release No. 1425, 1430.*

the American Bar Association after the Supreme Court had upheld the registration requirements, "are bent not on nullification or repeal but on compliance. To all these I pledge our wholehearted cooperation. We offer them an open door to our round table. We can meet success in this sector as we have in others." Round table techniques, involving section 11, failed dismally when applied to the largest, most important holding company systems. Even before the initial court decision, many reasonably compact systems had complied with section 11, usually through the acquisition of their subsidiaries' assets. After the *Electric Bond and Share* decision, the more sagacious companies abandoned the game. J. P. Morgan's United Corporation, reducing its holdings in all utilities to less than a 10 percent equity interest, became a respectable investment company. The more diversified companies, bound by huge investments and management ties, waited upon the commission and prepared for future litigation, even though the benefits of voluntary action had been revealed as early as December 1937, when the SEC blessed, with minor modification, a section 11 plan submitted by American Water Works and Electric Company. This substantial holding company was permitted to retain all of its utility properties, gas and electric, in four contiguous states, although the commission required the dissolution or merger of several intermediate holding companies in the system. Furthermore, American Water Works' coal and water properties and retail appliance businesses were found "reasonably incidental and economically appropriate" to the operation of an integrated system.[23]

Voluntarism did not appeal to other companies. During the summer of 1938, Douglas proposed and major portions of the industry accepted the formation of an integration committee,

23. William O. Douglas, address before the Section of Public Utility Law, American Bar Association, July 26, 1938, JFP, Series 1, Box 26; Securities and Exchange Commission, *Third Annual Report* (Washington, 1937), pp. 37–40; James Guthrie, memorandum to Douglas, February 14, 1938, JFP, Series 1, Box 3; *New York Times,* July 2, November 16, 1938; Securities and Exchange Commission, *Fourth Annual Report* (Washington, 1938), pp. 10–11.

but "weeks of effort with that committee," Frank said, "proved fruitless." Douglas tried another approach. He invited each company to file separate, confidential integration proposals. By the summer of 1939 the commission concluded that "none of them [the separate plans] met the requirements of section 11." In February and March 1940, after six months of hearings, the commission issued formal orders to nine major companies stating that they were not confined to a single integrated system and ordered that additional hearings be held to determine what action should be taken by the companies in order to meet the demands of section 11. Responding to the companies' request for a tentative statement of its own conclusions, the commission issued additional findings, opinions, and orders between January and August 1941. Here, the SEC set down important interpretations of section 11. "Many holding companies still want to employ dilatory tactics," Frank had told Roosevelt. "They are trying to make it appear, erroneously, that national defense needs will be impaired by integration." Some companies became even more dilatory after the commission's interpretation of section 11. Engineers Public Service Company maintained that section 11 did not preclude the retention of one integrated system in Virginia and adjoining states and one integrated system in Texas and adjoining states. The SEC read the section differently: additional systems were retainable only if located in the state or states of the principal system or in adjoining states. In addition, the commission informed United Gas Improvement Company that a single, integrated system could not include both electric and gas properties. These judgments were cold comfort to Electric Bond and Share, Commonwealth and Southern, North American, and four other major companies.[24]

24. Jerome Frank to Thomas Swift, August 27, and September 28, 1940, JFP, Series 1, Box 13; Frank to FDR, November 20, 1939, JFP, Series 1, Box 12; Securities and Exchange Commission, *Holding Company Act* Release No. 2897; Robert Blum, "SEC Integration of Holding Company Systems," *Journal of Land and Public Utility Economics* 17 (November 1941): 423–39.

World War II did not deter the commission, despite the plea of Samuel W. Murphy, president of Electric Bond and Share, for a moratorium on section 11. Without further litigation, United Gas Improvement accepted the SEC's tentative opinions and filed a voluntary integration plan that included divestment of all additional systems outside of southeastern Pennsylvania and portions of northern Delaware and Maryland. "The long resistance," Ganson Purcell rejoiced, "seems to be crumbling. The early verdict on section 11 must have delighted President Roosevelt as much as it dismayed retired Congressman George Huddleston. No one, however, was more pleased than the SEC's new chairman, Edward C. Eicher of Iowa, who thought he had lost a congressional battle in 1935 but who won the administrative war six years later.[25]

The SEC's early administrative experience with the Public Utility Holding Company Act demonstrated that it was far easier to help in the creation of new private economic organizations than to tear down old ones. Many members of the financial community could see immediate, concrete benefits in the development of a National Securities Dealers Association or in reorganization of the New York Stock Exchange. They actively assisted the SEC in these endeavors because they would continue to share substantial decision-making power with the commission. Cooperation of this nature was at best sporadic under the 1935 act. The SEC labored without encouragement from the financial community and implemented the statute only through the application of grinding legal pressure. It was some time before the leaders of the utility world recognized that positive economic benefits followed geographical integration.

25. Jerome Frank to FDR, February 4, 1941, JFP, Series 1, Box 10; Blum, "SEC Integration of Holding Company Systems," pp. 430–39; Securities and Exchange Commission, *Seventh Annual Report* (Washington, 1941), pp. 77–81; Ganson Purcell to FDR, December 31, 1942, PPF 1820, FDRP.

9

Securities Regulation and the New Deal

At the end of Franklin Roosevelt's second term, federal efforts to regulate corporate finance had gained wide, and occasionally enthusiastic, support from pivotal sections of the business community. "While investment bankers have been reluctant to welcome the great measure of control which your commission has over our business," one banker told James Landis, "I think that many of us are aware of the necessity of supervision and perhaps our greatest fear has been the possibility of supervision by a body in which we have not got confidence." Numerous considerations nurtured this support. Above all, legislation and administration had eschewed radicalism. In addition, legislation and administration conferred benefits upon regulated groups by proving to be compatible with many of their own aspirations, including revived business activity. "The SEC," IBA president Jean Witter said, "is evidencing the desire to cooperate with our business. Every member of this Association has, in turn, an obligation to reciprocate this attitude and help the Commission in performing its function. We must do our part. This cooperation from all interests provides a great opportunity to work out procedures that will help to reopen the capital markets."[1]

With the exception of the Public Utility Holding Company Act, regulation had not forced drastic organizational changes upon corporations or redesigned the basic machinery by which

1. Joseph R. Swan to James M. Landis, October 28, 1935, JMLPLC, Box 13; Jean Witter, as quoted in *Investment Banking* 9 (April 1939): 6.

securities were underwritten, distributed, and traded. Proposals that looked in these directions, including fresh accounting methods, segregation of broker and dealer functions, or novel margin requirements, floundered before congressional hostility, entrenched business habits, the reluctance of administrators to disturb existing economic relationships during a period of depression, and genuine uncertainty about the long-range social and economic benefits of the innovations.

Frankfurter's opinion, expressed in 1933, that investment bankers had nothing to fear from the Securities Act, seemed acceptable to many members of the profession by 1940. The reduction of civil liabilities through formal amendment and the modification of accounting requirements were major factors in winning acceptance for the statute, but so, too, was a growing recognition that the law, effectively enforced, assisted financial operations by policing marginal elements within the industry and by promoting minimum standards of disclosure. During 1934–35, SEC stop orders discouraged private issues, the majority of them fraudulent, aggregating over $20 million. The figure reached $155 million in 1938–39. "Responsible members of the [investment banking] profession," T. H. Sanders concluded, "have less fear that competitors will take business away from them by using less exacting standards . . . calculated to make the preparation of the issue cheaper for the issuer, and . . . presented to the public in a more favorable light than they really deserve. . . . Many members of the . . . profession would be greatly disturbed if adverse court decisions should tend to destroy the salutary influences of the Commission." Minimum standards of disclosure and continuous protection against dubious promotions were important benefits, even though the 1933 statute did not, as many investment bankers desired, simplify the mechanics of national distribution. SEC registration requirements were accepted reluctantly, if at all, by state commissions.[2]

2. Securities and Exchange Commission, *First Annual Report* (Washington, 1935), pp. 67–70; *Fifth Annual Report* (Washington,

A high degree of self-regulation reduced opposition from stock exchanges and over-the-counter dealers to the Securities Exchange Act. In addition, the scope of the SEC's responsibilities under both statutes imposed a coherence upon financial activities that decades of private organization had been unable or unwilling to provide. Before the New Deal many investment bankers outside of New York City had looked upon the New York Stock Exchange as inscrutable and somewhat irrelevant to their own endeavors. Few held such primitive ideas in 1940. The Securities and Exchange Commission drew together and made more intelligible the hitherto chaotic activities of underwriting, distribution, and trading. After 1939, for the first time, representatives of the IBA, the National Securities Dealers Association, and the stock exchanges were conferring through permanent, institutionalized committees sponsored by the commission. The SEC helped to professionalize many corporate functions. "In one month," an accountant noted with astonishment, "the SEC has set . . . standards . . . for the profession, which years of futile committee work within the professional societies have not been able to produce or even begin to produce."[3]

Frankfurter, following passage of the Public Utility Holding Company Act, had told Roosevelt: "If you don't look out, you will ruin these fellows into prosperity." At about the same time, Cohen remarked upon "how calm brokerage opinion has become regarding the effects of the Holding Company Act." He attributed this response to the knowledge that the market value of holding company stocks depended primarily upon the earning power of operating subsidiaries. Should a holding company be compelled to divest some of its subsidiaries, the common stock would be distributed among the holders of the

---

1939), pp. 191–93; T. H. Sanders, "Accounting Aspects of the Securities Act," *Law and Contemporary Problem* 4 (April 1937): 193–94.

3. "Accounting Exchange," *Accounting Review* 10 (March 1935); 100–02.

parent company's securities. By 1938, *Fortune* magazine could predict, somewhat heretically, that holding companies would "come out of the operating room with safer, sounder, more durable capital structures than they went in with." Investors shared this assessment. The commission's standards for geographical integration and corporate simplification did not produce bankruptcy or financial morbidity. A reduction of net assets usually meant divestment of scattered, undigested properties which, while dynastically impressive, had become an economic burden upon the entire system. United Gas Improvement, International Hydro-Electric, and Electric Power and Light, three companies that initially felt the impact of section 11, saw their outstanding securities make remarkable and lasting market gains.[4]

Finally, members of the business community came to realize that a regulatory commission and its members, while dedicated to financial probity, were not on that account opposed to business institutions or the profit motive. Indeed, commissioners and staff members looked upon the SEC as an extension of business enterprise. "The work is fascinating, and the commission a most interesting and capable one," Chief Counsel John J. Burns told Frankfurter. "There is in this job a grand opportunity to grow in practical knowledge of the most important phase of our industrial civilization." Burns left the commission in 1938 after helping the government win its initial suit under the Public Utility Holding Company Act. He became chief counsel for J. P. Morgan's reorganized United Corporation. Burns was not opposed to the New Deal, nor was he a captive of Wall Street or a traitor to the commission. His attitude and actions were entirely consistent with the SEC's philosophy, as expressed by Frank: "whenever a man trained at the commission goes into private practice, either at the Bar or

4. Felix Frankfurter to FDR, March 13, 1936, FFPH, Roll 3; Benjamin V. Cohen to James M. Landis, September 12, 1936, JMLPLC, Box 9; "Washington and Power," *Fortune* 17 (February 1938): 45–46; Ganson Purcell to FDR, January 15, 1943, PPF 1820, FDRP.

in corporate finance, the problem of mutual understanding between business and the commission is to a great extent simplified. Such a man can acquaint his . . . client with procedures and practices of the Commission usually much better than a person who has not had the benefit of that experience."[5]

Federal securities regulation did not, as many of its supporters assumed, transform a nation of speculators into a nation of cautious, sober investors. Between 1934 and 1940, the Securities and Exchange Commission, utilizing full disclosure, investigations, stop orders, stock exchange surveillance, and participation in utility reorganization, only reduced opportunities for corporate theft and restricted the methods by which individuals, while inflicting pecuniary damage upon one another, could derange the entire economy. Franklin Roosevelt and his New Dealers did not find the magic key to recovery. They did, however, fashion political tools like the SEC that held the possibility of more orderly, enduring economic growth in the future. This was their lasting achievement.

5. John J. Burns to Felix Frankfurter, August 8, 1934, FFPH, Roll 10; Jerome Frank to Alfred Benjamin, April 19, 1941, JFP, Series 1, Box 2.

Bibliography

Manuscript collections contributed significantly to the preparation of this study. The Franklin D. Roosevelt papers, including the President's official files (OF) and personal files (PPF) contain indispensable correspondence and memoranda to and from FDR on both the legislative and administrative aspects of securities regulation. Correspondence from business and financial leaders is particularly important because it reveals their diverse opinions and often conflicting strategies. The Roosevelt collection is uneven. Because of the President's intense personal interest, both the OF and PPF files contain abundant material on electric utilities, holding companies, and their regulation. Material relating to the 1933 and 1934 legislation is less extensive. Chapter 3 profited immeasurably from the voluminous material on foreign debts and international finance in the diaries of Henry Morgenthau. The papers of Morris L. Cooke, maintained with the Roosevelt collection, provided valuable background on the problems of utility regulation.

The papers of Felix Frankfurter, hitherto unused by historians, contributed greatly to my understanding of the administration's policies and the legislative progress of those policies. Much of Frankfurter's impact upon the New Deal came during informal conversations with FDR, administration leaders, and congressmen. Informality has reduced the density of material in some areas. Frankfurter's papers contain a precise account of the legislative struggle over the Securities Act. Teaching regularly at Harvard, he maintained written contact with the daily situation through letters and telegrams from Landis, Cohen, and Corcoran. Frankfurter's active participation in New Deal affairs declined during his short visit to England in 1933–34 and a written record of his important role in the final Holding Company Act compromise is limited by the fact that he was a frequent guest at the White House during the summer of 1935. The collection contains excellent material on Frankfurter's earlier contributions to Roosevelt's public utility program in New York State.

James M. Landis kept an extensive record of the legislative history of the Securities Exchange Act, including drafts of the different bills, correspondence, and memoranda. Benjamin Cohen's files in the records of the National Power Policy Committee contain comparable material on the Public Utility Holding Company Act. Mr. Cohen kindly consented to an interview, which enhanced my perception of the economic and political problems confronting the draftsmen on the major bills.

With the exception of the Carter Glass and Hiram Johnson collections, I found very few congressional manuscripts of striking importance. The records of individual House and Senate committees, while occasionally of great physical size, did not contain new revelations. On the 1934 Exchange legislation, however, Glass's papers provided new insight into the senator's strategy and the role of the Federal Reserve Board. Senator Johnson's diary, in the form of weekly letters to his son, contributed to my understanding of the controversy surrounding Title II of the Securities Act.

The papers of Jerome Frank contain a fascinating record of many issues confronting the Securities and Exchange Commission during the years 1938–40. The collection contains valuable material on the administrative attitudes of William O. Douglas and Frank in addition to extensive correspondence dealing with the Holding Company Act and the reorganization of the New York Stock Exchange.

Public documents made an important contribution to this study. Congressional hearings, the *Congressional Record,* and reports by administrative agencies, when used with caution, are indispensable for examining public and private attitudes on regulatory issues. I found the hearings frequently verbose but also amazingly candid on vital legislative matters. The correspondence which often supplements the formal hearings displayed the diversity and rivalry within the American financial community. Two reports, above all, assisted my awareness of complex regulatory issues: the Senate Banking and Currency Committee's investigation of stock exchange practices and the Federal Trade Commission's inquiry into the utility industry. Both reports include excellent summary volumes.

Professional journals, general periodicals, and newspapers helped not only to supplement unpublished materials on legislative and administrative issues, but provided important data on the activities of specific interest groups. The annual proceedings and monthly *Bulletin* of the Investment Bankers Association enabled me to follow the association's regulatory strategy between 1912 and 1941. The *Journal of Accountancy* and the *Accounting Review* provided comparable material on the accounting profession. The esoteric quality of many law journals has led those untrained in the law to ignore their importance as a guide to legislative and administrative history. This is unfortunate because American political debate, at least in the modern period, has often revolved around complex questions of corporate law. Legal journals enriched my general knowledge of business and governmental relations and increased my perception of many technical issues involved in securities legislation. Finally, all historians of recent America owe a substantial debt to the national political and financial reporters of the *New York Times* and the *Wall Street Journal*.

I derived limited benefit or inspiration from existing secondary literature. Although comprehensive from the lawyer's point of view, Louis Loss's *Securities Regulation* (Boston: Little, Brown, 1951) remains a technician's manual. It lacks historical and political depth. Contemporary accounts, including Ferdinand Pecora's *Wall Street under Oath* (New York: Simon and Schuster, 1939) and William O. Douglas's *Democracy and Finance* (New Haven: Yale University Press, 1940), although fascinating chronicles of entrepreneurial misdeeds, seldom rise above the polemical level. Alfred L. Burnheim and Margaret G. Schneider, eds., *The Security Market* (New York: Twentieth Century Fund, 1935) is a restrained and dull inventory of regulatory needs. A recent volume by Ralph F. De Bedts, *The New Deal's SEC: The Formative Years* (New York: Columbia University Press, 1964) suffers from three defects. De Bedts used few manuscript sources, failed to discuss crucial administrative issues, and ignored entirely the pervasive influence of private interest groups upon regulatory policies.

Manuscripts and Unpublished Records

Capital Issues Committee. Record Group 158, Federal Records Center, Suitland, Maryland.

Department of Commerce (Secretary's File). Record Group 40, National Archives.

Morris L. Cooke Papers. Franklin D. Roosevelt Library, Hyde Park, New York.

Jerome Frank Papers. Yale University.

Felix Frankfurter Papers (microfilm). Harvard Law School Library.

Felix Frankfurter Papers. Library of Congress.

Carter Glass Paper. University of Virginia.

Leon Henderson Papers. Franklin D. Roosevelt Library, Hyde Park, New York.

House of Representatives. Committee on Interstate and Foreign Commerce. 73 Congress 1 Session, through 74 Congress 1 Session. Record Group 233. National Archives.

Hiram Johnson Papers. University of California (Berkeley).

James M. Landis Papers. Harvard Law School Library and Library of Congress.

Henry Morgenthau Papers. Franklin D. Roosevelt Library, Hyde Park, New York.

National Power Policy Committee Records (Cohen File). National Archives.

James H. Rogers Papers. Yale University.

Franklin D. Roosevelt Papers. Franklin D. Roosevelt Library, Hyde Park, New York.

Senate. Committee on Banking and Currency. 73 Congress 1 Session, through 75 Congress 3 Session. Record Group 46. National Archives.

———. Committee on Interstate Commerce. 74 Congress 1 Session. Record Group 46. National Archives.

Henry L. Stimson Papers. Yale University.

Huston Thompson Papers. Library of Congress.

Treasury Department (Secretary's File). Record Group 56. National Archives.

Louis B. Whele Papers. Franklin D. Roosevelt Library, Hyde Park, New York.

Public Documents

Biographical Directory of the American Congress, 1774–1961. U.S. Government Printing Office, 1961.

U.S. *Congressional Directory.* 73d Cong., 1st sess. U.S. Government Printing Office, 1933.

———. 74th Cong., 1st sess. U.S. Government Printing Office, 1934.

————. 75th Cong., 1st sess. U.S. Government Printing Office, 1936.

U.S. *Congressional Record*. 63d Cong. 2d sess. U.S. Government Printing Office, 1914.

————. 65th Cong., 2d sess. U.S. Government Printing Office, 1918.

————. 66th Cong., 1st sess. U.S. Government Printing Office, 1921.

————. 67th Cong., 1st sess. U.S. Government Printing Office, 1922.

————. 72d Cong., 2d sess. U.S. Government Printing Office, 1932.

————. 73d Cong., 1st sess. U.S. Government Printing Office, 1933.

————. 73d Cong., 2d sess. U.S. Government Printing Office, 1934.

————. 74th Cong., 1st sess. U.S. Government Printing Office, 1935.

————. 74th Cong., 2d sess. U.S. Government Printing Office, 1936.

————. 75th Cong., 3d sess. U.S. Government Printing Office, 1938.

U.S. Federal Power Commission. *Annual Report*. U.S. Government Printing Office, 1921–40.

U.S. Federal Trade Commission. *Annual Report*. U.S. Government Printing Office, 1934–35.

————. *Utility Corporations*. Summary Report of the Federal Trade Commission. Senate Document no. 92. 70th Cong., 1st sess. U.S. Government Printing Office, 1935.

U.S. House of Representatives. *Report of the Capital Issues Committee*. 6th Cong., 3d sess. Document no. 1485. U.S. Government Printing Office, 1918.

————. *Final Report of the Capital Issues Committee*. 65th Cong., 3d sess. Document no. 1836. U.S. Government Printing Office, 1919.

————. Judiciary Committee. 66th Cong., 1st sess. *Federal Blue Sky Law*. U.S. Government Printing Office, 1921.

————. Committee on Interstate and Foreign Commerce. 67th Cong., 1st sess. *Blue Sky Bill*. U.S. Government Printing Office, 1921.

————. Committee on Interstate and Foreign Commerce. 67th

Cong., 2d sess. *Blue Sky Bill*. U.S. Government Printing Office, 1922.

———. Committee on Interstate and Foreign Commerce. 73d Cong., 1st sess. *Federal Securities Act. House Report* no. 85 and no. 152. U.S. Government Printing Office, 1933.

———. Committee on Interstate and Foreign Commerce. 73d Cong., 2d sess. *Stock Exchange Regulation. House Report* no. 1383 and no. 1838. U.S. Government Printing Office, 1934.

———. *Report of the National Power Policy Committee*. 74th Cong., 1st sess. Document no. 137. U.S. Government Printing Office, 1935.

———. Committee on Interstate and Foreign Commerce. 74th Cong., 1st sess. *Public Utility Holding Companies. House Report* no. 1318 and no. 1903. U.S. Government Printing Office, 1935.

———. Committee on Interstate and Foreign Commerce. 74th Cong., 2d sess. *Unlisted Securities. House Report* no. 2601. U.S. Government Printing Office, 1936.

———. Committee on Interstate and Foreign Commerce. 75th Cong., 3d sess. *Regulation of Over-the-Counter Markets. House Report* no. 2307. U.S. Government Printing Office, 1938.

U.S. Securities and Exchange Commission. *Accounting Series Releases*. U.S. Government Printing Office, 1935–40.

———. *Annual Report*. U.S. Government Printing Office, 1935–45.

———. *Decisions and Reports*. U.S. Government Printing Office, 1938–45.

———. *Holding Company Act Releases*. U.S. Government Printing Office, 1935–45.

———. *In the Matter of Richard Whitney et al.* 3 vols. U.S. Government Printing Office, 1938.

———. *Proceedings before the Securities and Exchange Commission in the Matter of the Institute of International Finance.* U.S. Government Printing Office, 1935.

———. *Proceedings before the Securities and Exchange Commission in the Matter of the Readjustment of the External Obligations of the Republic of Peru.* U.S. Government Printing Office, 1935.

———. *Proceedings before the Securities and Exchange Commis-*

sion in the Matter of Foreign Bondholders Protective Council. U.S. Government Printing Office, 1935.

———. *Report on the Feasibility and Advisability of the Complete Segregation of the Functions of Brokers and Dealers.* U.S. Government Printing Office, 1936.

———. *Report on the Government of Securities Exchanges.* 74 Congress 1 Session. House Document no. 85. U.S. Government Printing Office, 1935.

———. *Report on the Study and Investigation . . . of Protective and Reorganization Committees.* U.S. Government Printing Office, 1937.

———. *Report on the Study of Investment Trusts and Investment Companies.* U.S. Government Printing Office, 1938.

———. *Securities Act Releases.* U.S. Government Printing Office, 1934–40.

———. *Securities Exchange Act Releases.* U.S. Government Printing Office, 1934–41.

———. *Trading in Unlisted Securities.* U.S. Government Printing Office, 1936.

U.S. Senate. Committee on Banking and Currency. 63d Cong., 2d sess. *Regulation of the Stock Exchange.* U.S. Government Printing Office, 1914.

———. Committee on Banking and Currency. 73d Cong., 1st sess. *Securities Act. Senate Report* no. 47. U.S. Government Printing Office, 1933.

———. Committee on Banking and Currency. 73d Cong. 2d sess. *Stock Exchange Regulation. Senate Report* no. 792. U.S. Government Printing Office, 1934.

———. Committee on Banking and Currency. 74th Cong., 2d sess. *Trading in Unlisted Securities upon Exchanges. Senate Report* no. 1739. U.S. Government Printing Office, 1936.

———. Committee on Banking and Currency. 75th Cong., 3d sess. *Regulation of Over-the-Counter Markets. Senate Report* no. 1455. U.S. Government Printing Office, 1938.

———. Committee on Finance. 72d Cong., 1st sess. *Sale of Foreign Bonds or Securities in the United States. Senate Report* no. 41. 73d Cong., 1st sess. U.S. Government Printing Office, 1933.

———. Committee on Interstate Commerce. 74th Cong., 1st sess. *Public Utility Holding Company Act. Senate Report* no. 621. U.S. Government Printing Office, 1935.

Published Letters, Memoirs, and Other Documentary Sources

American Bar Association. *Reports*. Chicago, 1912–40.
Foreign Bondholders Protective Council. *Annual Report*. Washington, D.C., 1935–43.
Freedman, Max, ed. *Roosevelt and Frankfurter: Their Correspondence, 1928–1945*. Boston: Little, Brown, 1967.
Investment Bankers Association. *Proceedings of Annual Convention*. New York, 1912–42.
Lilienthal, David E. *Journals: The TVA Years*. New York: Harper and Row, 1964.
National Association of Railroad and Utility Commissioners. *Proceedings of Annual Convention*. Chicago, 1925–40.
National Association of Securities Commissioners, *Proceedings of Annual Convention*. New York, 1920–40.
National Conference of Commissioners on Uniform State Laws. *Handbook and Proceedings*. New York, 1920–33.
New York State Bar Association. *Bulletin*. New York, 1929–34.
New York Stock Exchange. *Report of the President*. New York, 1920–40.
———. *Yearbook*. New York, 1920–40.
North Carolina Bar Association. *Reports*. Raleigh, 1926–30.
Ohio Law Reporter. Columbus, 1915–25.
Roosevelt, Elliott, ed. *F. D. R.: His Personal Letters*. 3 vols. New York: Duell, Sloan and Pearce, 1950.
Roosevelt, Franklin D. *The Public Papers and Addresses of Franklin D. Roosevelt, 1928–1936*. 5 vols. New York: Random House, 1938.

Newspapers Cited

Atlanta Constitution.
New York Herald-Tribune.
New York Times.
Wall Street Journal.
Washington Post.

Business, Professional, and Popular Journals

Accounting Review, 1925–40.
Business Week, 1933–40.
Certified Public Accountant, 1933–35.

Commercial and Financial Chronicle, 1933–40.
Financial Age, 1933–35.
Harper's Weekly, 1911–13.
Investment Bankers Association, *Bulletin*, 1920–41.
Investment Banking, 1933–41.
Journal of Accountancy, 1925–41.
Law Notes, 1920–23.
Public Utilities Fortnightly, 1925–45.

Court Cases Cited

Public Utilities Commission v. *Attleboro Steam and Electric Co.*, 273 U.S. 83.
Caldwell v. *Sioux Falls Stock Co.*, 61 U.S. (L. ed.) 495.
William R. Compton Co. v. *Allen*, 216 Fed. 547.
Electric Bond and Share Co. v. *SEC*, 303 U.S. 419.
Hall v. *Geiger-Jones Co.*, 61 U.S. (L. ed.) 480.
Merrick v. *Halsey*, 61 U.S. (L. ed.) 498.

Articles

Ashby, Forrest B. "The Influence of Securities Regulation upon Standards of Corporation Financing." *Michigan Law Review* 26 (1928): 876–84.
Ayres, Arthur V. "Governmental Regulation of Securities Issues." *Political Science Quarterly* 28 (December 1913): 586–92.
Barnett, George E. "The Securities Act of 1933 and the British Companies Act." *Harvard Business Review* 13 (October 1934): 1–14.
Berle, Adolph A., and Frederick S. Fisher, Jr. "Elements of the Law of Business Accounting." *Columbia Law Review* 32 (April 1932): 573–622.
Blum, Robert. "SEC Integration of Holding Company Systems." *Journal of Land and Public Utility Economics* 17 (November 1941): 423–39.
Brach, Gilbert E. "The Blue Sky Law." *Marquette Law Review* 3 (1918–19): 140–48.
Breed, William C. "Public Regulation in the Origination and Distribution of Securities." *Investment Banking* 3 (February 21, 1933): 186–96.
Brown, Carey E. "Fiscal Policy in the 'Thirties: A Reappraisal." *American Economic Review* (1956): 857–79.

Brown, Montreville J. "The Minnesota 'Blue Sky' Law." *Minnesota Law Review 3* (February 1919): 156–62.

Buchanan, Norman. "The Origins and Development of the Public Utility Holding Company." *Journal of Political Economy* 44 (1936): 31–53.

Danielian, N. R. "Gas, A Study in Expansion: The Case of Associated Gas." *Atlantic Monthly,* July 1933, pp. 481–97.

Dawson, Mitchell. "Blue Sky Blues." *American Mercury* 25 (March 1932): 353–61.

Douglas, William O., and George E. Bates. "The Federal Securities Act of 1933." *Yale Law Journal* 43 (December 1933): 190–201.

Eicher, Edward C. "Consumers and the Public Utility Holding Company Act." *Journal of Business* (University of Iowa) 21 (March 1941): 11–23.

Fernald, Henry B. "Accountants' Certificates." *Journal of Accountancy* 47 (January 1929): 18–19.

Finlayson, Ranald A. "The Public Utility Holding Company under Federal Regulation." *Journal of Business* (University of Chicago) 19 (July 1946): 1–19.

Flexner, Bernard. "The Fight on the Securities Act." *Atlantic* 153 (February 1934): 232–37.

Fournier, Leslie T. "Simplification of Holding Companies under the Public Utility Act of 1935." *Journal of Land and Public Utility Economics* 13 (1937): 138–52.

Frankfurter, Felix. "The Early Writings of O. W. Holmes, Jr." *Harvard Law Review* 44 (November 1931): 710–21.

———. "Mr. Hoover on Power Control." *New Republic,* October 17, 1928, pp. 241–42.

———. "Mr. Justice Brandeis and the Constitution." *Harvard Law Review* 45 (November 1931): 44–64.

———. "The Task of Administrative Law." *University of Pennsylvania Law Review* 75 (May 1927): 614–21.

———. "The Young Men Go to Washington." *Fortune* 13 (January 1936): 61–63, 109–11.

"Geographical Integration under the Public Utility Holding Company Act." *Yale Law Journal* 50 (1940): 1045–55.

Harbeson, Robert W. "Railroads and Regulation, 1877–1916: Conspiracy or Public Interest?" *Journal of Economic History* 27 (1967): 230–42.

Hatfield, Henry R. "What Is the Matter with Accounting?" *Journal of Accountancy* 44 (October 1927): 271–76.

Hawley, Ellis W. "Hoover and the Bituminous Coal Problem." *Business History Review* 42 (Autumn 1968): 247–70.

Healy, Robert E. "Advantages of Self-Regulation." *Investment Banking* 9 (April 1939): 19–23.

"High Finance in the 'Twenties: The United Corporation." *Columbia Law Review* 37 (May 1937): 785–816, (June 1937): 936–80.

Jennings, Richard W. "Mr. Justice Douglas: His Influence on Corporate and Securities Regulation." *Yale Law Journal* 63 (May 1964): 934–49.

Karl, Barry D. "Presidential Planning and Social Science Research: Mr. Hoover's Experts." *Perpectives in American History* 3 (1969): 347–409.

Kennedy, Joseph P. "Securities and Exchange Commission." *Certified Public Accountant* 14 (August 1934): 453–54, (December 1934): 722–23.

Klapbrunn, Hans. "Regulation of Interstate Security Sales." *University of Chicago Law Review* 1 (May 1933): 86–92.

Kohn, Harry F. "The Blue Sky Law." *Technical World* 17 (March 1912): 36–45.

Landis, James M. "Business Policy and the Courts." *Yale Review* 27 (December 1937): 1–23.

———. "Crucial Issues in Administrative Law." *Harvard Law Review* 57 (May 1940): 1077–1102.

———. "The Legislative History of Securities Act of 1933." *George Washington Law Review* 28 (October 1959): 29–49.

———. "The Place of Administrative Law." *Connecticut Bar Journal* 13 (April 1939): 71–81.

———. "Shifting Postulates in Modern Legal Development." *Proceedings and Reports of the Associated Harvard Clubs* (April 14–16, 1939): 76–81.

———. "Symposium on Administrative Law." *American Law School Review* 9 (April 1939): 181–84.

"The Legend of Landis." *Fortune* 10 (August 1934): 28–31, 109–11.

Mathews, George C. "Your Interest—Our Needs." *Investment Banking* 8 (November 20, 1937): 34–35.

May, George O. "Uniformity in Accounting." *Harvard Business Review* 17 (Autumn 1938): 1–8.

Means, Gardiner C. "The Diffusion of Stock Ownership in the United States." *Quarterly Journal of Economics* 44 (August 1930): 561–600.

Meeker, Edward J. "Preventive vs. Punitive Securities Laws." *Columbia Law Review* 26 (March 1926): 318–28.

McCall, Ambrose V. "Comments on the Martin Act." *Brooklyn Law Review* 3 (April 1934): 197–203.

Reed, Robert R. "Blue Sky Laws." *Annals of the American Academy of Political and Social Science* 88 (March 1920): 176–83.

Ripley, William Z. "Public Regulation of Railroad Issues." *American Economic Review* 4 (September 1914): 541–64.

Rodell, Fred. "Douglas over the Stock Exchange." *Fortune* 17 (February 1938): 118–19, 120–26.

Roose, Kenneth D. "The Recession of 1937–1938." *Journal of Political Economy* 56 (June 1948): 239–48.

Sanders, T. H. "Accounting Aspects of the Securities Act." *Law and Contemporary Problems* 4 (April 1937): 190–99.

"SEC." *Fortune* 21 (June 1940): 31–33, 125–31.

Sharfman, Leo. "Commission Regulation of Public Utilities." *Annals of the American Academy of Social and Political Science* 53 (May 1914): 1–18.

Shaw, William B. "Progressive Law-Making in Many States." *Review of Reviews* 48 (July 1913): 85–90.

Simpson, Lawrence P. "The New York Blue Sky Law and the Uniform Act." *New York University Law Quarterly* 8 (March 1931): 465–74.

Smith, Frank P. "Accounting Requirements of Stock Exchanges, 1933." *Accounting Review* 12 (June 1937): 145–53.

———. "The Future of Small Securities Exchanges." *Harvard Business Review* 14 (Spring 1936): 360–70.

Steig, Olga M. "What Can the Regulatory Securities Act Accomplish?" *Michigan Law Review* 31 (April 1933): 780–89.

Stoddard, William L. "Blue Sky Situation." *Outlook,* January 27, 1926, pp. 147–50.

Thompson, Huston. "International Trade Commission." *American Bar Association Journal* 8 (1922): 509–10.

———. "Regulation of the Sale of Securities in Interstate Commerce." *American Bar Association Journal* 9 (1923): 57–59, 140–41.

"Uniform Sale of Securities Act." *Columbia Law Review* 30 (December 1930): 1189–98.

Untermeyer, Samuel. "Speculation on the Stock Exchanges and Public Regulation of the Exchanges." *American Economic Review* 5 (March 1915): 22–25, 50–61.

Vanderlip, Frank. "What about the Banks?" *Saturday Evening Post,* November 5, 1932, pp. 3–4.

Washburn, Watson. "Anti-Fraud Legislation." *Michigan Law Review* 31 (April 1933): 765–74.

"Washington and Power." *Fortune* 17 (February 1938): 45–46, 119–25.

Waterman, Merwin H. "The Financial Policies of Public Utility Holding Companies." *Michigan Business Studies* 5 (1932): 1–168.

Wright, Warren. "Public Utility Management Fees." *Journal of Land and Public Utility Economics* 6 (November 1930): 1–16.

Books

Alsop, Joseph, and Robert Kintner. *Men around the President.* Garden City: Doubleday, 1939.

American Institute of Accountants. *Fiftieth Anniversary Celebration.* New York: American Institute of Accountants, 1938.

Ashby, Forrest B. *The Economic Effects of Blue Sky Laws.* Philadelphia: University of Pennsylvania Press, 1926.

Atkins, Willard E., et al. *The Regulation of the Security Markets.* Washington, D.C.: Brookings Institution, 1946.

Berle, Adolph A. *Studies in the Law of Corporation Finance.* Chicago: Callaghan, 1928.

———, and Gardiner C. Means. *The Modern Corporation and Private Property.* New York: Commerce Clearing House, 1932.

Bernheim, Arthur L., and Margaret G. Schneider, eds., *The Security Market.* New York: Twentieth Century Fund, 1935.

———. *Stock Market Control.* New York: Twentieth Century Fund 1934.

Blum, John M. *From the Morgenthau Diaries: Years of Crisis, 1928–1938.* Boston: Houghton Mifflin, 1959.

———. *From the Morgenthau Diaries: Years of Urgency, 1938–1941.* Boston: Houghton Mifflin, 1965.

Bonbright, James C., and Gardiner C. Means. *The Holding Company: Its Public Significance and Its Regulation.* New York: McGraw-Hill, 1932.

Braeman, John, and Robert H. Bremner, eds. *Change and Continuity in Twentieth-Century America.* Columbus: Ohio State University Press, 1964.

Brandeis, Louis D. *Other People's Money.* New York: Harper Torchbook, 1967.

Cochran, Thomas C. *The American Business System.* Cambridge, Mass.: Harvard University Press, 1957.

Cushman, Robert E. *The Independent Regulatory Commissions.* New York: Oxford University Press, 1941.

De Bedts, Ralph F. *The New Deal's SEC: The Formative Years.* New York: Columbia University Press, 1964.

Deinzer, Harvey T. *Development of Accounting Thought.* New York: Holt, Reinhart, 1965.

Dewing, Arthur S. *Corporation Finance.* Rev. ed. New York: Ronald Press, 1935.

————. *Corporation Securities.* New York: Ronald Press, 1934.

————. *The Financial Policies of Corporations.* 3d ed. New York: Ronald Press, 1934.

Douglas, William O. *Democracy and Finance.* New Haven: Yale University Press, 1940.

Eccles, Marriner. *Beckoning Frontiers.* New York: Alfred A. Knopf, 1951.

Edwards, George W. *The Evolution of Finance Capitalism.* New York: Longmans, 1938.

Flynn, John. *Graft in Business.* New York: Harcourt, 1931.

————. *Investment Trusts Gone Wrong.* New York: Harcourt, 1930.

————. *Security Speculation.* New York: Harcourt, 1934.

Frank, Jerome. *Law and the Modern Mind.* New York: Coward-McCann, 1930.

————. *Save America First.* New York: Harper, 1938.

Freidel, Frank. *Franklin D. Roosevelt: The Triumph.* Boston: Little, Brown, 1956.

Fusfield, Daniel R. *The Economic Thought of Franklin D. Roosevelt and the Origins of the New Deal.* New York: Columbia University Press, 1956.

Galbraith, John K. *The Great Crash.* Boston: Houghton Mifflin, 1955.

Haber, Samuel. *Efficiency and Uplift: Scientific Management in the Progressive Era, 1890–1920.* Chicago: University of Chicago Press, 1964.

Hawley, Ellis W. *The New Deal and the Problem of Monopoly.* Princeton: Princeton University Press, 1966.

Hays, Samuel P. *Conservation and the Gospel of Efficiency.* Cambridge, Mass.: Harvard University Press, 1959.

Karl, Barry D. *Executive Reorganization and Reform in the New Deal.* Cambridge, Mass.: Harvard University Press, 1963.

Kirkendall, Richard S. *Social Scientists and Farm Politics in the Age of Roosevelt.* Columbia: University of Missouri Press, 1967.

Kolko, Gabriel. *The Triumph of Conservatism: A Reinterpretation of American History, 1900–1916.* New York: Free Press, 1963.

————. *Railroads and Regulation.* Princeton: Princeton University Press, 1965.

Kurland, Philip B., ed. *Of Law and Life and Other Things That Matter: Papers and Addresses of Felix Frankfurter, 1956–1963.* Cambridge, Mass.: Harvard University Press, 1963.

Landis, James M. *The Administrative Process.* New Haven: Yale University Press, 1938.

Link, Arthur S. *Wilson: The New Freedom.* Princeton: Princeton University Press, 1956.

Loss, Louis. *Securities Regulation.* Boston: Little, Brown, 1951.

————, and Edward M. Cowett. *Blue Sky Law.* Boston: Little, Brown, 1958.

Lowenthal, Max. *The Investor Pays.* New York: Alfred A. Knopf, 1933.

May, George O. *Twenty-Five Years of Accounting Responsibility, 1911–1936.* New York: American Institute of Accountants, 1936.

Meyers, Charles H. *The Securities Exchange Act of 1934.* New York: Francis Emory Fitch, 1934.

Moley, Raymond. *After Seven Years.* New York: Harper, 1939.

————. *The First New Deal.* New York: Harcourt, 1966.

Morison, Elting E. *Turmoil and Tradition: A Study of the Life and Times of Henry L. Stimson.* Boston: Atheneum, 1964.

Pecora, Ferdinand. *Wall Street under Oath.* New York: Simon and Schuster, 1939.

Polenberg, Richard. *Reorganinzing Roosevelt's Government, 1936–1939: The Controversy over Executive Reorganization.* Cambridge, Mass.: Harvard University Press, 1966.

Ramsay, Marion L. *Pyramids of Powers.* Indianapolis: Bobbs-Merrill, 1937.

Reed, Robert R. *Blue Sky Laws: Analysis and Text.* New York: Clark, Boardman, 1920.

Ripley, William Z. *Main Street and Wall Street.* Cambridge, Mass.: Harvard University Press, 1926.

Romasco, Albert. *The Poverty of Abundance: Hoover, the Nation, the Depression.* New York: Oxford Univerity Press, 1965.

Schlesinger, Arthur M., Jr., *The Coming of the New Deal.* Boston: Houghton Mifflin, 1959.

―――. *The Politics of Upheaval.* Boston: Houghton Mifflin, 1960.

Sloan, Lawrence H. *Corporate Profits: A Study of Their Size, Variation, Use and Distribution in a Period of Prosperity.* New York: Harper, 1929.

Sobel, Robert. *The Big Board: A History of the New York Stock Exchange.* New York: Free Press, 1965.

―――. *The Great Bull Market.* New York: W. W. Norton, 1968.

Soule, George. *Prosperity Decade: From War to Depression, 1917–1929.* New York: Harper Torchbook, 1968.

Stein, Emanuel. *Government and the Investor.* New York: Oxford University Press, 1941.

Taylor, William H. *Financial Readjustment of Utility Corporations since 1929.* Urbana: University of Illinois Press, 1934.

Twentieth Century Fund. *Electric Power and Government Policy.* New York, 1948.

Waterman, Merwin H. *Investment Banking Functions.* Ann Arbor: University of Michigan Press, 1958.

Weissman, Rudolph L. *The New Wall Street.* New York: Harper, 1939.

Wiebe, Robert H. *Businessmen and Reform: A Study of the Progressive Movement.* Cambridge, Mass.: Harvard University Press, 1962.

―――. *The Search for Order.* New York: Hill and Wang, 1967.

Willoughby, William. *The Capital Issues Committee and War Finance Corporation.* Johns Hopkins Studies in History and Political Science, vol. 52. Baltimore: Johns Hopkins Press, 1934.

Index

on need for high margin requirements, 129; and Glass
amendment to stock exchange
bill, 136; on preference for
FTC, 139–40; and utility regulation in New York, 152–53;
appoints National Power Policy
Committee, 153; and abolition
of public utility holding companies, 154, 155, 158; denounces
Rayburn compromise on holding company bill, 166; skeptical
of Frankfurter-Barkley compromise, 176; appointments to
SEC, 179; on need to reassess
Securities Act of *1933*, 188; and
bankers' conspiracy against Securities Act, 189–90; and
amendments to Securities Act,
195. *See also* Frankfurter, Felix; Johnson, Hiram; Landis,
James M.; Securities and Exchange Commission; Title II

Roosevelt, Theodore: on financial
regulation, 3; and use of experts, 58

Roper, Daniel C., 195; and Securities Act of *1933,* 44; proposals for stock exchange regulation, 114, 114 n., 115 n.; on
Cohen stock exchange bill, 122
n.; and committee to study Securities Act of *1933,* 189; and
modifications of Securities Act,
193

Rosenblatt, William, 88 n., 107

Ross, James D., 179

Rublee, George, 84 n.; writes
Colombian petroleum law, 79;
progressive career of, 80 n.; on
meeting with Hiram Johnson,
82–83; and bondholders advisory council, 83; and Raymond B. Stevens, 88 n., 89 n.;

opposes Johnson on Title II (Securities Act of 1933), 88; FDR's
opinion of, 92; urges banker
support for private bondholders
council, 93; and Foreign Bondholders Protective Council, 94.
See also Feis, Herbert; Foreign
Bondholders Protective Council; Johnson, Hiram; State Department; Stevens, Raymond;
Stimson, Henry

Sachs, Alexander, 128 n.

Sanders, T. H.: on SEC accounting standards, 204–05; on benefits of SEC regulation, 229. *See
also* Accountants; Securities
and Exchange Commission

Sauthoff, Harry, 171

Securities Act of *1933*, 3, 42, 177,
185; attitude of investment
bankers and lawyers toward, 71;
amended by Hiram Johnson,
73; reasons for passage of, 112;
and Hundred Days, 112; administration of given to SEC,
136; compared to Securities Exchange Act of *1934*, 142; private investment and revision of,
186–87, 197; attacked as obstacle to recovery, 187–88; revision of opposed by Landis, 191;
amendments to, 192–94; and
concessions to bankers on, 195–
96; and recession of *1937–38,*
198–200; and accountants, 200,
202–03; acceptance of by investment bankers, 229. *See also*
Cohen, Benjamin V., Corcoran,
Thomas G.; Frankfurter, Felix;
Landis, James M.; Moley, Raymond; Rayburn, Sam; Thompson bill; Thompson, Huston

Securities Exchange Act of *1934,*